The Other Side of Paradise: Tourism, Conservation, and Development in the Bay Islands

Susan C. Stonich
Associate Professor
Department of Anthropology
Environmental Studies Program
University of California
Santa Barbara, CA 93106

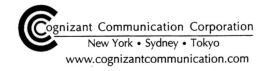

Cognizant Communication Corporation
New York • Sydney • Tokyo
www.cognizantcommunication.com

The Other Side of Paradise:Tourism, Conservation, and Development in the Bay Islands

Cognizant Communication Offices:

U.S.A.	3 Hartsdale Road, Elmsford, New York 10523-3701
Australia	P.O. Box 352 Cammeray, NWS, 2062
Japan	c/o OBS T's Bldg. 3F, 1-38-11 Matsubara, Setagaya-ku, Tokyo

Library of Congress Cataloging-in-Publication Data

Stonich, Susan C., 1944-
    The Other Side of Paradise:Tourism, Conservation, and Development in the Bay Islands / Susan C. Stonich.
        p. cm. — (Tourism dynamics)
    Includes bibliographical references and index.
    ISBN 1-882345-30-4 — ISBN 1-882345-31-2 (softbound)
        1.Tourism—Economic aspects—Honduras—Islas de la Bahââ. 2. Tourism—Environmental aspects—Honduras—Islas de la Bahââ. 3. Islas de la Bahââ (Honduras)—Social conditions. 4. Islas de la Bahââ (Honduras)—Economic conditions. I. Title. II. Series.

G155.H6 S76 2000
338.4'7917283'150453—dc21   99-054930
                                                    CIP

Printed in the United States of America

Printing: 1 2 3 4 5 6 7 8 9 10 Year: 1 2 3 4 5 6 7 8 9 10

Cover designed by Lynn Carano

Dedication

To Jerry

Contents

Chapter 4. Tourism, Demography, and Environment

List of Figures

List of Photos

List of Tables

Preface

In late October 1998, Hurricane Mitch developed into a catastrophic, Category 5 hurricane with wind speeds in excess of 200 miles per hour and took deadly aim at Honduras. Described as the most destructive Atlantic storm in the last 200 years, it stalled with its eye over the Bay Island of Guanaja for 39 hours before it made landfall along the Honduran North Coast (Figure P.1). While lingering off the coast for several days, Mitch absorbed enormous amounts of water from the ocean. Even after wind speeds diminished and it was downgraded to a tropical storm, it dropped as much as 5 feet of rain in some places as it moved south across Honduras and Nicaragua before turning west and passing over El Salvador and Guatemala. The intense rainfall caused major flooding in lowland areas and in river basins and brought about deadly landslides on deforested mountainsides. The power of the floods was so great that new maps will have to be drawn to reflect the altered topography of Honduras. Estimates of the dead approach 10,000 for the entire Central American region and 7,000 for Honduras alone. In addition, an estimated 12,000 persons remain missing, presumably dead. In Honduras, some 2 million people (over one third of the population) were left homeless and estimates of the number of people who will require resettlement range from 100,000 to 1 million. Destruction of roads, bridges, electrical plants and grids, water and sewage systems, and communication systems was far-reaching. An estimated 70% of Honduras' physical infrastructure was seriously damaged, including 169 major bridges, all major highways, and most secondary roads. Total monetary losses for the region are estimated at about US$6 billion, while loss estimates for Honduras alone are US$4 billion (Oliver-Smith, 1999).

For several weeks after the disaster, dramatic scenes of death and destruction appeared daily on TV screens throughout the world. But those early scenes were only the first act in the unfolding of this catastrophe. Approximately a month after the hurricane, the government of Honduras was compelled to declare a national medical emergency. Extensive flooding inundated large areas and the standing fresh water caused serious outbreaks of water-borne infectious diseases, including an estimated 200,000 cases of amoebic dysentery, 30,000 cases of malaria, and 20,00 cases of cholera (Oliver-Smith, 1999). Lack of communications and destruction of transportation networks left many communities isolated and without access to medical care with which to combat these maladies. The death toll of Hurricane Mitch grew for many weeks after its initial impact.

The Honduran people are beginning to address the awesome task of rebuilding their country. Their burden is exceedingly difficult in light of the economic impacts of Hurricane Mitch, which seriously constrains the ability of the nation to recover. In addition to sweeping away people, homes, and entire villages, massive

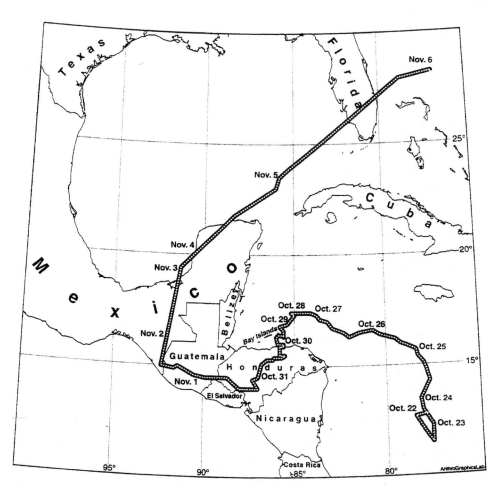

Figure P.1. The path of hurricane/tropical storm Mitch from October 22 to November 6, 1998.

flooding also destroyed industrial and commercial sites while simultaneously depositing a wide variety of chemicals and other toxic materials in the soils and aquifers as well as in coastal and marine environments. Vast areas of agricultural land were flooded, destroying at least 80% of agricultural crops, both those grown for domestic consumption and for export. An estimated 20% of Honduras' most important export crop—coffee—was lost, but actual losses were much higher because damage to roads hampered carrying out the coffee harvest or prevented the transport of harvested coffee to markets. Bananas, which rank second in providing foreign exchange to Honduras, were harder hit with loss estimates of US$800 million. Virtually all banana plantations along the North Coast were completely flooded, reducing production to about 5% of normal and creating as much as 80% unemployment in the industry for the foreseeable future. Honduras' third most important export crop—cultivated shrimp—also suffered devastating losses (approximately US$150 million) due to both inundation and contamination that affected the majority of shrimp farms along the Gulf of Fonseca in southern Honduras. Small and medium-sized hillside farms, largely cultivated by peasant farmers, fared no better than larger export-oriented farms and plantations. Hillside farms were stripped of topsoil by heavy rainfall and landslides, and many farms located in highland valleys were buried under deep layers of debris and sediment. In addition to the economically devastating loss of foreign exchange brought about by the destruction of export crops, enormous unemployment throughout the agricultural sector will significantly impede the ability of Honduran families to recover. Economic recuperation from the household to the national level will take decades even with debt relief and immense international assistance.

The government of Honduras (GOH) is attempting to begin to address the formidable task of rebuilding through changes in its economic strategies as well as through political means. The steep drop in production of its major agricultural exports will place them well below tourism and the *maquila* sector (offshore production facilities most of which produce textiles) as generators of much needed foreign exchange for the next several years. In light of this, the GOH has enhanced its efforts to promote and expand these two economic sectors. During the recent visit to Central America of U.S. President Clinton, the presidents of the regional republics urged that their textile industries receive enhanced benefits under the Caribbean Basin Initiative—equivalent to those enjoyed by Mexico under the North American Free Trade Agreement (NAFTA). In Honduras, however, earnings from tourism (US$143 million in 1997) rank third behind coffee and bananas in generating foreign exchange and significantly exceed earnings from *maquilas* (US$16.6 million in 1997). It is conceivable that tourism may be Honduras' major source of foreign exchange for the next several years—provided that ways can be found to bring tourists back to Honduras.[1]

Hurricane Mitch was a two-edged sword with respect to tourism in Honduras. On the one hand it demonstrated the vulnerability of tourism to natural disasters. On the other hand, the two most important tourist destinations in Honduras (the Bay Islands and the archeological site of Copan) were spared the brunt of the storm. Even the Bay Island of Guanaja over which Hurricane Mitch hovered for almost 2 days appears to be recovering its tourist capacity. According to reports by Guanaja business owners, the final major resort to reopen on the island did so by early February 1999. Government and private sector estimates of the damage to the tourism industry are about US$100 million. The apparent lesser impact of Hurricane Mitch on the tourism sector than on other sectors of the economy has motivated substantial efforts to rescue the industry by both the public and the private sectors as a means of advancing Honduran economic recovery. The Honduras Institute of Tourism (IHT), a government agency, established a Hurricane Mitch Response Team almost immediately after the storm. Shortly thereafter, the GOH engaged the services of the U.S.-based public relations firm, Egret Communications, to carry out the strategy of the IHT through evaluating the tourism situation, creating a marketing plan, and handling post-Mitch, public relations' damage control. Among the IHT's major objectives was to inform international travelers that tourist operations in Honduras were little affected by Mitch and most of the tourist facilities were open for business shortly after the storm. Egret created a Web site (http://www.hondurasmitch.com) to provide current information on Mitch's impact on tourism in Honduras. The site included summary updates on the effects of the storm, impacts by various areas of the country (including each of the Bay Islands), press releases by government officials and business owners, road and travel information, and links to the Honduras Institute of Tourism. By visiting this site, a potential tourist could find out detailed information on the damage and status of individual lodgings, link to that specific hotel or resort's Web site, and send an electronic mail message directly to the tourist business. In addition to providing current information, the site also entreated potential visitors to help in the efforts to rebuild Honduras by becoming a tourist:

> With much of our economy severely damaged by Hurricane Mitch, the tourism industry plays a very important role in the recovery of our nation. The dollars spent in Honduras by our guests will enable the 45,000 people who depend on tourism for their livelihood to rebuild their lives, feed their families, and continue in pursuit of their dreams. . . . We hope you will consider a vacation or dive trip to Honduras in the next year. (Egret Communications, 1999)

The GOH also has attempted to augment tourism through political means. Most significantly, it accelerated passage of the reform of Article 107 of the Honduran Constitution by the National Congress. This highly controversial measure makes it legal for foreigners and foreign corporations to purchase lands and own infrastructure on the Caribbean and Pacific coasts and on all islands. Previously the purchase and granting of clear title to foreigners in these areas was prohibited by the constitution. According to the Honduran Minister of Tourism, the reform is estimated to generate approximately US$500 million in foreign investments, primarily in the form of hotel and resort construction on the Bay Islands and the North Coast. The widespread sentiment of the owners of tourism-related businesses toward the reform was clearly expressed by a well-known owner of a tourist hotel, "Article 107's reform will enable Honduras to become a player in the world tourism arena" (Rosenzweig, 1999). Other broader political changes stimulated by Hurricane Mitch also will likely affect the tourism sector. These include accelerating the processes of political decentralization originally initiated by the Municipal Reform Law of 1990 in order to delegate some reconstruction activities to municipal authorities and of privatization of several state-owned industries such as telecommunications, energy, and major port facilities.

Dealing with the aftermath of Hurricane Mitch also spurred local-level responses in tourist areas, most notably on the Bay Islands. Resorts and hotels have offered significantly reduced rates, increased their presence at international travel and tourism trade shows, and augmented their affiliations with international travel and tour companies. One of the important efforts to date was the founding of a new Bay Islands Tourism Association (BITA) established by business owners who wanted to respond quickly to what they considered to be erroneous images of devastation portrayed by the media. The group has applied for legal status as a nongovernmental, nonprofit organization. BITA established 12 committees to work on various tourist-related concerns and issues (e.g., security, health, legal, financial, beautification, and so forth) and it is attempting to integrate information regarding tourism on the Bay Islands through a common Web site that will link all tourism-related businesses.

It remains to be seen whether these government and private-sponsored initiatives will succeed in sustaining, let alone expanding, the tourism sector and thus contribute more significantly to the Honduran economy. There may be a unique opportunity for the growth of tourism in the aftermath of Hurricane Mitch. However, with much of the country's infrastructure gone or badly damaged, with risks to human health considerable, and with access to adequate and safe water and food major concerns, several serious impediments to the industry also exist. After growing significantly between 1960 and the mid-1970s, the tourism sector throughout Central America went into steep decline during the widespread political violence of the late 1970s and the 1980s. It has only been in the last several years that tourism has regained its economic importance in the region. It may be, at least for Honduras, that sector vulnerability due to natural disasters is as far-reaching and long lasting as vulnerability due to political upheaval.

The decision by the GOH to make tourism one of the pillars of economic recovery in the aftermath of Hurricane Mitch is understandable given the mounting importance of tourism to the global economy. Tourism is the world's largest industry, the greatest generator of jobs, and an increasingly important sector of the economies of many countries (World Travel & Tourism Council, 1998a). In 1998, the industry contributed 11.6% to the global gross domestic product (GDP); this figure is predicted to increase to 12.5% by 2010 (World Travel & Tourism Council, 1998b). Between 1995 and 2000, worldwide spending on travel is estimated to increase from US$3.4 trillion to US$4.2 trillion, capital investments in all travel-related industries are projected to rise from US$645 billion to US$828 billion, and global employment in all tourism-related industries is expected to grow from 232 million to 250 million (Crossette, 1998). In 1996, 595 million tourists visited foreign destinations annually. By 2020, 1.6 billion of the world's 7.8 billion people will take a foreign trip according to predictions by experts from the World Tourism Organization (World Tourism Organization, 1997a). In the Third World, the contribution of the travel and tourism sector to GDP is substantial, it is frequently the primary source of foreign exchange earnings, and it has proven to be a crucial source of income and employment for many people. However, a number of the social, cultural, economic, and environmental consequences of tourism have attracted concern and led to a vigorous debate about the extent to which tourism actually has the ability to sustain rural livelihoods, communities, cultures, and environments. Tourism also has provoked consequential local-level strife in the areas in which it has expanded. Hostility often involves the loss of critical natural resources on which local people depend for their livelihoods. The Bay Islands of Honduras are one of the clearest examples of community-level discord associated with the spread of tourism. Conflicts surrounding the social, cultural, economic, and environmental impacts of tourism have been so great, in fact, that the Bay Islands were one of three Latin American cases examined in a recent study on conflict management in coastal zones conducted for the Inter-American Development Bank (IDB) (Rijsberman, n.d.).

The Other Side of Paradise: Tourism, Conservation and Development in the Bay Islands uses a political ecology perspective to examine the linkages between tourism development, local conflict, and environmental conservation initiatives in the Bay Islands, Honduras. It is based on the belief that understanding the origins of current threats to the people, environment, and natural resources of the Bay Islands requires analysis of the historical evolution and political dynamics of international and state-sponsored development and conservation policies operating in collaboration with the interests of the islands' elite. Of particular interest are the ways in which these policies have tightened state and elite control of resources at the expense of a substantial portion of island residents and their customary use rights.

One of the book's major goals is to reveal the factors that are vital to equitable development and conservation initiatives in the context of significant expansion of the tourism sector. It explores comprehensively the implications of embracing community-based approaches to development and conservation too uncritically and too quickly. While cautiously advocating community-based conservation as a potential way to protect environments, rural livelihoods, and cultures, it also demonstrates the significant political, economic, social, and cultural obstacles to achieving effective community-based development and environmental conservation. It scrutinizes the relationships between power, rural livelihoods, class, ethnicity, gender, community participation, and environmental conservation in the context of the recent boom in tourism in the Bay Islands. In so doing, it delineates the linkages between the local and the global, as people, communities, and regions are articulated into the global economy through the expanding tourism sector and into the increasingly complex institutions of global environmental governance through conservation projects funded by multilateral and bilateral donors. The book examines the cultural, ethnic, social, gender, economic, and other kinds of conflicts that this integration engenders. The book also is concerned with providing a methodological framework for conducting social science research that can significantly contribute to effective community-based participation in tourism development and conservation efforts and to realistic policy recommendations in complex social, cultural, and political contexts. As much as possible, the book attempts to present recent changes on the Bay Islands from the perspective of the local people most affected by these changes—especially island people whose voices so far have not been heard and who have not participated in the decisions that profoundly affect their own destinies. How do they view the significant changes that are occurring on the islands? What are their needs, aspirations, and hopes for the future? How would they like to share in the benefits of tourism? In light of the probable post-Mitch growth of the tourism industry on the Bay Islands, it is crucial that the local-level impacts of tourism development be understood, not only to ameliorate current problems but also to ensure that future development does not exacerbate an already contentious situation.

This book is based on 10 years of interdisciplinary research that involved many participants including several hundred Bay Island residents. Special thanks are due to Dr. Becky Myton, Professor of Biology at the National Autonomous University of Honduras and formerly technical advisor to the Honduran Ministry of the Environment; Dr. Gus Salbador, former Director of the St. Luke's Cornerstone Mission on Roatán; Dr. Jackie Woods, former Director of the Roatán Hospital; and Cheryl Galindo, Irma Brady, and staff of the Bay Islands Conservation Association (BICA). I am particularly grateful to the many U.S. and Honduran student and project volunteers for their efforts in collecting and analyzing the data. I am also thankful to David Lawson, Senior Graphic Artist at the University of California-Santa Barbara, Anthropology Graphics Laboratory, for his help in processing the maps and photos used in this book. Funding for the research on which this book is based came from the University of California Academic Senate, the University of California Research Expeditions Program, and Earthwatch International.

Notes

[1]According to reports from the Bay Islands, tourist arrivals stopped almost entirely immediately after Hurricane Mitch, picked up somewhat over the Christmas holidays, then plummeted thereafter.

Chapter 1

Introduction

> The perfect islands in the eye of your dreams could not surpass the scenic beauty and special appeal of the Bay Islands of Honduras. Tucked away in a corner of the Western Caribbean and protected by the hush of time, the Bay Islands are the classic portrayal of forgotten tropical isles—unspoiled, sensuous, and totally irresistible. (Honduras Tourist Board, 1985)

To most tourists who visit the Bay Islands, they are "Paradise"—remote tropical islands with pristine diving sites, coral reefs, and palm fringed beaches that rival any in the world (Figure 1.1). But there is another side of this tropical Eden that most tourists seldom comprehend. This underbelly of paradise encompasses degraded natural environments, human societies and cultures at risk, and escalating, sometimes violent, conflicts.

In June 1997 the Honduran government formally declared the Bay Islands National Marine Park, more than a decade after the idea of the protected area first was proposed. Instead of reacting with enthusiasm to the news, many of us who know the Bay Islands well reacted with cynicism. Skeptics asked many questions: What difference would a park make now—after more than a decade of unbridled growth in tourism? Would a park ameliorate the significant declines in the quality of the natural environment, the culture, and the society of the islands, and the escalating human conflicts that have occurred recently? Would the park enhance the quality of life and the standard of living of the majority of the islands' ethnically and culturally diverse residents as well as conserve the environment and contribute to the cultural survival of the islands' peoples?

The Other Side of Paradise: Tourism, Conservation, and Development in the Bay Islands addresses these questions by examining the links between tourism development, conservation initiatives, and their human and environmental outcomes. The analysis is historical, investigating how tourism development and conservation strategies are consolidating control over the islands by the Honduran state, functioning in collaboration with members of the island elite and at the expense of the majority of island residents. Couched in the framework of contending local, national, and international power relations, it demonstrates the relative benefits and costs arising from current patterns of tourism development for various social actors—by divisions of nationality, ethnicity, class, and gender. It shows how deteriorating human and environ-

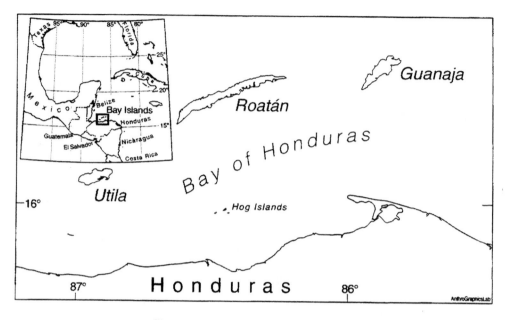

Figure 1.1. Map of the Bay Islands.

Photo 1.1. "Paradise!" West Bay Beach, one of the most important tourist attractions on Roatán.

mental conditions are exacerbating long-term social and cultural conflicts and creating new ones.These conflicts are over material resources—access to land, marine resources, and jobs—but also over maintaining cultural and ethnic identities.The book identifies significant obstacles to achieving the integrated goals of community-based conservation and development and suggests ways in which these formidable constraints can be overcome.As such, the book has application beyond Honduras and Central America to other areas of the Third World where tourism is growing and where national parks and reserve systems have been proposed as solutions to environmental and human problems.

I first visited the Bay Islands in 1980, part of a long tradition of foreign explorers, pirates, castaways, adventurers, revolutionaries, mercenaries, smugglers, and fugitives who encountered the Bay Islands since Christopher Columbus came across them in 1502. I have returned to the islands many times, first as a tourist and then as a researcher. I've seen the Bay Islands through different lenses: as a lone anthropologist in need of a break after conducting long periods of difficult fieldwork on the Honduran mainland; as a wife and mother on vacation with her children; and as a principal investigator directing the efforts of dozens of students and volunteers. In turn, the islands' residents have perceived me in various guises.

In the 1980s, the islands were the place of choice for a little "rest and relaxation" for many of us who worked in the "real" Central America.There was an audible sigh of relief as we exited the rickety planes that we chartered to fly us the short distance from La Ceiba, on the mainland coast, to Roatán, the largest of the Bay Islands.These sighs came not only from having survived the flight but also from the relief we felt in being able to escape temporarily the poverty and the escalating violence that characterized the Central American mainland. Memories of snorkeling in the royal blue water teeming with multitudes of fish and other sea creatures, eating lobster and conch stew, drinking *Cuba Libres* and cold beer, and reading trashy novels remain cherished memories of those days. You could drink the water too with little risk of contracting dysentery or other gastrointestinal diseases.The islands' residents were friendly and, according to most measures of health, education, and income, significantly better off than their fellow citizens on the Honduran mainland despite the absence of widespread electricity, telecommunications, and comprehensive drinking water and sanitation systems.There were risks, of course, especially from malaria, dengue fever, and the painful bites of millions of sand flies, but trips to the islands generally were idyllic interludes from the harsh realities of life on the mainland.The contradictions between life on the islands and on the Honduran mainland were stark and the irony of escaping the hardships of Honduras by visiting her most isolated and distinct region was noted by many of us.We saw in the relationship of the Bay Islands to Honduras one of the many examples of uneven development that characterize Honduras, Central America, and the Third World more generally.

Since the early 1980s the Bay Islands have changed remarkably, especially after improvements to the airport on Roatán were completed in 1988. During the last 10 years, the full-time resident population grew from less than 20,000 to more than 30,000 people with much of the increase due to the in-migration of desperately poor ladinos from the mainland who came in search of work in the tourist sector. During the same time, the number of tourists skyrocketed from less than 10,000 annually to more than

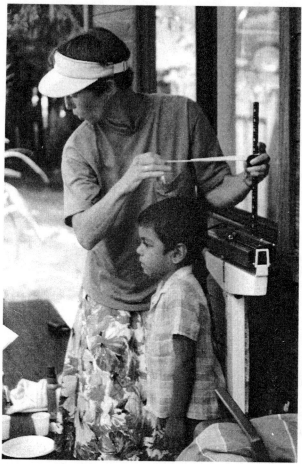

Photo 1.2. Weighing and measuring ladino boy as part of this project.

90,000, the estimated number of tourists who currently visit the islands each year to dive the coral reefs and enjoy the white sand beaches. Unfortunately, the recent boom in tourism largely has been unregulated. Paved and unpaved roads now dissect the islands, especially the largest island, Roatán. Most of these new roads are unstabilized and promote widespread erosion, siltation, and deterioration of watersheds. Tourist facilities have been constructed with little heed to their environmental consequences. Hundreds of wells have been dug indiscriminately in order to meet the needs of the growing human population. Despite this escalating population, the islands, as yet, do not have potable water or sanitation systems. As a result, much of the islands have been deforested, many crucial habitats have been degraded, and the quality of both sea and fresh water has declined to dangerous levels. In sum, the islands' biophysical environment is at risk. The impacts on human livelihoods and health are considerable, especially on women, the poor, and children. Evidence of substantial economic investment and the implementation of large development and conservation projects funded by powerful multilateral and bilateral donors such as the Inter-American Development Bank (IDB) and the United States Agency for International Development (USAID) suggest that the problems do not stem from lack of money alone. A number of international environmental organizations also have been active on the islands and although a number of environmental projects have been implemented, these efforts have emphasized seemingly nonpoliticized, environmental education and clean-up projects rather than attempts to address the root causes of environmental degradation and associated human conflicts on the islands. The few marine reserves that have been designated on the islands by local municipalities have generated considerable local conflict.

While it may be easy to point to mounting numbers of tourists and immigrants as the heart of the islands' problems, such a conclusion oversimplifies a much more complex set of interrelated phenomena. These processes have at their core the unregulated development of tourism within the context of the Bay Islands' history, contending cultures, power structures, and relationship to the mainland. Tourism development, controlled by powerful government, public, and private interests, has significantly altered relationships among various power holding groups with interests in the islands that have, in turn, changed previous patterns in access to and use of crucial natural resources and in household economic survival strategies. While it is the more powerful social groups who have garnered the greatest benefits of tourism development it is the less powerful people on the islands who feel that they have borne the greatest costs.

It is not only the islands' natural environment that is at risk. Equally jeopardized are the cultures of the Bay Islanders, the Afro-Caribbean and Anglo-Caribbean peoples who constituted the majority population of the Bay Islands until recently. Although politically part of Hispanic, Spanish-speaking Honduras, the Bay Islands have remained one of the English-speaking enclaves in the Western Caribbean and have figured substantially in more than 400 years of Anglo-Hispanic conflict in the region (Davidson, 1974). The Bay Islanders maintained their cultural, social, and economic ties with other English-speaking enclaves (especially Belize, the Cayman Islands, and the U.S.) and retained the English language and Protestantism. Thus, the Bay Islanders insulated themselves fairly successfully from Hispanic, Honduran influences even after the Wykes-Cruz Treaty transferred sovereignty of the islands from Great Britain to Honduras in 1859. Recently, however, Hispanic and islander histories have clashed once again and island culture and society are being challenged by external actors as well as by members of their own communities. It appears that recent efforts of the Honduran government to promote tourism may be the most successful attempt to integrate the islands into the mainland polity, economy, society, and culture. The response of the native, Afro-Caribbean, Bay Islanders has been to vigorously resist this integration by attempting to demonstrate their unique ethnic and cultural identity and to use this newly found unity to affect political action. The recent formation of their own grassroots nongovernmental organizations (NGOs) and their subsequent designation as one of Honduras' "indigenous" peoples are evidence of their relative success in this regard.

This chapter begins with a discussion of current trends in the promotion of international tourism as a paramount economic development strategy in Central America—the

latest in a series of development initiatives that have been promoted in the region. It
then surveys current thinking about participatory, community-based development and
conservation, especially in the context of enhanced tourism development. Finally, it
concludes with a presentation of political ecology as a framework for analyzing the
complex, interrelated human and biophysical phenomena related to tourism, equitable
community-based development, and environmental conservation.

The Growth of International Tourism in Central America

International tourism in Central America has grown unevenly since the 1960s (Figure
1.2). From 1960 to 1970 the number of tourists visiting Central America grew more
than 600%, from 124,000 to 744,000, part of the worldwide trend in the growth of
international tourism during that period. Between 1970 and 1975, annual tourist
arrivals to the region rose from 744,000 to 1.7 million (230%), an increase that surpassed the rate of growth of international tourism globally (134%), to the Americas
(118%), and to Mexico (143%) during the same period (calculated from data in World
Tourism Organization [WTO], 1993). Between 1975 and 1985, however, total tourists
to the region dropped to 1.1 million annually, in response to the well-publicized
escalating violence throughout the isthmus (Chant, 1992). This decline was most
conspicuous in Guatemala, Nicaragua, and El Salvador (the sites of the most widespread
and violent conflicts) but also occurred to a lesser extent in relatively peaceful Costa
Rica (Figure 1.3). International tourist arrivals to Honduras remained relatively low, but
consistent, during the same time period. Simultaneously, arrivals to Panama increased by
approximately 30%, largely due to the inclusion of U.S. military personnel and their
families in national tourist statistics.

Since the end of the "lost decade" of the 1980s, Central American governments have
been trying to strengthen their economies through new avenues of economic development designed to integrate their economies, diversify exports, promote foreign investment, and increase foreign exchange earnings (Stonich, 1993). One of the most important

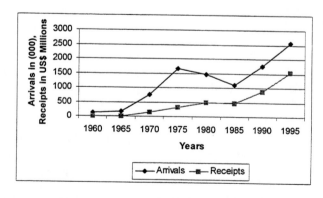

Figure 1.2. Central American tourist arrivals and receipts: 1960–1995. Source:
1960 to 1965 (Ritchie et al., 1965); 1970 to 1995 (WTO, 1993, 1994, 1996).

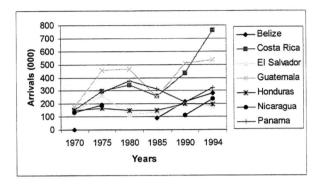

Figure 1.3. Tourist arrivals to individual Central American countries: 1970–1994. Source: WTO (1993, 1994, 1996).

of these development strategies is the promotion of international tourism, which has grown in tandem with increased political stability in the region ("Central American Presidents," 1996; "Presidents Push for Tourism Integration," 1996). Between 1987 and 1991, tourist arrivals and receipts to Central America grew at average annual rates of 11.5% and 16.8%, respectively—exceeding the average rates of tourism growth globally, in the Third World, and elsewhere in the Americas during the same period (Stonich, Sorensen, & Hundt, 1995). In 1991, 2.1 million international tourists visited Central America, surpassing the previous high of 1.7 million tourists reached in 1975 before the outbreak of widespread regional violence. During the 1990s, more than 2 million international tourists visited Central America annually of which about 25% visited Guatemala, 24% Costa Rica, 13% Panama, 11% Belize, 10% El Salvador, 10% Honduras, and 7% Nicaragua. With the exceptions of Costa Rica and Belize, where most international tourists arrive from the U.S., the majority of international visitors to Central America arrive from other Central American countries (42%), while 29% arrive from the U.S., 12% from Europe, and 2.4% from elsewhere in the world (calculated from WTO, 1993).

In 1996, more than 2.6 million tourists visited Central America and tourism contributed approximately US$1.6 billion to foreign exchange earnings ("Central American Presidents," 1996; "Presidents Push for Tourism Integration," 1996). It should be noted, however, that although the rate of tourism growth in Central America is significant, Central America's market share of tourism to the Americas, in terms of arrivals (2.12%) and receipts (1.4%), remains relatively small (computed from WTO, 1993). Although Central America's portion of the American tourist market may be relatively insubstantial, the tourism sector is making an increasingly important contribution to the export-dependent economies of Central America (Table 1.1, Figure 1.4). As evident in Table 1.1, between 1987 and 1994, for Central America, the percentage of international tourist receipts to total export receipts was surpassed only by that of the Caribbean countries and more than double those of the world, developing countries, the Americas, North America, and South America. Figure 1.4 shows the changes in tourism receipts as a percentage of total export receipts in the various Central American countries between 1973 and 1995.[1] It illustrates the increasing contribution of tourism to export earnings

Table 1.1. Tourist Receipts as a Percentage of Total Export Receipts

	World	Developing Countries	Americas	North America	South America	Central Caribbean	America
1987	6.9	8.4	9	8.2	6.3	23.7	12.9
1988	7	8.7	8.6	8	5.6	24.8	13.6
1989	7	8.5	0	8.5	5.1	24.4	15
1990	7.7	9.5	10.3	9.9	6.6	25	18.1
1991	7.9	8.8	11	10.4	7.8	26.5	20.4
1992	8.4	9.7	11.5	10.9	8.2	30.7	21.3
1993	8.6	9.9	11.7	10.9	8.7	36.7	22.8
1994	8.4	9.6	10.8	9.9	9.1	35.8	20.5

Source: For 1987–89, WTO (1993); for 1990–94, WTO (1996).

since the mid-1980s for Central America as a whole, as well as for individual Central American countries. In the mid-1990s, tourism and travel made the greatest contribution to the economies of Belize (48% of total export receipts), followed by Costa Rica (27%), Guatemala (11%), Nicaragua (10%), El Salvador (9%), and Honduras (7%). It is notable that the two countries in which the tourism sector contributes most to the

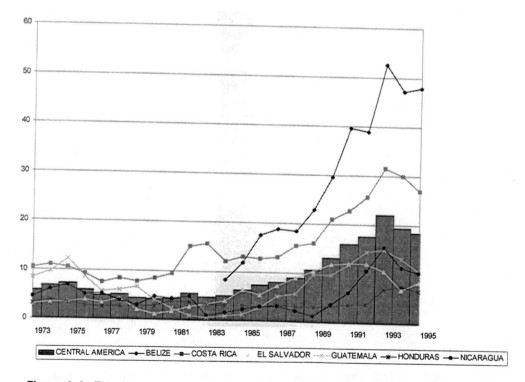

Figure 1.4. Travel as a percentage of exports: 1973–1995. Source: International Monetary Fund (various years).

national economies (Belize and Costa Rica) generally are viewed as the two most peaceful and politically stable countries in the region. In 1997, foreign exchange earnings from tourism ranked first among all sources of foreign exchange in Costa Rica and Belize, second only to coffee in Guatemala, and third (behind coffee and bananas) in Honduras (Rosenzweig, 1998). With the exception of Costa Rica, recent assessments of tourism in Latin America have tended to overlook or underestimate tourism's growing importance to the economies of Central America (Chant, 1992; Getino, 1990; Gormsen, 1988). In reality, Central America's governments and development planners have recognized the potential of the tourism industry to confront the economic and social problems of the region and have taken steps over the last decade to realize that promise. As recently shown by Hurricane Mitch, however, tourism promoters do so in a context of significant vulnerability to natural disasters common to the region (hurricanes, earthquakes, volcanic eruptions, fires, and floods), to risks from a wide variety of infectious diseases, and to increased incidences of violent crime.

Incentives to Promote International Tourism in Central America

In May 1996, Central American presidents signed the *Declaration of Montelimar II*, which designated the tourism industry as the paramount economic growth strategy within the isthmus. The declaration emphasized the necessity for joint efforts among Central American countries and the promotion of the Central American region as a single tourism location rather than as several separate national destinations ("Central American Presidents," 1996; "Presidents Push for Tourism Integration," 1996). The promotion of international tourism is being facilitated by a number of international and national incentives. International development donors, especially the World Bank, the IDB, the United Nations (UN), and USAID, have played key roles in the expansion. Financial assistance from these institutions has helped fund a number of international and national tourism initiatives in the region. These include collaborative efforts among international donors, NGOs, national governments (primarily Central American, Mexican, U.S., and European), and private investors; a more important position for tourism in international trade policy; and economic incentives for potential international and national investors (Stonich et al., 1995).

One of the earliest attempts to promote regional tourism was the cooperative effort of the Central American governments of Belize, El Salvador, Guatemala, and Honduras, under the leadership of Mexico, to create *El Mundo Maya* (The Mayan World) with the financial assistance of interests in the U.S. and Europe.[2] In March 1988, the presidents of Belize, El Salvador, Guatemala, Honduras, and Mexico signed a joint tourism promotion pact and established *El Mundo Maya*. Their main goal was to secure technical and financial aid from the European Community (EC) for the development of the regional Mayan World Project aimed at expanding both the public and private tourism sectors in the five countries. The objective, according to Mexico's Minister of Tourism, was "to showcase the history and culture of the entire region as one entity without borders" and "to promote the Mexican resort of Cancun as the international 'doorway' to the Mayan world" ("Neighbors to Aid Mayan Ruins," 1991). With initial financing of US$1 million from the EC, the first phase of the program began in 1991. Three kinds of tourism were promoted in each country: cultural tourism (some aspect of archeology, ethnography, and/or history); coastal tourism (sun, sand, and sea); and eco/adventure tourism.A total of 14 tourism circuits was established in the five participating countries (Rivas, 1990). Originally, Honduras had two circuits—the Copan ruins (archeology) and Roatán Island, the largest of the Bay Islands (coastal beach tourism). Subsequently, a third circuit was added—*la Mosquitia*/the *Rio Platano* Biosphere Reserve (eco/adventure tourism).There is considerable satire in including the Bay Islands and *la Mosquitia* in The Mayan World because neither the prehistoric, historic, nor contemporary inhabitants of either area are, or were, Maya. In addition to creating integrated tourism circuits, other development plans included infrastructural improvements (roads, airports, and marinas); new hotel construction; archeological projects in El Salvador and Chiapas, Mexico; and extensive international marketing (through brochures, travel publications, airline inflight magazines, environmental/conservation journals, newspapers, and travel trade shows).As part of the Mayan World project, the Bay Islands were the subject of many articles featuring the islands' attractions (e.g., Basch, 1992; Gordon, 1993; Olson, 1994; Sletto, 1993; Stephens, 1989;The Caribbean Islands of the Maya World, 1994;Yost, 1992).

At the national level, the governments of Central America are attempting to promote tourism in a number of ways, including the creation and/or expansion of national tourist offices/ministries; the improvement of necessary infrastructure (generally with international financial assistance); and economic incentives for potential investors such as access to credit at preferential rates, tax abatements, and deferring or waiving import duties.While there has been no comprehensive regional evaluation of these incentive programs, a preliminary examination of such efforts in Costa Rica identified several issues and made several recommendations.According to Coffey (1993), such efforts should encourage: 1) expanded linkages (beyond hotels) to additional types of tourist-oriented businesses; 2) better coordination with broader economic development goals; 3) greater domestic (rather than foreign) investment through reduced interest rates for national investors; and 4) expanded monitoring incentive programs to prevent overdevelopment of the industry.

Efforts to Promote Tourism in Honduras

Tourism has been recommended as a viable means of economic development for Honduras for several decades (e.g., Checchi, 1959; Ritchie, Fothergill, Oliver, & Wulfing, 1965). It was only in the early 1980s, however, that the government of Honduras (GOH) aggressively began promoting tourism as a national development strategy—emphasizing the important Mayan archeological site of Copan, the scenic beaches and colonial history of the North Coast, and the relatively pristine coral reefs of the Bay Islands. Since 1980, the GOH has promulgated a series of laws that established a number of specified "Tourism Zones" and provided generous tax and import incentives to attract foreign capital investment.As part of its augmented embrace of neoliberal economic policies and associated emphasis on the promotion of so-called "nontraditional" exports, these measures have accelerated since 1990, especially with the establishment ofTourism Free Zones (1992 Decreto Numero 84-92), which gave investors in the tourist industry the same fiscal benefits as the private Export Processing Zones.These incentives include 100% foreign ownership; the right to operate without paying federal and municipal taxes; the right to import free of all duties and taxes any equipment needed to build, furnish, supply, and run a business (including motor vehicles, boats, yachts, and airplanes); and the right to replace old and worn equipment tax free. Potential foreign investors also have access to para-statal organizations such as the Foundation for Investment and Development of Exports (FIDE), which assists foreign companies seeking to develop investment and sourcing programs in Honduras. With access to advanced information technologies (i.e., its recently created World Wide Web homepage [http://www.hondurasinfo.hn] and electronic mail address [fide@hondutel.hn]) FIDE advertises itself globally as "Your One-Stop Office of Investment." In an effort to integrate investment and tourism efforts, the Industrial Development Group—Honduras (IDGH) (a division of FIDE) and the Honduran Institute of Tourism (IHT) opened a joint office in Miami in 1997. Until Hurricane Mitch, attempts to expand the tourism sector met with some success and, by 1997, only coffee (US$330 million) and bananas (US$239 million) generated more foreign exchange earnings than did tourism (US$143 million). In an attempt to further augment the contribution of tourism to the economy of Honduras, the IHT was restructured in early 1998 and became part of a ministry level secretariat, the Ministry of Industry, Commerce, and Tourism. Significantly, the first director of the new Ministry of Tourism was a former president of FIDE.

Human and Environmental Issues Related to Tourism Development in Central America

The significant expansion of tourism as economic development in Central America raises several critical concerns. Many of these focus directly or indirectly on issues of social and economic equity and environment. For example, how will economic gains measured at the macroeconomic level (e.g., through the increased contribution of tourism earnings to foreign exchange) affect the local level, socially, economically, and environmentally? How successful will tourism development be in raising the incomes and quality of life for the majority of Central Americans given the disastrous social, economic, and environmental consequences of previous economic development schemes in the region?[3] Will tourism development promote social equity in the region or, like previous development models, enhance regional inequalities and promote social conflict? To this end, which segments of society will benefit and which will pay the price for the current patterns of tourism being promoted in the region?

In light of a number of critiques of environmental protection efforts in Central America (e.g., Annis, 1992; Barzetti & Rovinski, 1992; Thrupp, 1990; Utting, 1994), one of the most important concerns is whether or not environmental protection initiatives associated with the promotion of tourism sustain local livelihoods as well as protect crucial environments and critical ecologies. In general these criticisms conclude that a significant number of past efforts have forced a trade-off between environmental protection and human welfare. Further, they have undermined not only local livelihoods but also precluded the possibility of achieving environmental objectives. Utting (1994) concludes that what is needed in Central America is a more integrative approach to environmental protection that simultaneously addresses the failure to site environmental initiatives within a broader development framework and the failure to integrate concerns for environmental protection with the rights and needs of local people.

These considerations are being investigated by a limited, but growing, number of studies scrutinizing the effects of tourism in Central America. Although most assessments of *El Mundo Maya* have been done from the perspective of business management (e.g., Thomlinson, 1994), a few evaluations of the project's social and cultural repercussions have begun to appear. According to Gunson (1996), critics of *El Mundo Maya* include Maya organizations such as the Kekchi Council of Belize and other Mayan cultural groups. Critics maintain that Maya archeological sites and existing villages are being transformed into a regional theme park in which local people have little decision making and are used mainly as low-cost labor, and in which Maya culture, past and present, is increasingly commodified (Gunson, 1996). According to a Quiche Maya who is an officer of one such group, "They [the directors, managers, and staff of *El Mundo Maya*] see us as an obstacle to development. . . . They just want to build big hotels for the tourists. They're the ones who benefit, not us" (quoted in Gunson, 1996). In a revealing statement made by a Belizean journalist, "If you go to a meeting of *El Mundo Maya* you won't find a Maya there, except maybe serving dinner."[4]

The most comprehensive assessment of the various human and environmental aspects of the expanding tourism industry in the region has been done for Costa Rica (Castonguay & Brown, 1993; Chant, 1992; Coffey, 1993; Evans-Pritchard, 1993; Hill, 1990; Jukofsky, 1993; Laarman & Perdue, 1989; Thrupp, 1990). Hill (1990), for example, in her discussion of the history of the tourism sector there, stresses the interdependence of national policy, natural resources, and local communities as they are integrated into the international tourism industry. She points out the paradox of the government promoting tourism as a strategy for sustainable development while at the same time being burdened with one of the world's largest per capita foreign debts. In a general way, she emphasizes the need to identify and to take into account both the winners and the losers among various stakeholders affected by the industry. Thrupp (1990) more directly brings up issues of social equity in her analysis of natural resource management initiatives and environmental predicaments in Costa Rica. She concludes that tourism development (especially the emphasis on wilderness protection through the creation of parks and preserves) primarily serves the interests of privileged upper middle-class people—primarily tourists and scientists from the North. In addition, in a context of increasing landlessness within Costa Rica, she finds incompatible the preservation of large areas of parkland for use by tourists. Further, she points out that a number of studies, in addition to her own, have found that many poor Costa Ricans are not interested in tourism and/or parks, largely because they do not have access or financial ability to enjoy such ventures. Moreover, she suggests that recent attempts to include the rural poor into environmental conservation and tourism enterprises are insufficient and often misdirected.

The effects of expanding tourism on local communities also are best documented in a Costa Rican case, in connection with the establishment of Tortuguero National Park, located along a relatively remote area of the Caribbean Coast (Bjorndal & Bolten, 1992; Bjorndal, Bolten, & Lagueux, 1993; Bjorndal & Carr, 1989; Jacobson & Lopez, 1994; Jacobson & Robles, 1992b; Lee & Snepenger, 1992; Place, 1988, 1991, 1995). Tortuguero National Park was created in 1975 to protect the last remaining major nesting beach in the Western Caribbean of the endangered green sea turtle (*Chelonia mydas*) and was one of the first national parks established in Costa Rica (Place, 1995). Despite its isolation the number of tourists to Tortuguero climbed from about 2,000 annually in the mid-1980s to 20,000 by the early 1990s (Place, 1995). In her analysis of the local-level impacts in Tortuguero, Place (1988, 1991, 1995) identifies several "costs" associated with the expansion of tourism including: increased socioeconomic differentiation of the local population; the relegation of local people to menial jobs; inflation; increased foreign ownership of local resources; related reductions in access to local beaches and other natural resources on which locals depended for their livelihoods; and environmental destruction associated with pollution and declining water quality. She also concludes that the members of the local community who benefited most from tourism were the wealthier residents who could take advantage of emerging opportunities. She determined that most income from village-based tourism was distributed among four families who operate small cabins and restaurants. She concludes that the Costa Rican government has been much more effective in protecting the park's natural environment than facilitating the successful integration of the local community into various ecotourism ventures. Lee and Snepenger (1992) document the enhanced nonlocal and/ or foreign ownership of large luxury tourist lodges that did not support the local economy, as well as the growing economic dependence of local people on the tourism industry. In 1990, 57% of households had at least one person employed directly in the industry, most at low-paying, part-time jobs. At the same time, the community was without public water, sewage, and refuse collection systems as well as a resident physician. The trend toward foreign-owned luxury tourism in Tortuguero also significantly altered village demography (Place, 1995). By 1993, several hundred new residents had immigrated into the village in search of employment in the tourism sector, in effect doubling the population of the village, while simultaneously several longtime residents left the village. These demographic changes have contributed to the individualistic character of the community in which residents relate to each other competitively rather than cooperatively, making more difficult any concerted attempt to promote community-based tourism initiatives (Place, 1995). Significant tensions exist within the community as illustrated by the recent controversy over the construction of a 30-meter-wide and 3-kilometer-long road through a biological corridor connecting Tortuguero National Park and the Barra del Colorado Wildlife Reserve. The road project was generated by the local municipality without the authorization of the national government and was intended to link the village of Tortuguero (accessible only by boat or plane) to an already existing road. The municipality maintained that it was unfair to deny local residents the right to a road that would increase residents' access to schools, medical care, markets, and other services not available in the isolated community. Environmentalists argued that the road would increase illegal logging, plantations, and hunting within the protected areas and make the park easily accessible to an uncontrollable number of tourists. Community residents were seriously divided over the issue. Some, generally those with economic interests in the tourism industry, saw the road as a potential threat to the natural resources crucial to maintaining a viable tourism industry. Farmers and others who did not benefit directly from the tourism industry tended to be more in favor of the road (Escofet, 1996; Harris, 1996). Thus, although Tortuguero National Park generally is regarded as a qualified conservation success because of the continued threats from poaching and illegal logging (Jacobson & Lopez, 1994; Jacobson

& Robles, 1992a), local-level impacts cannot be evaluated so positively. Place concludes that if tourism is to benefit local residents the means must be found to facilitate local participation in the industry. At a minimum this will require appropriate training and access to capital (Place, 1995). According to Boo (1992), many tour operators and lodge owners have come to realize that having the added dimension of local involvement is appreciated by tourists and also affords a significant marketing opportunity.

A number of studies have considered the impacts of tourism (principally ecotourism) on local communities in Belize, which has rhetorically embraced community-based tourism as a national priority (Alexander & McKenzie, 1996; Holtz & Alexander, 1995; Horwich, 1990; Horwich & Lyon, 1998; Lindberg & Enriquez, 1994; Lindberg, Enriquez, & Sproule, 1996; Norris, Wilber, & Marin, 1998). Looking primarily at ecotourism's contribution to local economies measured in terms of the percentage of households that receive income from tourist-related jobs, Lindberg and Enriquez (1994, pp. 29–32) conclude that tourism makes a significant economic contribution to communities near their Belizean case study sites, Hol Chan Marine Reserve, Cockscomb Basin Wildlife Sanctuary, and Manatee Special Development Area. Similarly, residents of the seven villages located at the Community Baboon Sanctuary earned a total of US$8,417 in 1992 from tourism at the sanctuary, although 55% of this total was earned by residents of only one community (Bruner, 1993). Unfortunately, thorough examinations of the social and cultural impacts of tourism were not included in these analyses.

Based on their involvement with the Community Baboon Sanctuary (CBS) since its founding, Horwich and Lyon (1998) identify several problems associated with community-based tourism development that could have been ameliorated had the community been more involved with the sanctuary since its inception. These problems included continuous battle for control of CBS and its financial benefits, personnel problems, mismanagement of funds, lack of record keeping and other poor management practices, and lack of financial accountability. Moreover, the CBS engendered an unproductive competitive attitude between villages and participants as well as facilitated the spread of drug (crack cocaine) and alcohol problems. Currently, the CBS also is at risk due to the emergence of noncommunity-based tourism enterprises in the area. Competition from noncommunity-based tourist enterprises also is a factor in the community-based efforts in the Toledo region of Belize (Norris et al., 1998). Norris et al. suggest several steps necessary for effective community-based efforts in tourism and conservation. The most important of these is integrating economic benefits for the local community with environmental conservation goals. That serious local repercussions can occur in Costa Rica and Belize, by most measures the most affluent and democratic countries in the region, points to the need to examine similar issues in other far less prosperous and less democratic areas of Central America, such as Honduras.

Although the above studies do not explicitly examine the consequences of employment in tourism on gender arrangements, such an investigation was carried out in Barbados (Levy & Lerch, 1991). The results have implications for the Bay Islands given that the Afro-Antillean population of the Bay Islands is part of a similar cultural and social milieu. Levy and Lerch show that women tourism workers in Barbados tend to be in lower status, lower paid, and more temporary jobs and that they must often juggle the demands of domestic and wage labor. Moreover, they conclude that women participate in larger and more complex financial and social networks than do men. Finally, the authors advise that women's participation in the industry would be enhanced with private and public programs designed to provide flexible work hours, increased training, and enhanced support for women entrepreneurs.

Community Participation, Development, and Conservation

Participatory approaches to development are in vogue once again, reanimating the community development strategies of the 1950s and 1960s and continuing the "basic needs" development philosophies of the 1970s (Annis & Hakim, 1988; Bulmer, 1985; Cernea, 1985; Cernea, 1992; Chambers, 1993, 1994a, 1994b; Chambers & McBeth, 1992; Christensen & Robinson, 1980; Cohen & Uphoff, 1977; Goodenough, 1966; Rahnema, 1993; Roberts, 1979; Schwartz, 1981). Although rooted in earlier paradigms, local or community participation acquired enhanced importance during the 1970s as disenchantment with expensive, large-scale, and top-down development programs grew. Local participation was linked to a new regard for the rural poor, many of whom had not benefited from the prevailing development paradigm. The approach was bolstered by the so-called McNamara Doctrine of the World Bank and the New Directions Mandate of the USAID that were part of a broader burgeoning of ideas and practices aimed at defining and implementing social change by, and with, the people affected and in accordance with their wishes. Ensuing policies, programs, and projects focused on the poor majority in developing nations and on alternatives to capital-intensive development efforts that primarily benefited the elite and the urban, industrial sector (Horowitz & Painter, 1986). Development agencies postulated that local communities had to be actively involved in designing and implementing programs if the poor were to benefit. Development practitioners such as Robert Chambers and Norman Uphoff were at the forefront in advocating local participation in development (e.g., Chambers, 1983; Uphoff, 1985). Since then, local participation has been used as a vehicle in many avenues of Third World development including agriculture, forestry, water management, education, and health. However, despite the expanding number of projects and the considerable rhetoric devoted to local participation, the reality often was quite the contrary. Many rural development efforts continued to incorporate very little meaningful participation by local populations. In many instances under the precept "local participation," external agencies continued to design and manage projects while the local community merely "participated" in their implementation. Recently, environmental conservationists, who perceive in local participation a potential means of achieving conservation goals, have applied the concept in communities, especially those composed of indigenous peoples living in, or adjacent to, national parks and other protected areas (Ghimire & Pimbert, 1997; McNeely, 1995; Primack, 1998; Western, Wright, & Strum, 1994).

In its current renaissance, participatory development often is linked to the rise of popular social movements and civil society and to processes of democratization (Chambers, 1995; Love, 1991). Some promote local participation in development as a means of countering dwindling international foreign assistance while others claim the superiority of "local" communities to sustain natural resources and the livelihoods of the poor (Chambers, 1995). Belief in the advantages of participatory development has given rise to a proliferation of "participation initiatives" by major international development agencies including the Inter-American Foundation (IAF), the Canadian International Development Agency (CIDA), the International Fund for Agricultural Development (IFAD), the IDB, the Organization for Economic Cooperation and Development (OECD), the United Nations Development Programme (UNDP), the USAID, and the World Bank. These institutions have produced a large number of handbooks aimed at facilitating community participation as well as methodologies for conducting related participatory research (Inter-American Development Bank [IDB], 1997b; World Bank, 1996).

Ideally, participation implies the power of local people to influence the design, implementation, monitoring, and evaluation of development efforts that affect their lives and resources. However, similar to community development approaches of the past, participation often remains central to the rhetoric of agencies, institutions, and government without generating meaningful local involvement. Although "participatory development" may be ubiquitously advocated both as a philosophy and as a mode of development, significant gaps remain between rhetoric and practice, and it may be in danger of becoming just the latest development fad (Rahnema, 1993).

While achieving meaningful local participation in development initiatives presents considerable challenges, these obstacles are exacerbated when combined with conservation objectives. Notwithstanding the difficulties, local, community-based conservation is now at the center of conservationist thinking. Many of the same international donor agencies that embraced the concept of "local participation," along with international environmental organizations (e.g., World Wildlife Fund [WWF], Conservation International [CI], and the Nature Conservancy [NC]) and private foundations (e.g., Ford Foundation and the MacArthur Foundation), have espoused the rhetoric, policy, and practice of community-based conservation.

Despite the enthusiasm, locally managed community-based conservation only recently has been invoked in conservation programs, and considerable debate exists about how it can be accomplished or how it should be evaluated. There may be highly contested compromises between development and environmental goals, especially in contexts of widespread poverty and pressing short-term needs (Western & Wright, 1994). In addition, both community-based development and conservation strategies may directly conflict with the interests of the state and those of local and national elite. Often, conservation groups augment the capacity of Third World states or state agencies to protect fragile and critical environments and resources. Some states, however, co-opt the conservation concerns of environmental groups as a means of strengthening state control over productive natural resources. A number of studies have documented how Third World states, often in collaboration with local and national elite, have used conservation ideology to justify coercion in the name of conservation—often by using violence (Hitchcock, 1995; Neumann, 1992; Peluso, 1992, 1993; Peluso, Vandergeest, & Potter, 1995; Vandergeest, 1996; Vandergeest & Peluso, 1995). The state's mandate to protect natural resources and its monopolization of legitimate violence combine to facilitate social control. Sanctioned violence in the name of resource defense also facilitates the control of people, especially recalcitrant, marginal, and minority groups who challenge the state's claims to resources as well as authority in other matters.

Some international environmental organizations, while advocating community-based approaches, may also justify (sometimes inadvertently) coercive protective measures on the basis of their anticipated outcomes—such as the preservation of biodiversity, forests, coral reefs, endangered species, and so forth. This is more apt to occur in situations where the power relations and politics of environmental conservation are overlooked or minimized. Conservation initiatives, including such actions as the establishment of protected areas, national parks, marine reserves, and other restricted zones, essentially involve the establishment of new social structures and mechanisms for controlling the allocation, access, and use of natural resources (Little, 1994).

These concerns raise a number of key questions, foremost of which are: Who participates? and What constitutes participation? These core questions lead, in turn, to debates over various meanings of "community" and "local"; then to an examination of the expanding roles of NGOs in participatory development and conservation initiatives; and finally to considerations of "representation" and the "accountability" of individuals and organizations to act as spokespersons for particular communities or segments of those communities.

Who Participates? Issues of Locality and Community

Even though the terms "local" and "community" frequently are central to discussions of participation, there is no consensus about their meanings (Schwartz, Deruyttere, Huntley, Stonich, & Kottak, 1996). Increasingly, however, realistic assessments of what constitutes the "local" and the "community" are viewed as essential to meaningful local-level participation (Little, 1994). Moreover, while participatory development is assumed to take place among local populations, focusing exclusively on the "local" is seen as problematic for several reasons. Although the "local" has its own reality embedded in a specific place and time, this reality always is part of wider spatial, social, temporal, and other spheres. The local community is intimately connected with external actors at many levels including the national, international, and transnational. The need to conceptualize the "local" in terms of linkages and flows within these broader arenas is being recognized as fundamental to effective participation (Li, 1996; Rahnema, 1993).

Similarly, use of the term "community" requires careful examination because participation is contingent upon assumptions made about communities. Yet, according to Peter Little, "Community is a commonly misused term that can invoke a false sense of tradition, homogeneity, and consensus. Anthropological research during the last twenty years has confirmed that most rural communities are not free of conflict nor are they homogeneous" (1994). Analysis of much of the existing literature on local participation and conservation reveals an underlying assumption of the meaning of "community" as consisting of small, spatially bounded, socially homogeneous groups using locally evolved norms to live with nature harmoniously, managing resources sustainably and equitably (Ascher, 1995; Ghimire & Pimbert, 1997; Stevens, 1997; Western et al., 1994). Despite considerable empirical evidence that communities and indigenous peoples have complex histories and behaviors that do not necessarily preclude overexploitation and destruction of natural resources, a recent compendium of projects on community-based conservation begins with, "Communities down the millennia have developed elaborate rituals and practices to limit offtake levels, restrict access to critical resources, and distribute harvests" (Western et al., 1994). Similarly, another recent study is introduced with, "The survival and quality of forests in most developing countries depend on the strength of community forest organizations formed by the people traditionally involved in forest use" (Ascher, 1995). Indigenous, folk, local communities now appear to be the heroes of conservation rather than the destroyers of nature as they were earlier (Lynch & Talbott, 1995).

Such visions of community provide its advocates substantial symbolic means to pose alternatives to state or market-oriented remedies for conservation. However, few existing communities conform to this commonly held vision, and a number of studies have shown that internal differentiation within communities often presents formidable obstacles, as well as potential incentives, to effective participation and conservation (Brown & Wyckoff-Baird, 1992; Kottak, 1995). Unwarranted adherence to the concept of community as homogeneous obscures the identification of the multiple social interest groups and legitimate stakeholders that exist within communities as well as the differential access to power, resources, and influence that various actors enjoy. Moreover, it obfuscates an examination of the processes of collaboration and coalition building engaged in by various stakeholders in most development and conservation situations. Here the structure of power relations among various community stakeholders is very relevant because those relations can not only affect the outcome of coalition building but also preclude collaboration from being initiated.

Overcoming stereotypical notions of "community" in order to enhance local participation is particularly essential, as well as difficult, in tourism contexts. In *Imagined Communities*, Benedict Anderson (1991) explains how "communities" exist principally in the imaginations of scholars, foreigners, patriots, and (for purposes here) tourists, NGOs, developers, and development/conservation specialists. Stereotypes persist, in part, because of these imaginings. The concept of the "imagined community" is essential to the tourist industry regardless of the locale being promoted. One need only look at any travel magazine, brochure, World Wide Web site, or other advertising medium to see this. Tourism advertising generally attempts to obscure reality by selectively focusing on the charming, the beautiful, or some other marketable quality of a tourist destination. When local people are portrayed at all, they usually are shown as quaint or picturesque components of the place being advertised. In an attempt to sell tourist places to potential consumers, international tourist advertising frequently depicts Third World societies in an unrealistic, and often demeaning, manner, substituting an imagery of paradise for any sense of reality (R. Britton, 1979; Enloe, 1989). This idealized imagery clearly is founded on the economic interests of promoters as well as on the desires of consumers. Environmental conservation also figures prominently in the advertising strategies of public and private sector stakeholders concerned with promoting their nations, locales, or facilities as environmentally friendly, ecotourism destinations.

Tourism communities are imagined not only through advertising but also through the reports and project documents generated by the myriad of consultants, government officials, and development planners concerned with the potential of promoting tourism in a specific locale. These too represent reality from specific perspectives, and can be used to legitimize and justify particular tourism development policies and projects. For example, the project documents generated in connection with *El Mundo Maya* emphasize the regions' acute poverty, undernutrition, and illiteracy. These depictions, which differ significantly from the images of the region provided to tourists, are used to legitimize tourism development initiatives. To date, the extent to which such contending representations of reality and "imagined tourism communities" affect development and conservation programs largely remains unexamined.

The Role of NGOs: Issues of Representation and Accountability

Efforts to promote participatory development and conservation frequently are dependent on the existence of local institutions and/or NGOs that are important stakeholders at the community level (Little, 1994). In the prevailing international political context that includes restricting the role of the state and enhancing civil society, combined with sharp declines in foreign assistance, the prevalent strategy of aid donors has been to work through NGOs. This has contributed to a proliferation of these organizations at the local as well as at the national and international level (M. Edwards & Hulme, 1992a, 1992b, 1996a; Hulme, 1994; Princen & Finger, 1994). This increase has stimulated considerable research on the role of NGOs in participatory development. This work has demonstrated their diversity in terms of ideologies, values, structures, goals, objectives, and strategies. Some NGOs have been shown to be narrowly focused and short lived while others have grown into effective transnational players, gaining access to international organizations and influencing political agendas and outcomes. Burgeoning studies of NGOs have demonstrated how they have been able to link the local and the global in new ways and how they have created and exploited new niches in political action and diplomacy (Princen & Finger, 1994).

Recent studies also have raised serious concerns over issues of representation, accountability, and evaluation (M. Edwards & Hulme, 1992b, 1996b; Uphoff, 1996). While some NGOs may attempt to be truly representative of the people they purport to serve, others may act as agents of powerful local and extra-local stakeholders and interest groups. Given the heterogeneity that exists within most communities, it is crucial that the potential of NGOs in achieving effective participatory development and conservation be thoroughly assessed within the context of contending community and extra-local stakeholders. Many criticisms also have been raised concerning the power and role of international environmental NGOs, which have been particularly cited for attempting to implement First World perspectives on environmental problems and conservation on the Third World (Guha & Martinez-Alier, 1997; PANOS, 1995). As discussed earlier, these may result in so-called coercive conservation efforts.

Community-Based Tourism Development

The inability of local people to participate in, and to benefit from, the expansion of tourism into their locales is well documented ("Breaking Out of the Tourist Trap—Part One," 1990; "Breaking Out of the Tourist Trap—Part Two," 1990; "The Touris Trap—Who's Getting Caught," 1982; Wells, Brandon, & Hannah, 1992; West & Brechin, 1991). Even in

Costa Rica and the Galapagos Islands in Ecuador, where tourism (especially ecotourism) has been unusually successful, local communities have little capacity to provide the goods and services tourists demand and have gained little from tourism development (Southgate, 1998).[5] In response to this deficiency, a number of models for participatory, community-based tourism development have been suggested (Blank, 1989; Jamal & Getz, 1995; Murphy, 1985; Reed, 1997; Selin & Beason, 1991). Much recent research on community tourism, however, has a distinctly North American bias and often is based on the assumption that stakeholders have relatively equal access to resources and power (Murphy, 1985). As such, these studies have limited utility for application in the Third World where power among relevant stakeholders can be very asymmetrical and protected by force, and where critical resources and political networks often are controlled by the elite. Some researchers, however (Blank, 1989; Jamal & Getz, 1995; Reed, 1997), do stress the importance of considering the role of power relations in facilitating and hindering community-based tourism. For example, Jamal and Getz (1995, p. 190) urge that power relations be addressed at every stage of the collaborative process from problem framework through implementation. They offer recommendations for facilitating participation through sharing, allotting, and/or redistributing power. While such studies conclude that power relations are an integral element in establishing effective community-based tourism, they also point out that attempts to balance or disperse power among stakeholders is likely to be highly contested. Traditional power-holding groups may resist its redistribution, thereby hindering efforts aimed at collaboration among all legitimate stakeholders within a community. These relations are not simply obstacles to be overcome by creating better mechanisms or facilitating actions but should be considered as endemic to tourism development processes—as an explanatory variable that demonstrates why participation and collaboration succeed or fail (Reed, 1997).

The Political Ecology of Tourism and Conservation

Most social scientists now assume that conflict is inherent in most types of development involving resource use or conservation, especially when the stakes are high or when "winners" and "losers" clearly are present. Different social interest groups, or "stakeholders"—segments of the local "community" including rich and poor, women and men, ethnic groups, private companies, the state, international conservation groups, NGOs, and others—will have varied interests in resource use and conservation. While aims may be complementary at times, in many cases they are potentially or actively conflictive. Essentially, participation is a political process involving contestation and conflict among different people with diverse power, interests, and claims rather than a methodology or set of facilitating techniques. This general pattern should influence how local participation is structured and point to the different interest groups that must participate in the development and conservation activities.

Recent advances in political ecology are relevant to understanding the linkages between development, local participation, environmental destruction, and conservation in contexts of complex power relations (Blaikie & Brookfield, 1987; Schmink & Wood, 1987). Since the 1970s, political ecology has advanced as an interdisciplinary approach with which to analyze complex human–environmental interactions, especially those related to economic development in the Third World (Bryant, 1992; Peet & Watts, 1993). The well-known anthropologist, Eric Wolf, was among the first to use the term "political ecology" in his critique of cultural ecology and ecological anthropology in which he emphasized the need to contextualize local ecological realities within the broader political economy (Wolf, 1972). Although efforts to define the evolving field of political ecology are incomplete, researchers generally use the political ecology framework to understand how environmental and political forces interact to affect social and environmental changes through the actions of various social actors operating at different scales (Bryant, 1992). Scholars using this perspective typically couch their arguments in opposition to one or more of three popular, and often interrelated, explanations: overpopulation, economic irrationality, and technological inadequacy (Blaikie, 1985; Painter & Durham, 1995b; Stonich, 1989).

Embraced by anthropologists, geographers, political scientists, and historians, among others, political ecology is closely associated with the influence of Blaikie and Brookfield (1987) for whom political ecology combines a broadly defined political economy with the concerns of ecology. Political ecological analysis generally consists of an explanation of human–environmental interactions linked through different scales from the international/global through the local (Blaikie & Brookfield, 1987). Central to the analysis is the relative power of relevant social actors (stakeholders) that affect access to, and management of, natural resources. These stakeholders are then linked within and among levels of analysis through relations of power (Peet & Watts, 1993; Stonich, 1993). Political ecological analysis frequently integrates a number of essential components. First, an assessment of the various contested ideologies that directs the use of resources and influences which stakeholders benefit from and which are disadvantaged by those ideologies. Also vital is a determination of the various international interests involved, including donor agencies, organizations, and private investors that promote particular patterns of natural resource use. Increasingly of concern is the function of the global economy in advancing specific patterns in access to and use of natural resources. Crucial as well is the role of the state, particularly in terms of determining and implementing policies that favor the interests of certain social actors over those of others. Also central to the analysis is the relationship of class, ethnic, and gender structures to conflicts over access to productive resources; the interrelations among local resource users and groups of society who affect resource use; and diversity in the decisions of local resource managers (e.g., Rocheleau, Slayter, & Wangari, 1996; Stonich, 1993). Finally, political ecologists also agree on the significant role of historical analysis in understanding the development of social and ecological relations and their subsequent links to environmental degradation (Blaikie, 1985; Blaikie & Brookfield, 1987; Guha, 1990; Peluso, 1992; Stonich, 1993). Current efforts to develop a theory of political ecology center around understanding the ways in which the environmental arena reflects the structured relations of power and inequality in contemporary societies more broadly and in establishing the articulations between "the local" (however that might be conceptualized) and globalizing processes. Of significance here is the increased integration of various discursive approaches into political ecological analysis.

One major focus of research using a political ecology approach has emphasized human impoverishment and environmental destruction stemming from dominant development models (Faber, 1992; Little & Horowitz, 1987; Painter & Durham, 1995a; Stonich, 1989). A number of findings from these studies potentially can help understand deteriorating human and environmental conditions in other development contexts—including tourism development. First, environmental destruction identified with the economic production systems of the poor usually is an outcome of their impoverishment, either absolutely or relatively to other social classes. Impoverishment often is related to diminished access to land and other natural resources and to increased repression and violence at the hands of state authorities and more powerful individual and corporate interests engaged in land speculation. Second, as a consequence of their vulnerability and lack of power, smallholder producers often have received a disproportionate share of the blame for environmental decline (Stonich, 1989). In contrast, political ecological research has demonstrated that a great deal of land and other natural resources have been degraded by the activities of more powerful private, public, and corporate interests (Stonich, 1989, 1993). Large-scale enterprises that have acted destructively frequently have been granted land on concessionary terms by the state. This allows these more powerful stakeholders to treat land as a low-cost input, and makes it more economical to move elsewhere after the environment is degraded rather than try to conserve natural resources. Third, the same policies and practices that result in wealthy interests receiving land on favorable terms are responsible for the impoverishment of smallholders, because such policies institutionalize and exacerbate unequal access to resources. In sum, the political ecology approach applied to Third World development has shown that the crucial issue underlying environmental destruction and human poverty is blatant inequality in access to resources within a socially institutionalized context (Painter & Durham, 1995a).

Political ecological analysis provides the means to integrate several areas of tourism research, particularly studies done from the perspective of political economy and those concerned with the relationships between tourism and environmental quality. It also provides a potential framework for productively integrating tourism and development studies that heretofore have had only tenuous linkages (Brohman, 1996; Harrison, 1996). Although studies of tourism from an explicitly political ecological perspective are few, political economic analysis of international tourism has been a major approach (S. Britton, 1982, 1987, 1989; Brohman, 1996; Enloe, 1989; Lanfant & Graburn, 1992; Pleumarom, 1994). These studies point out a number of important characteristics associated with the expansion of tourism in the Third World that are central elements of political ecological analysis as well. These include the major part played by development assistance from multilateral and bilateral donors such as the World Bank, the United Nations, and regional development banks in promoting tourism development (Brohman, 1996; Lanfant & Graburn, 1992; Pleumarom, 1994); the interconnections among excessive foreign ownership, vertically integrated transnational tourism corporations, and foreign exchange leakages (S. Britton & Clarke, 1987; Brohman, 1996); the importance of Third World states in promoting tourism development as a means to improve and diversify economies through increased foreign exchange and investments (S. Britton, 1982; S. Britton & Clarke, 1987; Brohman, 1996); the linkages among various social actors (stakeholders) at various levels of analysis (scales) (S. Britton & Clarke, 1987; Brohman, 1996); the relative costs and benefits of tourism development along with the creation and/or exacerbation of existing social and spatial inequities (Brohman, 1996; Eadington & Smith, 1992; Tsartas, 1992); and growing social conflicts between stakeholders over control of local resources (S. Britton & Clarke, 1987; Brohman, 1996; Dieke, 1993; Oliver-Smith, Arrones, & Arcal, 1989; Poirier & Wright, 1993).

Over the last two decades, a burgeoning number of studies have focused on the impacts of tourism development on environmental quality, including effects related to diminished biodiversity, erosion, pollution, and degradation of water and other natural resources (Cohen, 1978; F. Edwards, 1988; Green & Hunter, 1992; Hunter & Green, 1995; Island Resources Foundation, 1996; Lindberg, 1991; Mathieson & Wall, 1982; Mieczkowski, 1995; Miller & Auyong, 1990, 1991; Nelson, Butler, & Wall, 1993; Pattullo, 1997; Pearce, 1989; Pigram, 1980; Trigano, 1984; United Nations Environment Programme: Industry and Environment, 1995; Wilkinson, 1989; Wong, 1993). Although the impetus for much of this research has been to document and understand instances of environmental destruction emanating from tourism development, there is no consensus among researchers that tourism is either essentially destructive or conservative of the environment. The more appropriate questions may be: Under what circumstances is tourism conservative or destructive to the environment? And what can be done to ameliorate or eliminate the environmental costs of tourism?

Considerable attention has been paid to the environmental consequences of tourism on coastal and marine areas and on small islands (Briguglio, Archer, Jafari, & Wall, 1996; Briguglio, Butler, Harrison, & Filho, 1996; Island Resources Foundation, 1996; Miller & Auyong, 1990, 1991; Wong, 1993). The Caribbean Environment Program of the United Nations Environment Program recently implemented a regional project to determine the level of coastal degradation in the Wider Caribbean and to promote actions to correct the environmental consequences of the tourism industry on coastal and marine resources (Island Resources Foundation, 1996).[6] Implemented through the Island Resources Foundation, the principal environmental costs identified by the study were declines in water quality and quantity, contamination from lack of adequate sewage and solid waste disposal facilities, loss of nonrenewable resources from sand and coral mining, and overharvesting of renewable resources including finfish, shellfish, mangroves, and corals. The study concluded that:

> Tourism impacts in the Wider Caribbean are extremely diverse, depending on differences among state economies, the relative and absolute size of the tourism sector, the rate of growth of tourism, and the nature of the tourism facilities involved . . . environmental degradation effects from tourism facilities in the coastal area are generally small, often dispersed, critically placed, and multi-faceted. Resolution of these effects are addressed by marshaling information and expertise from a wide range of technical resources in both the private and the public sector. (Island Resources Foundation, 1996)

Political ecology provides the means to conceptually and methodologically integrate the human and environmental consequences of tourism development and conservation strategies into a single analytical framework and to disaggregate these impacts by relevant social actors or stakeholders within the existing structure and relations of power. Political ecological analysis also illuminates the factors that are essential to effective local community participation by: 1) identifying the major interest groups or stakeholders; 2) examining the motives and behaviors that affect the use of resources by diverse interest groups; 3) exposing and confronting actual and potential conflicts among stakeholders; and 4) identifying potential winners and losers as a result of current or planned development and conservation initiatives.

The Scheme of This Book

The remainder of this book parallels political ecological analysis. Chapter 2 examines how the historical legacy of the Bay Islands set the stage for current patterns of tourism development, conflict, and conservation. It begins with a brief summary of the more than 400 years of Anglo-Hispanic conflict in the Western Caribbean involving the Bay Islands. It goes on to discuss the Bay Islands in the context of emerging global, regional, and national political economies and includes a history of "development" in the islands. In this context, it focuses on the emergence of the islands as ethnically and cultural diverse and the associated cultural and material tensions and conflicts that arose during this time. The chapter is especially concerned with the gradual evolution of a separate ethnic and cultural identity among the islands' black, Afro-Caribbean people.

Chapter 3 centers on the development of tourism on the islands. It first discusses the creation of the image of the Bay Islands as a tourist destination through the percep- tions, tales, and reports of adventurers, travelers, and others that visited the islands from the 1500s through the late-20th century. In this context, it details the emergence of the modern tourism sector beginning in the 1960s and the dynamic patterns in the con- temporary tourism industry. It shows the evolution of the islands from primarily an adventure tourism destination to one that is much more diverse and includes a variety of new forms of alternative tourism (e.g., ecotourism, academic/scientific, cultural, nature, diving, etc.) as well as mass tourism. The chapter is particularly concerned with the contradictions that accompany this contending array of types of tourism.

Chapter 4 links the boom in the tourism sector with its human demographic and environmental consequences within the context of ongoing conservation efforts. It begins with discussions of the legal and regulatory framework affecting the islands' environment and natural resources along with major conservation efforts. It goes on to introduce the perspectives of the islands' residents on the major environmental and other problems they currently confront. Within this background, it summarizes current patterns in human demography and settlement. It discusses critical demographic changes emanating from the significant increase in the human population due to the migration of ladinos from the Honduran mainland and the skyrocketing increase in the number of international tourists. It then reviews the impact of tourism development and these demographic changes on the islands' environment and resources, especially the effects on critical habitats, wildlife, forests, reefs, fresh/seawater, and other marine resources.

Chapter 5 examines the human consequences of the expanding tourism industry by divisions of nationality, ethnicity, class, and gender. It demonstrates the relative benefits and costs arising from current patterns of tourism in three communities on Roatán, the largest of the Bay Islands. It examines the profound effect of the expanding tourist industry on household economic strategies, consumption patterns, diet, nutrition, and health.

Chapter 6 synthesizes the analyses in previous chapters by specifying obstacles and incentives to community participation in development and conservation efforts. It begins with a discussion of the fundamental contradictions between recent tourism development and conservation initiatives. It continues with the identification of relevant local, national, and international stakeholders, including grassroots groups, NGOs, international donors, and conservation organizations. It then examines the associated social, ethnic, cultural, and economic conflicts among stakeholders over tourism and access to natural resources and to potential means of resolving conflicts. Particularly important is an examination of the relative power of these interest groups and the formation of contending coalitions around power relations. It then evaluates recent and ongoing "local" development and conservation efforts formulated by island-based NGOs and critiques the participatory strategies included in major internationally funded conservation projects. The chapter then evaluates the potential of the recently enacted Bay Islands National Marine Park to enhance development and conservation. The chapter culminates with a series of recommendations designed to resolve conflicts and move toward effective community-based tourism development and conservation. This discussion includes the feasibility of emergent ethnically based grassroots organizations and NGOs in enabling local participation in development and conservation initiatives.

Chapter 7 extends the analyses to consider obstacles to community-based tourism development and conservation in the Bay Islands and in the broader Central American and Third World context. It begins with a summary discussion of the political ecology of tourism and conservation in the Bay Islands. It then identifies major obstacles to community-based tourism development and conservation, and emphasizes the importance of taking into consideration history, existing power relations, and cultural survival in order to promote and democratize community participation. It evaluates the viability of tourism as a principal economic growth strategy in the Bay Islands, Honduras, and in Central America more generally, given the nature of the global economy and the presence of consequential constraints. The chapter concludes with a series of recommendations for a more informed and just tourism and conservation policy.

Notes

[1]Panama is not included in this graph for various reasons. First, in large part because of the presence of the Panama Canal, the Panamanian economy is very different from the economies of the rest of Central America, which are highly dependent on the export of a few primary agricultural commodities. Also travel/tourism statistics for Panama generally include the expenditures by U.S. military personnel and their dependents in the Canal Zone. These factors together distort the relationship between tourism receipts and total export receipts.

[2]With its own rapidly growing tourism industry, Costa Rica has not participated in joint tourism promotions with its Central American neighbors to any great extent.

[3]For comprehensive analyses of the repercussions of previous development efforts in Central America emphasizing the promotion of traditional and nontraditional agriculture see Conroy, Murray, and Rosset (1996), Thrupp (1995), and Williams (1986). For the Honduran case see Stonich (1989, 1991, 1992, 1993, 1995).

[4]For an important interdisciplinary perspective on the effects of tourism on the Maya of Quintana Roo, Mexico see especially Pi-Sunyer and Thomas (1997).

[5]Studies from Costa Rica and the Galapagos Islands show that even though under certain circumstances nature-based tourism can make significant contributions to the national economies, tourism still has not generated sufficient revenues for national park services to cover the costs of maintaining the parks they manage.

[6]For purposes of this study the "Wider Caribbean" was defined to include Caribbean Island states (Cayman Islands, Netherlands Antilles, Anguilla, Turks & Caicos, Aruba, Montserrat, British Virgin Islands, Antigua & Baruda, US Virgin Islands, Bahamas, St. Kitts & Nevis, Barbados, St. Lucia, Martinique, Guadeloupe, Grenada, St. Vincent & Grenadins, Dominica, Jamaica, Dominican Repubic, Puerto Rico, Trinidad & Tobago, Cuba, Haiti), Central American countries (Belize, Costa Rica, Panama, Nicaragua, Honduras, Guatemala), South American countries (Surinam, Guyana, Colombia, Venezuela, French Guyana), Mexico, and the U.S. Gulf Coast.

Chapter 2

The Historical Legacy: The Emergence of Bay Islander Identity

> We don't know where you came from. . . . We don't know who you are. . . . You have no history. (Honduran Minister of Culture, during a meeting with Bay Islanders in 1996)

> Is it fair to say that we are becoming strangers in our own land, while a wave of non-islanders are drowning our culture and threatening our identity? We must rise above the wave and claim the rights as a people with dignity and pride in our society. (Native Bay Islanders Professionals and Labourers Association [NABIPLA], 1995)

The statement by the Honduran Minister of Culture reflects the prevailing views held by Spanish-speaking Hondurans regarding Bay Islanders—that they are neither "Honduran" nor "indigenous." Although the GOH is mandated by its constitution to protect and preserve the cultures of its indigenous peoples, the minister's statement implies that the GOH does not recognize that responsibility in the case of the Bay Islanders. If the minister is alluding to the non-Hispanic and non-Central American origin of Bay Islanders' identity he is accurate, although it is quite incorrect to say that Bay Islanders have "no history." Like many peoples of the Caribbean they are a mix of relocated peoples—in this case with roots in the Cayman Islands, Belize, Jamaica, and elsewhere.

The Bay Islands are among the diminishing number of English-speaking enclaves in the Western Caribbean that lie on the periphery of Spanish-speaking Latin America.[1] They are part of the Spanish Main, that region of the Caribbean that was the nucleus of the Spanish empire, the site of the first tragic confrontations between Europeans and Native Americans, and the locus of centuries of violent conflicts among European powers (Sauer, 1966). Bay Islanders' identity has emerged in this marginality, shaped, in part, in terms of their relations to more powerful Spanish and subsequent Honduran mainland forces. Throughout the 19th century, well after they were formally incorporated into the Honduran national territory, the Bay Islands effectively persisted as a relatively autonomous economic and cultural entity. Despite the efforts of the GOH to extend its control throughout this century, the native people of the islands continue to regard themselves as having an ethnic and cultural identity that is quite distinct from the Spanish-speaking majority.

Geographical Setting

The Bay Islands are located in the western Caribbean Sea from 30 to 64 km north of mainland Honduras (Figure 2.1). The three major islands, Roatán (127 km²), Guanaja (56 km²), and Utila (42 km²) form a crescent that includes three smaller islands, Helene, Morat, and Barbareta, and 52 tiny keys with a total land area of approximately 258 km². The archipelago is circumscribed by spectacularly beautiful and diverse coral reefs that attract divers, snorkelers, and sport fishermen. In addition, the islands' wetlands and forests are home to a rich variety of wildlife including more than 120 species of resident and migratory birds that also have significant tourist appeal (Vega et al., 1993).

The Bay Islands became Honduras' most northern and sole insular department on March 14, 1872. The department is divided into four municipalities: the municipality of Roatán consists of the western half of the island of Roatán; José Santos Guardiola encompasses the eastern part of the island of Roatán and the small islands of Helene, Morat, and Barbareta; Utila comprises the island of Utila and adjacent keys; and the municipality of Guanaja includes the island of Guanaja and its nearby keys (Vega et al., 1993).

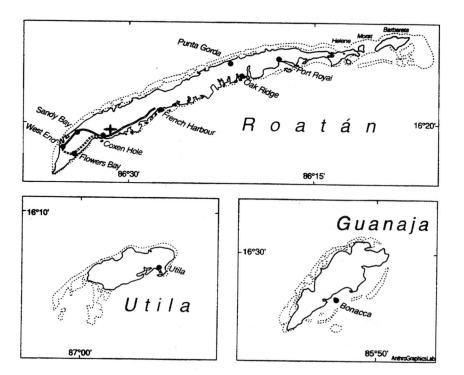

Figure 2.1. Map of Roatán, Utila, and Guanaja.

The Bay Islands are located south of the Bartlett Trough and rest upon the Bonacca Ridge, a discontinuous, undersea extension of the *Sierra de Omoa*, a mainland mountain range. Moving eastward from the low swampy areas of Utila to Roatán and Guanaja, the terrain grows steeper, more diverse in vegetation and wildlife, and more plentiful in freshwater resources. The predominant topographical characteristic of the islands is its many steep slopes. While most level areas of the islands are swampy, the greater parts of the islands possess slopes between 30% and 75% with some parts attaining slopes of 90%. The largest island, Roatán, has an elongated shape with a central ridge that divides the water drainage into north-facing and south-facing slopes. The watersheds are steep, narrow, and short. These characteristics result in swift, powerful currents that produce little standing water within the island and carry the majority of sediment directly to the sea (Vega et al., 1993).

Bioclimatically the islands do not differ significantly from one another. The islands all are located in the wet, subtropical forest life zone (Koppen terminology) with rainfall of at least 2,000 mm per year. The islands' only meteorological station on Guanaja reports a mean annual temperature of 27.5°C (range 25-29°C) over a 38-year period and an annual mean precipitation of 2,571 mm. The islands have marked dry and rainy seasons. While less than 100 mm of precipitation generally falls from February through June, the highest rainfall (46% of total annual precipitation) occurs during October and November (Vega et al., 1993). Because the islands lie in the trade wind belt, wind direction generally is from the east to southeast and wind velocity from 19 to 26 miles per hour. However, significant seasonal variation can occur. In August periods of up to 5 days of dead calm are common, while each winter about five North American cold fronts (*nortes*) reach the Bay of Honduras, bringing changes in wind direction to the north and west along with prolonged rainfall.

Hurricane Mitch was the latest of about 20 hurricanes that have affected the islands over the last century, approximately one every 10 years. The islands lie outside the paths of most Caribbean storms. Due to the islands' position relative to the mainland mountain barriers and the northwestward and northward path of most Caribbean storms, many hurricanes and tropical storms lose significant strength over mainland Honduras before striking the islands. The most destructive storms, such as Hurricane Francelia in September 1969 and Hurricane Mitch in October 1998, strike the islands from the open ocean.

Extensive fringing reefs enclose much of Roatán and Guanaja. The reefs provide food for a diverse array of sea creatures, protect the shores from wave action, and circumscribe relatively quiet lagoons such as at French Cay and Port Royal on Roatán and along the south coast of Guanaja. Within the reefs, depths vary greatly but generally are sufficient for the passage of small-draft watercraft. Narrow tidal inlets frequently intersect the north-side reefs. In a few instances, the edges of these reef openings extend to the shore, their coral margins lying immediately below the surface. Only along the central part of the south coast of Roatán where submerged valleys exist do deep waters reach the shore. It was in these areas of protected deep water and keys that the early Europeans selected sites for military posts and other early settlements. The various groups that inhabited the Bay Islands did not always settle in locations with good accessible harbors. Rather, a number of environmental, cultural, legal, and economic factors affected settlement, as will be discussed later in this chapter. Areas with good harbors, however, remain the largest urban centers and include the towns of Coxen Hole, French Harbour, and Oak Ridge, all on Roatán. Roatán, too, is the only island with extensive road and communication systems.

Spanish–Anglo Conflict in the Bay Islands

The thrilling history of the Bay Islands remains visible in prehistoric archeological sites, pirate hideaways, English fortresses, underwater shipwrecks, and an ethnically diverse population. Several distinct groups have occupied the islands at one time or another: pre-Colombian indigenous peoples most likely Paya, a group that also lived on the mainland; Spanish soldiers, pirates, and agriculturists; English buccaneers, sailors, and farmers; Garífuna (Black Caribs) from the island of St. Vincent in the eastern Caribbean who were marooned on Roatán by the British in 1797; Anglo-Caribbeans and Afro-Caribbeans from the Caymans and Belize who migrated to the islands starting in the 1830s; North American adventurers, fugitives, tourists, and retirees who began arriving around the turn of the century; Spanish-speaking mestizos/ladinos from the mainland of Honduras whose migration from the mainland has accelerated over the last two decades; and various European adventurers, castaways, travelers, tourists, and investors.

Although Columbus may not have captained the first European ship to visit the Bay Islands, he did stop there during his fourth and final voyage to the Indies (1502–1504) and accounts of his sailing provide the first known descriptions of the area. Columbus anchored off an island that he named *Isla de Pinos* (Pine Island) because of its many pines. This has been interpreted to be the island of Guanaja, where a small monument now commemorates his visit. His brother Bartholomew who went ashore briefly described a "very robust people who adore idols and live mostly from a certain white grain [maize or corn] from which they make a fine bread and the most perfect beer" (B. Columbus, 1505–1506, cited in Davidson, 1974, p. 26). Although the cultural relationships between the indigenous people of the Bay Islands and those of the mainland have been contested in the past, current thinking concurs that the aboriginal Bay Islanders were Paya and interacted quite extensively with Paya and other indigenous peoples living on the mainland.[2]

For almost 150 years after initial European contact, Spanish rule of the Bay Islands was virtually unchallenged and the islands experienced treatment similar to that of many Caribbean islands. The first known incident of slaving occurred in 1516 when Diego Velásquez sent licensed slavers to the Bay of Honduras and one of them raided the Bay Islands—killing those who resisted and capturing 300 native people. After being transported to Cuba to work in the mines, the slaves took over the slave ship in the Cuban harbor and sailed back to the Bay Islands where they attacked the Spanish garrison and forced the Spaniards to flee the islands. This incident was followed by a retaliatory raid commissioned by Velásquez that resulted in the killing of about 100 people and the capture of 400 natives from Utila. It was several years before the islands were again raided. By then, agriculture was replacing mining as the most important economic activity in the Caribbean and the Spanish government began questioning the consequences of eliminating native peoples and the labor shortages brought about by that policy. In 1516, Cardinal Cisneros initiated the Indian reform movement, the immediate result of which was the importation of African slaves to America (Sauer, 1966). This "reform" period was short-lived, and by 1520 Espanola decreed that all native peoples, on non-Christian islands (with a few exceptions) could be enslaved (Figueroa, 1520, cited in Davidson, 1974, p. 33). In the 1520s the islands were again subject to slaving raids that captured island peoples "for work in the mines, sugar cane, and fields, and to serve as shepherds" in Cuba (Gomara, 1966). Unlike many peoples of the Caribbean, the indigenous people of the Bay Islands survived the conquest to participate in the Spanish colonial system. Scant evidence suggests that after an initial period of sharp depopulation, the population stabilized at about 400 by 1639 (Davidson, 1974, p. 34). Under the Spanish *encomienda* system, the major elements of the indigenous economy—agriculture, fishing, and trade—persisted, with the addition of the production of crafts to meet Spanish needs (Davidson, 1974). By 1582, the islands produced sufficient foodstuffs beyond what was needed locally. Commodities raised on the islands, including corn, pork, chickens, plantains, pineapples, and yams, were transported to the major Spanish ports of Trujillo and Puerto Caballos (Puerto Cortez) on the mainland for use as provisions for return voyages to Europe (Davidson, 1974, p. 38).

The *Archipelago de las Guanajas* (the Bay Islands) was formally incorporated into the province of Honduras in 1528, at approximately the same time that the English, French, and Dutch began plundering the Caribbean Spanish ports and shipping lanes. The Bay Islands were situated strategically for such raids. The Gulf of Honduras contained the only Spanish ports (Trujillo and Puerto Caballos) between Panama and New Spain. Both routes of the Spanish Caribbean Fleet passed near the Gulf, one from Europe and the Greater Antilles to New Spain and the other (laden with gold and silver) from Cartagena and Panama to Havana and Europe. Fresh provisions for the raiders were not only available on the Bay Islands but also boats that could be appropriated. In addition, the excellent harbors on the south side of Roatán could serve as shelter for rendezvous and staging points for other raids within the region.

The French appeared in the western Caribbean by 1536 and the Dutch by 1594, but it was the English who eventually were the most successful in disrupting Spanish control of the Caribbean. Attempts to upset Spanish trade began in the Bay of Honduras in 1564 when a single English ship captured four Spanish frigates. It was to the Bay Islands that these British raiders or buccaneers sailed with their booty.[3] Historical records are brimming with incidents of English assaults during this period (Andrews, 1959, 1964; Wright, 1929, 1932, 1964). Over the next 200 years, incursions occurred so frequently that parts of the Caribbean, including the Bay Islands, eventually were considered British territory. Distraction with events in Europe and other parts of empire often diminished Spanish strength and authority in the Gulf of Honduras. During this time, British buccaneers frequently hid with their booty in the sheltered lagoons and harbors of the Bay Islands. Although there were many successful attempts to temporarily dislodge the British pirates from the islands, eventual Spanish relocations to the mainland facilitated the efforts of the pirates to regroup in their island strongholds. The buccaneers' treatment of the native Bay Island people often was violent—killing, burning settlements, and stealing boats and food were common (Wright, 1932). In the early 1640s, the Spanish exiled the remaining indigenous Bay Islanders to the mainland where they could be forced to produce provisions for the Spanish fleet without the risk of also supplying food to British pirates. The Spanish hoped that the strategy of depopulating the islands and eliminating the provisions would lead to the abandonment of the islands by the buccaneers. However, the opposite result occurred and, instead of ending British interference with Spanish trade, the depopulation led to enhanced British efforts to settle and politically control the islands.

The rivalry between England and Spain heightened in the western Caribbean between 1638 and 1782, and the Bay Islands, especially Roatán, became a major site for proving their respective powers. Attempts at colonization and pirate raids, frequently legitimized as privateering, were at the forefront of the English strategy. These efforts were followed by formal military occupation beginning in 1742. Although Spain's control of the Bay Islands often was disputed, Spain did not relinquish control permanently. Over 150 years, the cycle of English occupation, followed by expulsion by the Spaniards, eventual Spanish withdrawal, and reoccupation by the English was repeated three times and left significant vestiges of Anglo-Hispanic conflict on the islands (Davidson, 1974).

The first British attempt to settle permanently in the Spanish Bay Islands was under the authority of the Company of Adventurers of the City of Westminster for the Plantation of the Islands of Providence, Catalina, Henrietta or Andrea, better known as the Providence Company, that was organized in England by the leaders of the Puritan Party in 1630. The Company granted a formal patent to a North American colonist, William Claiborne, who brought several hundred colonists from Maryland and Virginia to Roatán in 1638 where he issued grants of land under the auspices of the Company. These initial colonists were followed by an unknown number of English immigrants who escaped the mother colony on Providence Island after the Spanish occupation in 1641 (Newton, 1914). In 1642, civil war in England temporarily severed formal contacts between England and the West Indies. After the demise of the mother colony on Providence and without protection from England, the colonists on Roatán were very vulnerable and by the end of 1642 were evicted by the Spanish.

In the late 1600s buccaneering reached its zenith in the Bay Islands and shipping was significantly disrupted throughout the Bay of Honduras. Before the first British military occupation in 1742, several famous pirate leaders, including Morgan, Jackson, Coxen, Sharpe, Low, and others, sought refuge in the islands at various times—to careen and refit ships, to cut logwood, to hunt wild hogs, to fish, and to capture turtles.

In 1742 a small force of 200 North American troops and 50 marines was dispatched by Admiral Vernon from Jamaica to Port Royal, Roatán where they constructed two small forts (Fort George and Fort Frederick) and two small settlements. The rationale behind this military settlement included providing a base from which to foment rebellion on the mainland; to ensure exclusive British control of the logwood trade; to facilitate illicit trade with Central America; and to provide refuge for English logwood cutters from Belize and the Mosquito Shore during periods of Spanish aggression (Watt, 1973). In order to ensure the success of the Roatán settlement, Governor Trelawny of Jamaica empowered its governor, William Pitts, to implement several inducements for prospective colonists. These included the establishment of a free port, liberal land grants, and 1-year's free subsistence for every immigrant and slave (Watt, 1973). Despite these enticements, the settlement did not attract colonists and most of the land grants were issued to members of the garrison. This may have been due to the justified fear on the part of prospective colonists that the British government would restore the island to Spain and British colonists would be evicted. This is precisely what happened in October 1748, when Britain and Spain signed the Peace of Aix-la-Chapelle and in November 1749 the British force left Roatán (Watt, 1973).

For 30 years following the British withdrawal there appears to have been no permanent British settlement on Roatán. From 1749 to 1779, relations between Spain and Britain in the Bay of Honduras were relatively calm (Brown, 1922). However, this did not totally distract English interest from the islands as suggested by the comments of Thomas Jefferys, Geographer to the King of England, who described Roatán in 1762:

> This is a plentiful island abounding with wild hogs, deer, Indian conies, wild fowl, quantities of turtle, and fin fish, etc. Its soil in the vallies is rich and fertile and will produce any thing in common with the rest of the West Indies. There is very good oak grows upon this island, as likewise pine-trees of sufficient bigness to make masts and yards for merchant ships. The south side is very convenient for shipping, having many fine harbours. The north side is defended by a reef of rocks that extend from one end of the island to the other, having but few passages through, and those but small note, being mostly made use of by the turtlers. This island is very well situated for trade both with the Spaniards at Guatimala and the Bay of Honduras. It is likewise very healthy, the inhabitants hereabouts generally living to a great age. . . . Port Royal the principal harbour on this island is naturally fortified with rocks and shoals; the entrance is so narrow that only a single ship can pass at a time. . . . This island in the last war was settled, and garrisoned by British troops from Jamaica; but at the sollictation of the court of Spain, was evacuated after the peace of 1748; and tho' then the Spaniards issued several placarts, inviting people to come and settle on the island, yet it is uninhabited; and the reason given by a Spaniard of great sense, and very large property on the continent, was, that they were all sensible that they could never expect any assistance or protection from their unwieldy government, and therefore must be defenseless and liable to be insulted and plundered by the

first enemy that comes, and that as long as they were a little more secure in their settlements on the main, it would never be worth the expense or hazard of any Spaniard to settle on the islands, which is a very cogent reason why all the islands on this coast and bay, as well as on the coast of Tierra Firma, are mostly uninhabited. (Jefferys, 1792/1970, pp. 51, 100)

Despite the Treaty of Aix-la-Chapelle, hostilities continued between the British and Spanish in the Bay of Honduras. By 1779, when British military strategists in Jamaica were planning an attack on the Spanish settlements on Lake Nicaragua, General John Dalling pointed out the strategic advantage of a military base in the Bay Islands:

The situation of the island of Roatán, its most noble harbour, its difficult access to an invading Enemy, renders it extremely eligible for a military post and to be the grand depot of Arms, Stores, etc. for all military operations going forth against Honduras, Guatimala or that part of Nicaragua to the Northward and westward of the Lake [Nicaragua], the climate is extremely healthy and free from those disorders to which the Sea coast of the Continent is subject. (Dalling, 1779)

When hostilities erupted in the Bay of Honduras in 1779, the former British military base on Roatán, Fort George (Old Port Royal), was reoccupied by British forces. In March 1782, over 600 Spanish regulars and militiamen under the command of the president of Guatemala assisted by 12 ships, including two men-of-war, began their attack on the last English stronghold at Port Royal. To prevent the Spaniards from entering the harbor the British sank their only ship, a brigantine, in the channel but to no avail. By the second morning of the battle, the British abandoned Fort George and sought refuge in the forest. The Spaniards captured 200 British soldiers and slaves, after which they demolished the fortifications, burned all of the buildings, and sailed to Trujillo (Davidson, 1974, pp. 61–62).

The Crown Colony of the Bay Islands

The period 1797–1859 saw the establishment of the first island settlements that persist until today. In March 1797, after the small Spanish military force on Roatán was expelled by English forces to Trujillo, approximately 5,000 dissident Black Carib (Garífuna) prisoners from the island of St. Vincent were marooned by the British at Port Royal (Davidson, 1974; Watt, 1973). The Spaniards considered this a British attempt to reoccupy the island and sent forces to recapture the island and remove the Garífuna to the mainland. Although most Garífuna readily accepted the offer to settle near Trujillo, a small number remained on the island and established a settlement on the north shore, Punta Gorda, that remains today (Davidson, 1974; Watt, 1973).[4]

Except for the Garífuna village at Punta Gorda and a few Spanish guards stationed occasionally at Port Royal, there appears to have been no large settlement of the islands during the first three decades of the 19th century. Orlando Roberts, an English trader in the Bay of Honduras from 1816 to 1823, traversed the south coasts of the islands from Guanaja, to Roatán, to Utila. He describes a virtually uninhabited paradise:

> We reached this island Guanaja . . . and landed opposite a watering place in an excellent harbour on the south side; the beach, above high watermark, was thickly covered by cocoa nuts; and near the watering place, innumerable tracks of the wild hog. The island contains hills of considerable elevation, thickly covered with trees; and it is said to contain beds of limestone, and some ores of zinc. . . . On Barbaratte, which is thickly overgrown with prickly plants and thick underwood . . . I found three or four sorts of wild grapes. Our fishers procured a large green turtle, and caught some very fine fish;. . . .
>
> Roatán . . . is moderately high, covered with wood, except at the west end, where there are some savannahs on which mules and other cattle used to be raised. . . . The woods abound in deer, wild hogs, gibeonites, pigeons, with millions of parrots and other birds . . . and the whole coast swarms with fish and turtle, both green and hawksbill . . . none of these fine islands are now inhabited.[5] . . .
>
> From Roatán the Island Utila is visible; and after a short run we landed at a low beach at the west end, where the water was perfectly smooth. The soil of all these islands is rich, and well adapted for the cultivation of cotton, coffee, etc; and the natural productions of each are similar. Innumerable flocks of parrots and pigeons were flying about; and cocoa nuts were so plentiful, that whole cargoes could be procured with very little trouble. (Roberts, 1827)

Despite the lack of additional settlements, the islands were not completely isolated, as demonstrated by the accounts of several officials of the British Navy and occasional reports of hunters, turtlers, and fishermen from both British and Spanish territory (Davidson, 1974, p. 75). At the conclusion of the Spanish–American revolution for independence, Honduras acquired the rights to the Bay Islands. Although the official English position was to recognize Honduran sovereignty, the English understood that the Bay Islands were strategically important militarily and commercially and a potential site for colonization as well as a shelter for English settlers from elsewhere (Davidson, 1974, p. 75).

At about the same time, Belize (British Honduras) was growing economically, and wealthy Belizean merchants, anxious that the Bay Islands not fall under the control of commercial rivals, urged a formal British takeover (Waddell, 1959). In 1838, the Commandant of Trujillo, the local representative of the Central American government, ordered that his nation's flag be hoisted on Roatán. In response to the appeal of the few English-speaking settlers living there, the Belize Superintendent, Colonel Alexander MacDonald, wrote a pointed note to the Commandant advising him that the sovereignty of Roatán had not been established. The British Foreign Office advised MacDonald that while he should not blatantly assert British sovereignty over the islands, British warships could be used to protect British subjects living there and to haul down any foreign flags found flying on Roatán. In April 1839, the *H.M.S. Rover* appeared at Belize with these instructions. MacDonald sailed with her to Roatán, hauled down the Central American flag and ejected the few soldiers garrisoned there (Waddell, 1959). MacDonald's action, along with his subsequent appointment of Belizean magistrates to the islands, and regular visits by ships of the British Navy affected the belief among potential colonists that the Bay Islands were British territory and thus appropriate and safe for settlement (Watt, 1973, pp. 62–63). Despite MacDonald's assertions of British sovereignty and the presence of Belizean appointed magistrates, the Bay Islands were not formally declared a British colony until March, 1852 (Waddell, 1959). By that time the U.S. was jockeying for power in Central America and the Caribbean. As such, the U.S. viewed the Bay Islands as a potentially strategic area and the establishment of a British colony there as an infringement of the Monroe Doctrine and the Clayton-Bulwer Treaty.[6] By 1855, the U.S. formally accused Britain of blatantly contravening the Clayton-Bulwer Treaty and the British Prime Minister, Claredon, disavowed the actions of the former Secretary of State for the Colonies, Earl Grey, who had recommended incorporation of the Bay Islands as a British colony. Finally, Britain agreed to return the islands to Honduras through the Wyke-Cruz Treaty of 1859. This was formally done in 1861 and in 1872 the *Islas de la Bahia* (Bay Islands) were incorporated as a department of Honduras (Waddell, 1959).[7]

The largest wave of 19th century immigration into the Bay Islands (1830s to 1859) coincided with the longest period of informal and formal British rule over the islands and with the serious social and economic dislocations that accompanied the abolition of slavery in the West Indies in 1834. Many modern communities on Roatán were settled between 1829 and 1831 when a few British-born colonists arrived via the Cayman Islands, Belize, and Jamaica.[8] Then in 1833 the Utila keys were settled by an Englishman and an American. In that same year, a few white colonists also settled on Guanaja. Immigration to the islands remained relatively low, however, until after 1844 when significant numbers of freed black slaves from the Caymans began coming to the islands. Between 1834 and 1850, the population of the islands grew from 50 to more than 1,800 inhabitants before stabilizing at around 1,600 for the rest of the decade (Figure 2.2).

Anticipating a loss of power after the emancipation of slaves who outnumbered white settlers five to one, white Cayman Islanders began migrating to other parts of the western Caribbean beginning about 1830. Belize and the Bay Islands were among the preferred sites for relocation. Between 1830 and 1855, approximately 650 Cayman Islanders settled on the Bay Islands and established many permanent towns. Although slavery officially ended in the Cayman Islands on August 1, 1834, owners could keep former slaves in a 4-year "apprenticeship." This precluded black emancipated slaves from migrating until at least 1838. Consequently, colonization of the Bay Islands by Cayman Islanders was divided ethnically as well as temporally. Between 1834 and 1843, about 24 white families migrated to the islands, while more than 20 times that number of black freed slaves arrived in the following 7 years (1844–1850) (Davidson, 1974, p. 76). The account of settlement written by a visiting British Naval Commander, John Mitchell, who visited the islands in mid-century, is the most thorough:

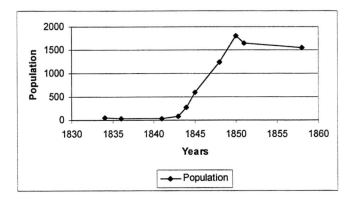

Figure 2.2. Bay Islands population: 1834–1858. Source: Waddell (1959), Watt (1973), and Davidson (1974).

The population is scattered in different parts along the whole sea shore of the island; from obvious reasons, they find these localities more convenient than the interior. They here erect their dwellings, in the midst of their palm and plantain groves, having their little vessels and fishing boats in quiet and sheltered nooks, and convey their produce and seek for their wants by water carriage. . . . At Coxon Hole, or Port McDonald, the greatest numbers seem located: there are here perhaps five hundred.

The origin of the mass of the population are liberated slaves from the Grand Cayman; and a small portion of the inhabitants are coloured people [whites or mixed], also natives of the islands, and formerly slave owners . . . they [the slave owners] emigrated and sought their fortunes on the unpeopled shores of Roatán. The slaves who had obtained their freedom, but could not procure labour in a small island, like the Grand Cayman, hearing of the success of their former masters, followed in their footsteps. . . .

Added to these two classes, a third and a much smaller one, must be named, which consists purely of Europeans. They are men who have tried various pursuits and professions of life, which they have given up for various reasons, have taken to others, and have become familiar with the hard usages of adversity; and they sought this remote island, some in their old and some in their middle age, either to commerce again, or to retrieve their broken fortunes, or to speculate in an imaginary construction of wealth. This class, though small in numbers, exercise a great influence over the minds of the community.[9] . . .

Each among the first settlers who came here from the Caymans, chose whatever land or spot he liked; which he appropriated to himself. From the few on the island no one disputed his possession, and his labour and occupation of the spot gave him a claim. In 1844, constant disagreements taking place, they convoked a general meeting amongst themselves - they agreed to hold possession of what each had at the time; that from and after that date every person might claim 300 yards of back land, with a frontage of 150 yards. . . . A public surveyor was invested with the power of measuring the land off, and a certain quantity of waste land was to lie between each property. Every man seems now to have his own plantation. (Michell, 1850, pp. 543–544)

Michell stresses the English character of the 19th century Bay Island settlers:

They speak the English language remarkably well. . . . They seem greatly to desire British protection, to be an English colony or settlement. . . . All their recollections and associations, their liberty and freedom, the knowledge they have attained, the independence they have gained, the wealth they possess, and their language and habits, are all English, and go to strengthen this assertion. (Michell, 1850, pp. 543, 545)

By mid-century, over 90% of the Bay Islands inhabitants were living near Coxen Hole (Michell, 1850, pp. 542–543). It is important to note that the concentration of settlement that led to the imposition of land regulations in 1844 also coincided with the beginning of colonization by black emancipated slaves from the Caymans. This may imply that the white settlers intentionally aimed to segregate the newer arrivals. The new law, together with the preference for sea front property, resulted in a linear settlement pattern adjacent to Coxen Hole, reportedly stretching for 2 miles by 1858, and the establishment of new communities by arriving freedmen to the west at West End, Flowers Bay, and Jobs Bight (Davidson, 1974).

By 1858, the Bay Islands were home to a diverse population of approximately 1,550 (Table 2.1). About 90% of the population lived on the largest island Roatán, 7% on Utila, 2% on Guanaja, and 2% on the smaller islands of Barbareta, Morat, and Helene. The largest numbers of residents were born in the Cayman Islands (42%), followed by native-born Bay Islanders (37%). Approximately 10% of island inhabitants were from the Mosquito Shore, 4% from Belize, 2% from Jamaica, 1% from England and Africa, and the remainder from various places throughout Europe, North America, and the West Indies. Although 79% of island inhabitants in 1858 have been categorized as "black," "colored," or "Negro" and 21% as "white," the ethic distribution on the islands varied significantly from one island to another (Table 2.2).[10] Negroes constituted 86% of the residents of Roatán and 84% of the smallest islands of Barbareta, Morat, and Helene, while white residents predominated on Guanaja (92%) and Utila (90%). On Roatán, white settlers were concentrated near Coxen Hole and French Harbour while Negro or black settlers were more dispersed, living in small communities along the western shoreline of Roatán, Morat, and Helene (Watt, 1973).

The colonial period also saw a boost in the general economy of the islands. In addition to subsistence activities based on farming, fishing, and turtling, the Bay Islanders produced a growing quantity of commodities for export. Between 1855 and 1859 the trade balance (the difference between the value of exports and the value of imports) grew from a net loss of £1,117 to a net gain of £2,711 (Davidson,

Table 2.1. Bay Islands Population: Place of Birth: 1858

Place of Birth	Roatán No.	Roatán %	Guanaja No.	Guanaja %	Utila No.	Utila %	Barbareta, Morat, Helene No.	Barbareta, Morat, Helene %
Cayman Islands	600	44	10	27	30	30	10	34
Bay Islands	488	35	9	24	62	61	13	45
Mosquito Shore	139	10			2	2	3	10
Belize	61	4			2	2	3	10
Jamaica	28	2						
England	14	1	4	11	2	2		
Africa	14	1						
USA	8	1	2	5	2	2		
Scotland	6		2	5				
Old Providence Island	7							
Nassau	6		9	24				
Ireland	2							
Cuba	2							
Germany	1				1	1		
Danish West Indies	1		1	3				
British North America	1							
Arabia	1							
Total	1379	100	37	100	101	100	29	100

Source: Davidson (1974, p. 81).

Table 2.2. Bay Islands Population: Ethnic Distribution: 1855 and 1858

	Roatán No.	Roatán %	Guanaja No.	Guanaja %	Utila No.	Utila %	Barbareta, Morat, Helene No.	Barbareta, Morat, Helene %	Total No.	Total %
1855										
Blacks	1,550	91	5	36	30	40	25	100	1610	89
Whites	155	8	9	64	45	60	0	0	209	11
Total	1705	100	14	100	75	100	25	100	1819	100
1858										
Blacks	1189	86	3	8	11	11	26	84	1229	79
Whites	190	14	34	92	90	90	5	16	319	21
Total	1379	100	37	100	101	100	31	100	1548	100

Source: Davidson (1974, p. 81).

1974, p. 85). Most of the increase was due to a doubling in the production of plantains, coconuts, and bananas, most of which were shipped to New Orleans. At the same time, production of coconut oil, fish, and yams, which were sold in Belize and on the Honduran mainland, declined. Not surprisingly, this change was tied to shifts in the primary export markets that demonstrated increased economic interaction with the U.S. In 1855, 58% of Bay Island products were exported to Belize while 41% were exported to the U.S. By 1859, 90% of Bay Island exports were shipped to the U.S. and only 9% to Belize. A similar pattern occurred for imports: in 1855, 85% of Bay Island imports came from Belize and 13% from the U.S.; by 1859, Belize accounted for only 37% of imports to the islands while 58% came from the U.S. (Davidson, 1974, p. 85).

The Postcolonial Bay Islands

The Bay Islanders considered the surrender to Honduras a great betrayal. In his analysis of the establishment and subsequent dissolution of the Colony of the Bay Islands, David Waddell concludes that:

> The whole episode must be regarded as an extremely discreditable one [for Great Britain] . . . an undoubted injustice to Honduras . . . a possible violation of the Clayton-Bulwer treaty . . . unfair to the islanders. . . . Up to the actual time of colonization the British settlers were on their own, and could expect no official help. An unequivocal renunciation of British claims leaving the inhabitants [of the Bay Islands] under Honduran sovereignty would before 1852 have been no injustice. But having extended protection and sanction by formal colonization the Colonial Office had created a quite different situation...As Henry Taylor put it "on the plea of protecting them we took possession of them, and . . . having possession of them, instead of protecting them, we have bartered them for those advantages and conveniences [of better relations with the United States]." . . . There can be no doubt that the cession was regarded as a great betrayal, and almost a century later travellers reported that some of the inhabitants were still hoping that Britain would some day resume her sovereignty. (Waddell, 1959, pp. 76–77)

The islanders sent several petitions to Queen Victoria urging their reinstatement as a British colony but received no comfort. According to Rose (1904):

> Deputations were sent and petitions made up, pleas and threats of all kinds were used to impress the Queen with the unwillingness of the islanders to serve any throne but her own: but the Treaty of Comayagua stood, and the islanders were deprived of the sovereignty which their ancestors had flaunted. (p. 56)

Some islanders, including several leaders, resorted to drastic measures to avoid transfer of the islands to Honduras. In early spring, 1860, a discontented group of islanders contacted filibusters in New Orleans and persuaded William Walker and his associates that, when the British left, the islanders would join him in his political designs over the Central American mainland (Waddell, 1959). Very likely, the islanders with whom Walker plotted were "white" islanders who wished to establish slavery on the islands.[11] Small groups of Walker's collaborators began arriving on Roatán. When the British flag was lowered, their scheme was to hoist the flag of the U.S. over the islands (Carr, 1963). The Walker threat was short-lived. While on his way to Roatán in 1860 he was caught by the British and handed over to the Honduran authorities to face a firing squad at Trujillo (Waddell, 1959). Walker's death ended all serious attempts by the islanders to resist the cession by force (Waddell, 1959). On June 1, 1861, Acting Lietuenant-Governor Thomas Price hauled down the Union Jack flying over Coxen Hole, Roatán and the formal, but tenuous, political bond between Great Britain and the Bay Islands was severed. That same day, the Bay Islanders sent their final petition to Queen Victoria. It read:

> Your excellency stated that we for the future must consider ourselves Hondurenians. With due submission to the dictum of Your Excellency, we still consider ourselves British subjects holding property in a foreign land, the which was taken possession of while under the protection of the British Crown, and therefore being British-born subjects, although residing in a Colony, the abandonment of which is quite unprecedented in the history of nations, we must still claim the protection of the British Crown, the same as any other of Her Majesty's subjects residing in a foreign land. As a last request we beg Your Excellency will forward this address to Her Majesty's Council in England, and with our latest breath we will ever shout in harmony, "God save the Queen."

The day-to-day lives of the Bay Islanders were not immediately affected by the change in governance. By the terms of the treaty, Bay Islanders were offered the option of accepting free Crown land and transportation to Belize if they wished. They were also allowed to retain all rights to land and assets they had claimed as British citizens and assured religious freedom. Local people also continued to hold municipal offices. Even after Spanish became the official language in 1872, the majority of Bay Islanders spoke English. Many of the Bay Islanders were slow to admit that their claims of British nationality were no longer valid and many island-ers assumed that they could continue to live under English Common Law (Lord, 1975, p. 34). These beliefs were reinforced by the relative disinterest of the GOH in their newest department. The de facto independence of the Bay Islands, however, ended with the visit of the British warship, *H.M.S. Psyche*, on July 18, 1902. Captain Cooker-Key was appointed to absolve Bay Islanders' unwavering claims of British citizenship. Cooker-Key stood up briefly and clearly declared that many of the people who were living in the Bay Islands and claiming British protection were not British citizens (Rose, 1904, p. 166). After reading the first article of the Wyke-Cruz treaty to the residents, he added:

> All British subjects that were living in the islands in 1861 when the latter were delivered to Honduras, are subjects of Honduras, they and their chil-dren, while they remain in this country; but beyond the limits of Republic they are British subjects. All British subjects, who settled in the islands after

Photo 2.1. Early adventure tourist and collector, Frederick Mitchell-Hedges, 1934.

the latter were ceded to Honduras, they are British subjects still; and as such
are entitled to privileges of British protection in or out of the country. (Rose,
1904, p. 167)

Despite this somewhat ambiguous proclamation, many islanders maintained their
assertions of British nationality long after incorporation into the Honduran polity.
Reporting on her trip to the islands in 1932 as companion to British amateur
ethnologist, sportsman, and adventurer, Mitchell-Hedges, Jane Houlson wrote that
the islanders "came unquestionably of the honourable line of buccaneers, speaking
English, and denying Honduranian nationality" (Houlson, 1934, p. 68). Similarly, in
1938 the British journalist, Peter Keenagh, reported that:

> Since the ratification of the Treaty of Comayagua there has been a continual
> struggle between Islanders and Mainlanders. The island families, for many
> reasons, consider that their British stock is superior to the confusion of
> Spanish, Indian, and Negro blood which populates the mainland, and there
> has never been the slightest feeling of subjection. . . . There is no common
> ground: islanders look down on mainlanders, and the Hondurans are in-
> clined to regard the island folk as pirates or half-savages on a par with the
> wild Carib tribes. The differences of race, language, and religion mitigate

Photo 2.2. Jane Harvey Houlson, companion of Frederick Mitchell-Hedges, 1934.

strongly against the formation of any kind of bond. (Keenagh, 1938, pp. 56, 72–73)

As late as 1955, when anthropologist Richard Adams visited the islands as part of his cultural survey of Central America, he reported that on Utila some residents still claimed British nationality even though both Honduras and Britain considered them to be citizens of Honduras (Adams, 1957, p. 640).

The Islands' Postcolonial Economy

The Export of Tropical Fruit

Most Bay Islanders chose not to accept the British offer of free passage and land grants in Belize. During the colonial period many had seen their enterprises in the production and export of tropical fruits (bananas, plantains, and coconuts) grow significantly. By the1870s, trade with the U.S., along with enhanced U.S. political and economic interests in the region, justified the appointment of an American consul for the islands—stationed first on Roatán then on Utila (Rose, 1904, p. 12). Increased competition from large mainland producers and a devastating hurricane in 1877, however, ended the boom in fruit production and export from the islands. It was several decades before the commercial production of tropical fruits once again became the dominant economic activity of the islands. By 1912–1913 earnings from the export of tropical fruits from the islands constituted over 5% of the total national export income (Davidson, 1974, p. 95).

Shortly thereafter (1917–1919), the efforts of the Tegucigalpa appointed governor of the islands, Lieutenant Colonel Rafael Barahona, to promote closer ties with the mainland contributed to the eventual collapse of the second boom in export production from the islands (Davidson, 1974, p. 95). Barahona appointed Spanish-speaking officials and enforced the Honduran law requiring instruction in Spanish by closing English-speaking schools and replacing them with schools staffed by Spanish speakers from the mainland. He also promoted policies that diverted the shipment of exports to the mainland rather than to the U.S. By the early 1930s, the majority of the islands' exports were being shipped to the mainland port of La Ceiba rather than to the U.S. In addition, total agricultural production declined to 10% of the amount exported to the U.S. around the turn of the century (Davidson, 1974, p. 95).

The production of tropical fruits remained an important economic option for Bay Islanders until the 1920s. However, after 1920 declining prices were followed by the devastating effect of the Panama fungus, or "sigatoka," and finally in 1929 the collapse of the market with the worldwide Depression. Workers both on the mainland and the islands were laid off and economic options were few. From 1929 to 1939, coconuts once again became an important crop for some islanders who manufactured copra and oil from cohune nuts.

Seafaring and Smuggling

At the time of the collapse of the second boom in export agriculture, the sea was furnishing increasingly important economic opportunities to Bay Islanders. The sea always had provided some means of subsistence, employment, and cash income. In the 19th century, Bay Island schooners engaged in some slave trade with the American south and ran guns to the Confederates during the American Civil War. In the latter part of the century fast two-masted schooners transported cargoes of fine Honduran mahogany north to the U.S. and returned loaded with supplies and manufactured goods for the scattered English-speaking settlements of the Western Caribbean (Parsons, 1954).

By 1900, the islanders dominated Honduras coastal trade using large dugouts (dories) hollowed by Garífuna boat builders and finished by individual island owners (Rose, 1904, pp. 36, 113). During the expansion of the tropical fruit industry a substantial number of trading networks were established throughout the Bay of Honduras. Smaller craft visited the western portion of Roatán and Utila where they picked up coconuts, plantains, and bananas from small producers. These were loaded onto larger vessels that transported the commodities between Utila and New Orleans. It was after 1905, however, when the United Fruit Company began to dominate almost all the shipping on the Nicaraguan and Honduran Atlantic coasts, that many Hondurans became sailors. Thousands were eventually employed by the Honduran Steamship Company, previously the shipping firm of the United Fruit Company (Griffin, 1998a).

With the simultaneous decline in agriculture and the enhanced importance of seafaring, smuggling took on greater importance in the islands. During the prohibition era in the U.S., swift Bay Island schooners ran cargoes of Jamaican rum to Florida. Disguised as fishing craft, these speedy vessels would load casks of rum in French Harbour and deliver them in 3 or 4 days to U.S. connections in Florida. If challenged by the U.S. Coast Guard, the Bay Islands captains ordered the heavy waterproof casks of rum tossed over the side, along with a number of fish pots, marking their location with small cork floats attached to lengths of light line. After being halted, boarded, searched, and cleared by the Coast Guard, crews hauled their cargo back aboard and met secretly with smugglers in secluded coves along the U.S. coast. After off-loading their cargo of rum they would put into Tampa or New Orleans and load their now empty holds with American cypress. The cypress, used for the construction of boats, houses, and water tanks, was then sold in French Harbour for a considerable profit (Evans, 1966, p. 46). Writing in the 1930s, Keenagh describes the smuggling of arms and humans, as well as rum:

> Most of the islanders lead a pleasant and easy life on the fruits of earth and sea: but those who have inherited something of the adventurous spirit of their fathers capitalize the revolutions which occur, with ridiculous regularity, among the Five Republics [of Central America]. The islanders carry arms and ammunition in their schooners, frequently for both sides at the same time. In this way, obviously enough, the Bay Islanders are a continued source of provocation to the Honduran Government. . . .
>
> Since most of the commercial activity of the island waterfront is best left uninvestigated, Port Royal is an ideal harbour and an eternal thorn in the side of the Honduran Customs office. Every house is a potential warehouse. . . . Smuggling and gun running in the Caribbean are lucrative occupations and do not seem to be fraught with any particular dangers. Central American governments are usually far too busy with internal affairs to devote ships and men to the suppression of smuggling. When a revolution is in the wind among the Five Republics, schooner after schooner steals away

from Roatán, and it sometimes happens that for several months most of the
men are gone. The leaders of the island have many contacts, in the outer
world, with those who are interested in the supply and demand for arms.
They always maintain a strictly neutral viewpoint themselves, for the politics
of Latin America do not affect their lives. . . .

Captain Macdonald, in fact, declared that it was not uncommon for a schooner to carry contraband weapons for both sides in the same shipment, leaving
half at one rendezvous and sailing on to deliver the other half somewhere
else. Even during the rare months when there is complete peace in the
Caribbean and no one is as much thinking of a revolution, an atmosphere of
contraband, which is justified by observation, seems to linger about Roatán.
Schooners appear and disappear in the night, carrying no cargo and no
passengers: cargo is discharged, as far as one can see, for years on end into
tiny warehouses from which nothing is ever taken. In addition the islanders
are for the most part far too well off to have earned their money entirely by
the selling of their half-hearted banana crops and copra.

Until the repeal of prohibition in the United States many of the schooners
occupied themselves with running rum from the Mexican coast, but in time
this became too dangerous, and only the most adventurous were not discour-
aged by the accurate marksmanship of the American Coast Guards. There
were still one or two craft lying near Roatán which were specially built when
rum running was at its height—fast launches with powerful engines—but
they were too expensive to run for other purposes. Captain Macdonald told
us also that a certain amount of money was made every year by smuggling
Chinamen into the United States. Only a small number of immigrant Orientals
are allowed into America every year, and many of those who are turned away
find their way south to the Caribbean Islands where they are willing to part
with as much as thirty or forty pounds to be landed secretly on the coast of
Florida. (Keenagh, 1938, pp. 59, 66–68)

Since the 1970s, illegal drugs, especially cocaine, have become the contraband of
choice being smuggled through the Bay Islands. Both the islands and the
Mosquitia have been identified as favorite trans-shipment points for drug smuggling through Honduras—which has replaced the tightly controlled Caribbean as
the Colombian drug barons' favored route ("Staging Post: Honduras," 1997). To
some extent, the old smuggling routes that were used to bring arms to the Contras
during the 1980s and drugs back to pay for them still operate. Recently, the lawyer
in charge of Honduras' antidrug efforts admitted that the islands and the long
Atlantic coastline are "awash with drugs" ("Staging Post: Honduras," 1997). There is
little that he can do because Honduras cannot afford to patrol adequately or
implement effective security measures, in part because of the involvement of high-
ranking military officers in drug trafficking. The more than 300 boats in the commercial fleet often go far afield—seemingly in search of lobster and shrimp but
capable as well of picking up consignments of carefully wrapped cocaine. Most
seafood is exported to the U.S. and containers supposedly packed with legitimate

exports often carry drugs as well ("Staging Post: Honduras," 1997). As will be discussed in subsequent chapters, problems associated with drug trafficking (e.g., drug dealing by otherwise unemployed island youth, increased addiction of islanders, rising crime, and the horrendous growth in the number of drug-related AIDS cases) are among the primary concerns of islanders.

Merchant Sailing and Fishing

By the 1940s, a new source of income and employment from the sea became available to male islanders—work on merchant ships—especially the U.S. merchant fleet. In 1940, the U.S. began leasing some of the larger United Fruit ships for use in defense duties. Many Bay Islanders, who were experienced sailors, served as crew on these ships. A large proportion of the adult male population of the Bay Islanders worked on company ships or on supply vessels used by the U.S. merchant fleet during the World War II; within the region, in Europe, and in the Far East. After the war ended, various U.S. shipping companies recruited seamen from the Bay Islands. Many seamen eventually obtained U.S. documents and settled in the U.S., especially in New Orleans and in New York (Graham, n.d.). During the 1960s and 1970s, islanders shipped out on Scandinavian as well as U.S. vessels to ports all over the world. Until recently, foreign merchant sailoring provided a major source of employment for islanders (Lord, 1975). According to islanders, a generation ago it was common for children to grow up without knowing their fathers, who were away at sea for long periods of time. The long absences of island men helped facilitate the Hispanicization of the islands that has occurred over the last 30 years (Graham, n.d.).

In the 1960s Bay Islanders increased their activities in commercial fishing and islanders with sufficient means purchased their own fishing boats. Shrimp, lobster, and conch were the major prizes. Most fishing boats in Honduras are part of the Bay Islands' fleet and most Honduran sailors are Bay Islanders or Garífuna. In the early 1990s, of the estimated 324 Bay Island boats engaged in industrial fishing, 56% were harbored in French Harbour, 27% in Oak Ridge, and 17% in Guanaja (Marin, 1993, p. 25).[12]

In the 1960s, ice and packing plants were opened in Guanaja and in Oak Ridge. These were followed by the construction of additional processing facilities in French Harbour and Oak Ridge during the 1970s. In the early 1990s there were five seafood packing plants on the islands of Roatán and Guanaja, as well as a large fishing fleet that operated off the islands. The processing plants have constituted a principal economic activity of the Bay Islands in recent decades. An estimated 250 persons, almost all ladino women, are employed in these plants (Marin, 1993). However, due to overexploitation and other poor fishing practices, fishing yields (catch per unit of effort) dropped by 50% between 1974 and the early 1990s, leading to bankruptcies and reduction in the operations of these processing plants. According to assessments made by consultants from the IDB, the general decline in fishing yields also led to greater pressure on fishing activity by small artisanal and subsistence fishers trying to maintain acceptable yields (IDB, 1992).

Bay Islander Ethnicity, Culture, and Identity

The more than 200 years of rivalry and armed conflict, during which England challenged Spanish supremacy of the Spanish Main, contributed to the sense of identity of the current Bay Islanders, even though few traces of fortifications and early settlements exist. Islanders speak proudly of their pirate ancestors and tell stories of the many pirates that sought refuge in the islands—Morgan, Coxon, Van Horn, Lafitte, and others. Tales of pirate gold abound, especially stories surrounding the reburial of pirate gold by aboriginal Bay Islanders in hideaways throughout the islands. Keys off Utila and French Harbour are believed to be haunted by the ghosts (or duppies) of pirates and Spaniards.[13] Several duppy folktales have pirate themes, including the stories of the "Gravel Man" dressed as a pirate who transforms himself into a dog and "Old One Foot," a peg-leg duppy who guards buried pirate treasure (Evans, 1966).

Piracy, smuggling, and evading customs duties were among the strategies of the English and their descendents in their defiance of Spanish and later Honduran authorities. Islander conceptions of pirates connote a certain bravery, independence, and resilience. Spaniards and Spanish-speaking Hondurans also perceive, and sometimes refer to, Bay Islanders as "pirates," usually in a derogatory sense that implies pirates as cutthroats, murderers, and thieves. Pirate imagery (and evidence of continual Spanish–Anglo antagonism and conflict) abounds in descriptions of Bay Islanders by travelers. For example, while in La Ceiba looking for a schooner to take him to the Mosquitia in 1936, British journalist, Peter Keenagh found Captain Macdonald:

> . . . a Bay Islander, descended directly from some of Morgan's pirates who had taken refuge among the Islands in the seventeenth and eighteenth century. Although we put very little faith in advice which came from the hotel proprietor [a ladino], we thought with nationalistic conceit that Macdonald was obviously our man. . . . We looked along the line of the bar and saw towering above the rest, an enormous man with a vast red face, wearing a singlet and a dirty blue deep-sea cap. He was drinking Irish whisky from a bottle. . . . He addressed us in perfectly good English . . . slapped us both on the back with a heavy great hand . . . "I'm Captain Macdonald, how d'you do?" (Keenagh, 1938, pp. 40–41)

Upon sailing to Roatán with Captain Macdonald, Keenagh wrote:

> That first night [on Roatán] we dined with Captain Dick, a swarthy pirate, one of three brothers who were the chief planters, navigators, and ship-wrights of the island . . . every room in Captain Dick's house was decorated with a picture of the King, and in the dining room a large Union Jack served honourably as a dignified and decorative tablecloth. . . . From talking to Captain Dick we gathered that the smouldering resentment against the mainland government had been slowly increasing during the last few years, and, he hinted darkly, if occasion arose the flame of revolt could easily be rekindled. . . . The rising heat of anti-mainland feeling on the islands is due,

with so many political disturbances, to taxation. The Honduran Government, it is held, does not keep its promises. For a number of years sums of money have been voted and set side for public works in the islands, and aerodromes, power stations and vast highways have been planned . . . but to this day no constructive step has been taken to spend any Honduran money on the islands. And, worse still from the islanders' point of view, even the money they pay out themselves in taxes is spent on the mainland. (Keenagh, 1938, pp. 69–72)

Who Are the Bay Islanders?

Answering the question, "Who are the Bay Islanders?" demands recognition of the fact that Bay Islanders are quite diverse. Particularly significant is the deep and longstanding division that exists between "white" and "Negro" or "colored" island-ers.[14] In his book, *The Historical Geography of the Bay Islands: Anglo-Hispanic Conflict in the Western Caribbean*, Davidson (1974) often fails to distinguish between Anglo-Antillean (white) and Afro-Antillean (Negro, colored, black) Bay Islanders, referring to both as "English." While it may be true that both groups refer to themselves as "English" in opposition to "Spaniards," "Hondurans," "ladinos," or "mainlanders," ethnic and cultural distinctions between these groups have played important roles in social and economic relations. The two groups also hold and exercise significantly different degrees of power. As discussed above, the two groups have been separated spatially, in terms of settlement pattern and the desirability of settlement location—although complete segregation has been possible in only a few instances (e.g., the Utila Cays, French Cay off Roatán, and Mangrove Bight on Guanaja). Conspicuous ethnic and cultural differences among Bay Islanders have been noted by several scholars (e.g., Adams, 1956, 1957; Jones, 1970; Jones & Glean, 1971; Parsons, 1954). The eminent anthropologist Richard Adams (1956), who conducted a comprehensive assessment of ethnic and cultural groups in Central America in the mid-1950s, distinguished between "Antillean Negroes" with "The Africo-Euro-American Cultural Tradition" and "white" residents of the Bay Islands who possessed "The Anglo-American-Islander Cultural Compo-nent." Approximately 20 years later, the geographer, David Jones (1970), also categorized as distinct "Creole" Bay Islanders ("Afro-Americans" whose "culture is basically derived from the British in the West Indies but who have lived for genera-tions on the Central American littoral") from "White Creoles" (the few white families living in the Bay Islands, Belize, and the Corn Islands). Jones notes that he classified this group separately because "White Creoles" generally would not accept the term "Creole" to describe themselves.

On the basis of interviews with "white" informants on Utila, Adams reported that, in 1955, the major Antillean Negro settlements in the islands were on Roatán where Negroes constituted 100% of the various settlements on the northwest coast of the island, 80% of the residents of Coxen Hole (Roatán), and 50% of the inhabitants of French Harbour and Oak Ridge (Adams, 1957, p. 636). At the same time "white" residents predominated on the island of Utila and comprised 100% of the population on the Utilian Cays. Adams does not take into consideration the proportion of ladinos on any of the islands. Jones and Glean (1971) reported similar settlement patterns to those encountered by Adams a decade earlier. In 1968, the principal settlements of white Bay Islanders on Roatán were French Harbour and Oak Ridge with a smaller population living at Jonesville and Port Royal. Whites predominated on Utila and three white families lived on Guanaja. Of the Roatán settlements only Coxen Hole and the strip of beachfront houses westward to Flowers Bay, together with the string of settlements on the north shore from West End to Sandy Bay, were predominantly colored. On Guanaja, the mainland settlements of Mangrove Bight and Savanna Bight were predominantly colored as was the town itself. Jones and Glean comment on the poor quality of housing of the colored population as well as their lack of political power in contrast to white islanders. They also indicated that a small number of Spanish-speaking families from the mainland were living in Coxen Hole. These families were engaged in commerce, teaching, and government administration. Also noted were the small Garífuna community of Punta Gorda on the north shore and the tiny Miskito community of Calabash Bight. On the basis of field observations in 1968 and 1970, Davidson estimated the percentages of various Bay Island population groups: Negroes, 42%; Whites, 27%; Colored or "Mixed" 16%; Garífuna (Black Carib), 4%; Ladinos, 7%; Indians, 1%; and Foreigners, 3% (Davidson, 1974, p. 130). He points out that the only Spanish-speaking ladino communities were located inland on Roatán—Corozal and Juticalpa—composed of residents who had emigrated from the mainland department of Olancho (Davidson, 1974, p. 108).

Interethnic social differentiation, class distinctions, and associated friction are manifest in the accounts of many travelers and scholars who visited the islands this century. For example, Jane Houlson comments that:

> . . . the Islanders . . . pride themselves in being white—another proof of the enterprise of Henry Morgan and the other pirates who made the Bay of Honduras their head-quarters. (Houlson, 1934, p. 65)

Referring to an unnamed village on the south side of Roatán (very likely Port Royal) she adds:

> Remote as it is, and having no communication with the mainland except by sailing-dories and schooners, it [the village] has its rigid strata of society which are unassailable. As one entered the harbour the first dwellings to be passed on the starboard side at the foot of the steep hills were a cluster of tumble-down primitive huts on a muddy piece of shore, having none of the appearance or convenience of the houses farther in, which were built neatly and solidly on piles with patches of garden about them. These first shacks were the habitations of the "coloured" people, who were looked down upon as an entirely different and quite inferior stratum of society by the rest of the population. They consisted of negroes, Caribs and mixtures of other dark blood, and kept to themselves. The rest of the village was very light of skin . . . and came unquestionably of the honourable line of buccaneers, speaking English, and denying Honduranian nationality. These people would have been mortally offended at the suggestion that they had a touch of

colour, even though they and their forefathers had lived and bred upon the islands for generations with the inevitable result. . . .

Even among these were class distinctions: "county" families who ruled with a feudal right unquestioned on the island, and owned schooners out of which they made a living; and "lower" classes—humbler beings who existed on the bounty of nature and their little fishing dories. (Houlson, 1934, pp. 67-68)

Thirty years later, in his study of the predominantly "white" community of French Harbour in 1961, Evans (1966) was very cognizant of ethnic heterogeneity and social stratification as well as related interethnic conflicts. Using villagers' self-identifications, he concluded that of the 581 residents, 354 (61%) regarded themselves as white, 221 (38%) as Negro, and 6 (1%) as Spaniard or ladino. He points out that in the British West Indies, most of the "whites" in French Harbour would be considered "colored" or "Creoles" (i.e., the descendants of Negro-white miscegenation that goes back a number of generations). He surmised that while most white villagers were aware of their mixed ancestry, this knowledge prompted them to attempt to separate themselves as far as possible from the Negroes in order to prevent further identification. He points out that Negroes who desired to enhance their status in the community continually pushed the social barriers erected to keep them in their place. He notes that although no rigid color line existed in public institutions, social and economic distinctions based on color were made daily. For example, groups were segregated spatially: whites lived on "the point" while Negroes lived on "the hill." There were also separate white and Negro sections of the churches and the movie theater. In addition, because most of the land in, and surrounding, the village was already owned by whites before the first of the freed slaves arrived from the Cayman Islands in the 1840s, very few Negroes owned property in French Harbour. Whites owned the plantations and Negroes worked for them (Evans, 1966, pp. 36-44).[15] According to one of Evans' white informants: "A black mon jus ain't no good lessen he's being told what ta do, and it ain't no white mon was made ta be told what ta do by no black . . . or by no Goddamned Spaniard neither fo dat matter" (Evans, 1966, p. 37).

Approximately a decade later, Lord (1975, pp. 106-119) documented even higher levels of interethnic segregation and animosity in another predominantly white enclave, Utila.[16] Quoting a native, white Utilian, "This is Little Rock, Arkansas," Lord inferred that his informant was referring to the fact that ethnic prejudices and stereotyping were the foundations of social relations on Utila (Lord, 1975, p. 107).[17] As in French Harbour, Negro Utilians arrived after whites and therefore did not gain access to the best properties. At the time of his research, Utila was divided into seven highly segregated barrios. Social as well as geographic boundaries between the several sectors of Utilian society were rigid and a conscious part of the daily interactions among islanders. Lord points out several examples of social stratification, based primarily on skin color, including marriage, residential, and linguistic evidence. He described separate dances for whites and coloreds/Negroes on Utila with a "colored folks dance" on Friday night followed by a "white folks dance" on Saturday (Lord, 1975, p. 115). There was also a strict precept to marry someone of the same ethnicity: 80% of all marriages were between people marrying within their own category (Lord, 1975, p. 111).

Conclusions

An examination of the historical emergence of a separate ethnic identity among the Bay Islanders reveals deep roots in the English-speaking Caribbean, within the context of longstanding antagonism and conflict with the Spanish, and later, the more powerful Honduran ladino majority. Also significant is the bifurcation of islander identity into distinct, and often hostile groups—Negro/colored and white islanders. Likewise notable has been the ability of some more affluent ladinos to become "white" through marriage while poor ladinos remain "Spaniards." While these distinctions may be based primarily on skin color they have significant socioeconomic and political implications. "White" and "colored" or "Negro" islanders hold significantly different amounts of power on the islands as well as with external interest groups such as the mainland government, foreign investors, and international organizations. While islanders have always felt peripheral to the mainland, recent events have triggered feelings of marginalization on the islands themselves. They also have increased tensions between "white" and "colored" islanders as several "white" islanders have been able to profit enormously from the recent boom in tourism.

Critically important in understanding island ethnicity and identity are the shared, preferred cultural characteristics of individualism, independence, and bravura stemming from the islanders' Caymanian and buccaneer history, and facilitated until recently by the lack of well-established communication between communities (Evans, 1966). The widespread belief in pirate ancestry is particularly noteworthy because it is highly unlikely that many, if any, of the current islanders actually have buccaneer forefathers. Despite this, one of Roatán's baseball teams calls itself "The Pirates," an interesting example of their own self-image because they compete with mainland teams.

Until recently, the islands' history reveals a lack of widespread or well-integrated community organization. These factors help explain the lack of organized response to efforts to Hispanicize the islands and to promote tourism in ways that many islanders judge to be detrimental to their ethnic and material survival. Also central is islanders' adherence to links with Britain and other English-speaking enclaves, particularly the Cayman Islands, Belize, and more recently the U.S. The islanders' staunch defense of their British ancestry, increasingly militant efforts to maintain the English language, and organized attempts to raise cultural consciousness are significant expressions of their perceptions of their own distinct ethnic identity. Long-used derogatory, ethnic slang terms have taken on new significance. Native Bay Islanders continue to refer to themselves as "British" or "English" and to mainlanders as "Spaniards," "*indios*" (Indians), or "natives." Mainlanders in turn refer to "white" islanders as "*caracoles*" (conch or snails), and to "colored" islanders as "*negritos*" (Negroes).

As will be discussed in subsequent chapters, the founding of a grassroots, nongovernmental organization composed principally of working and middle-class Afro-

Antillean islanders (The Native Bay Islanders Professional and Labourer Association [NABIPLA]) is evidence of current attempts to protect islander ethnicity and culture from several perceived threats.[18] The ultimately successful efforts of NABIPLA to have "English-Speaking Bay Islanders" recognized and included as members of the Confederation of Autochthonous Peoples of Honduras (CONPAH) was an important step in that direction. However, major risks to island ethnicity and culture remain. These stem from government attempts to further integrate the islands into the Honduran polity; a state agenda that emphasizes the significant expansion of tourism as a primary economic development strategy (i.e., control of the island economy); the massive migration of Spanish-speaking mainlanders who now comprise a majority on the islands; the loss of critically important land and marine resources; and the influx of large numbers of foreign investors, residents, and tourists.

As will be shown in the following chapters, Bay Islanders are attempting to protect their ethnicity and culture in many ways. These include: maintaining the English language; protecting and controlling natural resources; promoting islander rituals and other cultural practices; affecting biological reproduction through encouraging endogamy; the emergence of social movements to gain coordinated action among islanders and promote a unified political and economic agenda; and enhancing power among islanders by building strategic alliances. These efforts, however, are not an attempt to inhibit change but rather attempts to empower islanders to affect their own destinies.

Notes

[1] The English-speaking Western Caribbean generally is defined to include: Belize (formerly British Honduras), the Mosquito coast of Nicaragua and Honduras, the Isle of Pines, the Cayman Islands, Jamaica, the Corn Islands, and the islands of Providence and San Andres (Davidson, 1974; Parsons, 1954).

[2] Although there have been several archeological expeditions to the Bay Islands beginning in the 1920s, a comprehensive analysis of prehistoric settlement of the Bay Islands remains to be written. In 1933 an expedition to the islands funded by the Smithsonian Institution was headed by the well-known American archeologist, Duncan Strong (Strong, 1934, 1935). Brief discussions of the indigenous inhabitants in the context of pre-Hispanic lower Central America can be found in Stone and Lange (1984). A general discussion of the aboriginal cultural geography of the Bay Islands appears in Davidson (1974, Chapter 3).

[3] Several terms are used to describe these raiders: "Privateer" refers to a commander, crew, or ship that is privately owned and manned but authorized by a government during wartime to attack and capture enemy vessels; "pirate" describes someone who robs at sea or plunders the land from the sea without commission from a sovereign nation; "buccaneer" is used synonymously with "pirate" especially in reference to freebooters who preyed on Spanish shipping during the 17th century.

[4]The Garífuna with a population of more than 70,000 are the largest indigenous group in Honduras (Davidson & Counce, 1989). Although a small community persists on Roatán, the vast majority of Garífuna live in villages along the North Coast of Honduras. They have been very active in promoting indigenous rights in the country including both land and language rights. For more information on the Garífuna see Gonzalez (1969, 1979).

[5]Roberts evidently was not aware of the Garífuna village on the north side of Roatán.

[6]During the 1850s, the Caribbean and Central America were a venue for political rivalry between the U.S. and Britain. In April 1850 both countries signed the Clayton-Bulwer Treaty, in which they agreed that neither power was to fortify, occupy, or colonize any part of Central America. At that time Britain had plans to build a canal across the Central American isthmus—through Nicaragua. The U.S. hoped to construct an interoceanic railroad through Honduras.

[7]For a more thorough discussion of the colonial period see Waddell (1959). Waddell considers the treatment of the islanders by Britain to be relatively despicable. He explains the history of the Bay Islands Colony as the result of lack of communication between the British Colonial Office and the Foreign Office: that is, that the colonization was effected by the Colonial Office without the Foreign Office being informed and that the cession was effected by the Foreign Office without consultation with the Colonial Office.

[8]At the beginning of the Cayman immigration a few isolated settlements had been established along the south shore of the islands: two Americans on Suc-Suc Cay, Utila; two French families on the north shore of Port Royal harbor; a Spaniard on Barbareta; and two men on Sheen Cay, Guatemala (Davidson, 1974, p. 75).

[9]This comment by Captain Michell suggests the extent to which the Bay Islands historically have been the temporary or permanent residence (or hideout) of many adventurers and others seeking their fortunes or escape from the law.

[10]These are the classificatory terms that appear in the literature. Almost always these classes have been imposed by outsiders rather than islanders' own self-identification.

[11]According to Duncan (1990), "In the [U.S.] South he [Walker] was regarded as a hero. Part of his notoriety was due to his being an ardent proponent 'of the perpetuation and extension of the most solid, durable and beneficial, social and industrial system which exists in the world—the institute of negro slavery.' "

[12]Three categories of fishing occur in the islands: industrial, artisanal, and subsistence (Marin, 1993). In her study on the status of the natural resources in the Bay Islands for the Inter-American Development Bank, Mirna Marin defined "artisanal" fishers as individuals who fish full-time or part-time and who sell their catch. The results of her study show that, of these, 82% use hook and line, 24% use spears/harpoons, 16% use snares, and 22% use traps. She distinguishes "subsistence" fishers to include those who capture with hook and line enough fish to satisfy

their household needs but also occasionally sell part of their catch. Also categorized as "subsistence" fishers are the occasional fishermen who normally work as seamen in the merchant fleets of different countries.

[13]Many Bay Islanders continue to believe that the islands are inhabited by the spirits of the dead or duppies. Leach (1961) reports that the origin of the word duppy is West African, where it can mean either a ghost or a child. In the Bay Islands the term generally refers to ghosts rather than to children.

[14]Here, I am using terms that come directly from the literature and from the islanders themselves.

[15]Evans (1966, p. 42) determined a scale of social stratification based on skin color. In descending order, "socially superior" individuals included "white," white-negro (light), ladino, white-negro (dark), ladino-negro (reds or browns), while "socially inferior" persons were Negro.

[16]Lord (1975, pp. 106–108) characterizes Utila as having three major, locally recognized, social strata based on ethnicity with prestige gradations within each strata based on income and lifestyle. Highest in terms of social prestige is the so-called "white" population of Utila, who occupy the most important positions of local leadership and are the wealthiest. Like Evans, Lord concedes that "white" Utilians could conceivably have mixed ethnic backgrounds—although they would deny that possibility. Lord divides "white" Utilians into two subdivisions, the first consisting of persons with surnames of the founding families and the second, people with Spanish surnames who have married into founding families. Below "white" Utilians are "colored" persons with Negro ancestry. This group also is divided into two sectors. The first sector consists of Utilians who had what were considered to be Negro physical features and who were descended from the original colored settlers. The second includes those individuals with Spanish surnames who married colored Utilians. At the bottom of the social hierarchy are the "Spaniards," individuals from mainland Honduras who have Spanish surnames, speak little or no English, and work as common laborers.

[17]The white supremicist views of Utilians in the late 1960s also have been described by Jones and Glean (1971), who report that ethnic tension was greater on Utila than on any of the other islands at that time.

[18]The relative threats to the survival of white and Negro/colored islanders seem to differ in degree. In 1971, noting the decline in the white population of Roatán as people moved to the U.S., Jones and Glean (1971) predicted the disappearance of white islanders within one or two generations. However, not only have white islanders persisted, many have benefited significantly from recent economic opportunities (fishing, tourism, and perhaps drug smuggling) and have significantly augmented their fortunes. Many are the most successful ship owners, seafood processors, and resort owners. Exercising great power and being accustomed to doing as they please on the islands, their actions and financial success have provoked resentment (as well as some emulation) among Negro/colored islanders.

Chapter 3

Imagining the Bay Islands: The Expansion of International Tourism

The island was well watered, full of high hills and deep valleys. . . . Numerous fruit trees, such as figs, vines, and coconuts are found in the latter. . . . But the insects are so troublesome that I thought of endeavoring to get over to some of the adjacent keys in hopes of enjoying rest. . . . A small black fly [sandfly] creates such annoyance that even if a person possessed ever so many comforts, his life would be oppressive to him unless for the possibility of retiring to some small quay. (Philip Ashton's account of 16 months as a castaway on Roatán Island after escaping from pirates, 1722)[1]

Visiting Americans to Roatán often complain about insect bites and with reason. Insect repellents are sweated off; the sandfly is so small that window screens are ineffectual. . . . Measures will have to be taken to control insect pests. . . . Most annoying to tourists are sandflies. (Nance, 1970, p. 45)

We almost didn't get our passports in time. . . . We thought we were going to Roatán . . . paradise in the Caribbean. . . . We had no idea that Roatán was part of Honduras and that we needed a passport to go there. (Woman tourist from the U.S., Roatán, 1993)

Say the words *Central America* and a number of images come to mind, most of which have little to do with diving. (Dive Travel Directory, *Scuba Diving*, 1993)

Although considered politically strategic during the 18th and 19th centuries, the Bay Islands remained relatively remote until well into the 20th century. In part, because of their isolation and somewhat unsavory reputation, the islands attracted the attention of many renegades. One of the most famous of these was the American writer, William Henry Porter, better known as O. Henry, who spent several months of 1896 as a fugitive in Honduras. He had fled from the U.S. where he was about to be tried by a federal court on charges of embezzling from the bank by which he had been employed. At that time, Honduras was the only Central American country without an extradition treaty to the U.S. Porter spent some time in the port cities of Trujillo and La Ceiba (Long, 1949). According to islanders, he also visited the Bay Islands where he apparently cavorted with other fugitives, soldiers of fortune, and revolutionaries. The author's distinguished collection of short stories about Central America, *Cabbages and Kings* (Porter, 1904), is situated in the fictional country of *Anchuria* presumed to be Honduras. His description of the island of *Ratona* likely refers to Roatán:

> You must know that Ratona is an island twenty miles off the south of a South American republic. It is a port of that republic; and it sleeps sweetly in a smiling sea, toiling not nor spinning; fed by the abundant tropics where all things "ripen, cease and fall toward the grave." (Porter, 1904)

The islands also were visited by several of the adventurers, pseudo-archeologists, and explorers who traveled through Central America during the early part of this century (Wauchope, 1962). One of these was Mitchell-Hedges, who wandered the islands in the 25-ton yacht, *Amigo*, between 1929 and 1936 (Mitchell-Hedges, 1954). He described the islands:

> Roatán, Barbareta . . . Elena . . . Utila . . . Bonacca. . . . The names ring in my ears like the blare of bugles. . . . They are . . . the Bay Islands . . . emerald gems, in the Caribbean Sea, separated from the mainland by twenty-five miles of foul ocean on which a fine passage is hell, a bad one indescribable. (Mitchell-Hedges, 1954, p. 210)

In the words of one of Mitchell-Hedges' female traveling companions, Jane Houlson, her "Chief rambled the world for the sake of adventure" (Houlson, 1934). Although ostensibly working under the auspices of the British Museum and the Heyes Foundation in New York, Mitchell-Hedges' publications (e.g., *Battles with Giant Fish* [1923], *Land of Wonder and Fear* [1931], *Battles with Monsters of the Sea* [1937], and *Danger My Ally* [1954]) resemble romantic adventure tales much more than scholarly treatises. He appears to have spent as much time fishing, hunting, and looking for treasure as he did collecting artifacts for those who funded him. In his autobiography, *Danger My Ally* (1954), he credits himself with being named Chief of the Mule Division of the army by the president of Honduras and then saving Honduras from revolution by his intelligence and quick wit (Mitchell-Hedges, 1954, p. 117–120). Later in that same book, he concludes that the Bay Islands were part of the lost continent of Atlantis and that the Maya are the descendents of that "lost civilization." In his words:

> While exploring the island of Roatán we saw a narrow channel between the contorted roots of the mangroves. . . . Abruptly we were faced by a sheer cliff towering in majesty. . . . With difficulty we climbed the face of the cliff . . . found caves . . . during the following days in the floor of the caves we excavated painted pottery, stone implements, obsidian knives, jade and jadeite figurines, a stone metate and many other artifacts. . . . A continent was submerged [Atlantis] and . . . a remnant survived [on the Bay Islands], who destitute, terrified and overwhelmed, lived in isolated communities; and that

from these evolved, again through many millenia, the great Mayan civilization. (Mitchell-Hedges, 1954, p. 233–234)

The islands also were the object of more reputable scientific inquiry during this period, particularly by the renowned archeologist, Duncan Strong, whose 1933 Smithsonian expedition to Honduras included an archeological survey of the Bay Islands (Strong, 1934, 1935). Strong's findings remain significant in light of the limited archeological investigations conducted on the islands (Stone & Lange, 1984).

Although the islands may have been reachable to wealthy explorers, audacious scholars, and fugitives, they remained inaccessible to most travelers. British journalist, Peter Keenagh, described his ordeal traveling to the islands in 1937:

> A journey to the islands can be very uncomfortable and sometimes takes several days. The only craft going between the mainland and the islands are small trading schooners which sail irregularly and without warning so that the occasional traveler must consider himself far less important than a miscellaneous cargo of fish, fruit, and general merchandise. (Keenagh, 1937, p. 12)

Keenagh also noted the lack of visitors and tourist accommodations:

> There was a house they told us, belonging to a Captain Dick, which was always open for casual visitors, and it was there we were to stay. We asked a young islander how many people had visited Roatán in the last year; he said there had been five strangers come to interview the boatbuilders about building banana barges for use on the Mosquito Coast. (Keenagh, 1937, p. 14)

He refers as well to the continued antagonism between the islanders and the GOH and how these conflicts instituted intractable obstacles to "development" on the islands:

> One of their [islanders] chief grievances today is that the money they are obliged to pay to the Honduran Government in taxes is spent on improvements to the mainland. Relations with the Government have never been good and Honduran efforts to bring about a rapprochement have been discouraged. From time to time concerted drives have been made in this direction, with elaborate plans for the building of harbours, roads, landing fields, and wireless stations on Roatán and the other large islands, but few concrete results have received practically nothing, and their potential loyalty to an alien Government has been rather spoilt by the repeated prevarications of Tegucigalpa. . . .

> Small progress will be made in the development of the islands until there is a better understanding with the Honduran Government. Their nationalization will be a long and slow process; there is so little common ground, and the differences of race, language, and religion mitigate strongly against the formation of close bonds. Recently the Honduran Government has redoubled its efforts to encourage or force a rapprochement: English is

forbidden in the island schools, all posters and notices must be in Spanish only, and the governor of the islands, until recently an islander of British descent, has been replaced by a Spanish official from the capital of Honduras. (Keenagh, 1937)

Romantic, rustic, and somewhat savage images predominate in the accounts of the islands by travelers through the 1950s. Also ubiquitous are references to vast and secret pirate treasures. According to the Swedish adventurer, Tord Wallstrom, who visited the islands in the early 1950s:

A little way off the coast lie three small islands, Bonaccca, Roatán, and Utila with the common name of *Islas de la Bahia* in Spanish and Bay Islands in English. But those are merely their official names. In actual fact they are better known under the romantic and dramatic name: *Pirate Islands.* . . . I had heard a lot about the *Pirate Islands*: that they were inhabited by descendants of British Freebooters—fair headed, tough chaps, who spoke a queer antiquated English. I had heard about a people who "fished and cultivated coconuts, smuggled, and attended prayer meetings." About full-blooded beautiful women, devouring men. And much besides . . . quite a lot of pirate gold also has been found in caves and grottoes on the islands. (Wallstrom, 1955, p. 100–102)

Wallstrom goes on to observe the maintenance of ethnic and cultural distinctiveness and the continued prejudices of islanders toward Spanish-speaking residents:

We're all of English descent here, as you know. We don't live in the same way as the natives. We cannot live with them. They are all rough Spaniards. We live in decent homes, nice even though they are poor, with furniture, radio and piano. The natives have just their mud huts. They spit on the floor, we spit outside the door, that's what makes the difference you see (Elderly resident of Utila, quoted in Wallstrom, 1955).

The Emergence of the Modern Tourism Sector

Even after World War II, the Bay Islands (like much of the Western Caribbean) did not participate in the tourism boom that affected the Eastern Caribbean. Several factors inhibited the growth of the tourist sector on the islands including: the lack of transportation, infrastructure, and facilities; the political instability of Honduras; the image of "backwardness" of Central America in the minds of potential tourists; and the lack of concerted public and private efforts to develop the industry (Checchi, 1959, p. 90; Nance, 1970). Although the islands' tourism potential had been noted since the beginning of this century (e.g., Checchi, 1959; Rose, 1904; Webb Jr., 1954), significant tourism development only began in the 1960s after the initiation of regular airline service from the mainland (Davidson, 1974; Nance, 1970). In 1965, the islands were one of the five areas in Honduras selected for intensive tourist development by international economic consultants hired by the Central American Bank for Economic Integration (Ritchie et al., 1965, p. 72–74). According to their report:

> The tourist development of the Bay Islands is a foregone conclusion. No area of such beauty and such accessibility can remain undiscovered and unexploited. . . . Nature has not created comparable attractions along the Caribbean coasts of Guatemala, Nicaragua, or Costa Rica. The Bay Islands are a truly regional resource. (p. 72).

The consultants urged the immediate construction of improved landing strips and several longer term projects aimed at constructing an extensive road and harbor system. In 1965, the domestic carrier, Lansa Airlines, scheduled three flights a week between San Pedro Sula and Roatán in a Cessna 180. Before then visitors could either charter a plane from La Ceiba or San Pedro Sula, or endure the arduous 15-hour journey from La Ceiba to Oak Ridge aboard the weekly mail boat (Nance, 1970, p. 56). At that time, Evans (1966, p. 177) pointed out the absence of basic conveniences expected by many tourists—roads, hotels, hospitals, sanitary facilities, and a sufficient supply of potable water. Evans also recorded the skepticism of the Bay Islanders to the mounting efforts of the GOH to develop tourism. For islanders, enhanced tourism meant a greater ladino presence and control by the mainland (Evans, 1966, p. 179).

By the mid-1960s, the islands became the focus of a few newspaper and magazine accounts aimed at enhancing the tourist trade. These articles stressed the appropriateness of the islands for the adventurous traveler interested in sailing, diving, treasure hunting, and/or beautiful island women (Jackson, 1970; Kilbracken, 1967). Despite the recommendations of international consultants, initial efforts by the GOH to develop the industry, and some media attention, the islands had only five hotels: three on Roatán (two in Coxen Hole and one in Oak Ridge) and one each on Bonacca and Utila (Table 3.1). In 1967, transport to the islands was facilitated with the addition of daily flights between San Pedro Sula and Roatán and a few tourists began "discovering" Roatán (Nance, 1970). By 1969, three regularly sched-

Table 3.1. Growth in the Number of Bay Island Hotels: 1960–1996

Year	Bay Islands		Roatán		Guanaja		Utila	
	Hotels	Rooms	Hotels	Rooms	Hotels	Rooms	Hotels	Rooms
<1960	1		1					
1965	5		3		1		1	
1969			12	81				
1971	16		11		4		1	
1985	17	248	10	168	4	46	3	34
1992	35		27		6		2	
1994	46		30		9		7	
1996	80	954	39	603	17	152	24	199

Source: 1960, 1965, 1971: Davidson (1974, pp. 123–124); 1969: Nance (1970, p. 59); 1985: Honduras Tourist Bureau (1985); 1992: Vega et al. (1993); 1994: IHT (1995); 1996: Honduras Institute of Tourism/Mundo Maya (1996).

uled DC-3 flights arrived daily on Roatán. Visitors, however, often were confronted with harrowing landings on the island's only airstrip near Coxen Hole—a poorly maintained and unpaved field less than 500 meters long (Nance, 1970, p. 60). Pilots frequently had to make more than one attempt to land after first honking their horns in order to clear the landing field of chickens, donkeys, and other interlopers (Jackson, 1970).

Beginning in the 1960s, the islands also were "discovered" by Americans (many from the southern U.S. and California) who began "purchasing" ocean frontage land or acquiring long-term leases for as much as 99 years (Davidson, 1974; Nance, 1970). A few, such as the midwestern family that began building the islands' first resort, Cooper's Key Resort,[2] in Sandy Bay in 1964, developed their own resorts. Other speculators and private development companies (such as the Bay Islands Company from Birmingham, AL) acquired property to resell for private retirement homes and hotels (Davidson, 1974, p. 124). U.S. residents also established a number of other businesses including floating Laundromats, curio shops, bars, and repair shops (Davidson, 1974, p. 128). A few individuals acquired properties on the islands primarily for retirement or summer homes and did not engage in any further development activities (Davidson, 1974, p. 124).

The legality of the land transactions associated with these various activities remains equivocal—as does the current tenure of these properties—because the purchase and ownership of land on the islands by foreigners was prohibited by the Honduran Constitution. Article 107 of the Constitution stipulates that land situated in coastal and frontier areas within 40 miles of the Honduran border can only be owned or purchased by Hondurans. This includes all islands, cays, and reefs. Currently the Honduran Congress is attempting to reform Article 107, which will allow the purchase of lands anywhere within the 40-mile exclusion or border areas if the project is dedicated to tourism and is approved by the government.

Conflicting claims to island properties are one of the most significant problems on the islands and pit islanders, foreigners, and ladinos against each other in every possible permutation. For example, some foreign "buyers" were given land grants in the name of Queen Victoria, which are invalid in Honduras, while multiple individuals frequently claim ownership of the same parcel. One of the best known legal suits involved the present, islander owner of Cooper's Key Resort and the heirs of the U.S. citizen who acquired long-term leases and built the resort in the 1960s. Apparently the two men managed the business as partners and, according to the current owner, they were once "like father and son." At the death of the American in 1979, the present owner sued the heirs for debts he said had been accrued by the resort. The heir's family, who lived in the U.S., maintained that they had never learned of the suit. Except for publicly posted court filings in Honduras the principals weren't notified and therefore couldn't challenge the court decision that awarded 32 acres of property to the current owner. The family was unable to appeal the case because the case file was missing from the courthouse and without a file no appeal could be made (Johnson, 1994a). Another well-known incident involved the 1965 "purchase" of a 7-acre island off Guanaja by a Californian who planned to build a retirement home there. In 1992, the municipality of Guanaja claimed that it owned the land and expropriated the island in the Californian's absence. In this instance, the GOH intervened in response to pressure from the U.S. and returned the land to the American (Johnson, 1994a). The expropriation of land from foreigners is a serious concern, and the U.S. embassy has a staff to investigate the several dozen cases and attempt to recover property taken from U.S. citizens. According to a statement by a U.S. official, "To invest in Honduras or buy property is extremely risky. . . . When Americans come here to tell us they want to buy land, our immediate response is, 'Don't do it' " (Johnson, 1994a).

In addition to conflicts over land tenure, another notable consequence of enhanced speculation and investment in the islands in the 1960s was a significant increase in land prices. Between 1965 and 1967, land prices rose to 10 times their 1965 selling prices (Nance, 1970, p. 57). Further, the cost of a 1-acre waterfront lot that sold for about $75 in 1967 sold for $250–300 by 1970 (Davidson, 1974, p. 124).

By the late 1960s there appears to have been a change in the pattern of locating tourist facilities—away from preexisting settlements and toward more remote locations. These new resorts catered to higher paying clients and provided a number of tourist activities beyond room and board. By 1969, an estimated 900 tourists visited the islands and the number of accommodations grew to 12 (81 units) on Roatán: four (33 units) in French Harbour, three (24 units) in Oak Ridge, and one each in Sandy Bay (17 units), Coxen Hole, Port Royal (5 units), Punta Gorda, and Carib Point (2 units) (Nance, 1970, p. 59). Ten of the 12 hotels on Roatán were located on the south side of the island—nine on the 9-mile distance between French Harbour and Port Royal. Facilities consisted of five small guest houses, where island owners shared their home and meals; two hotels that provided rooms and food; two operating resorts (one in Sandy Bay and the other in Oak Ridge) that supplied facilities for diving, fishing, and boating in addition to food and lodging; and three resorts under construction at that time (Nance, 1970, p. 59). Potential tourists could choose from a range of accommodations. At Cooper's Key, guests stayed in individual cottages each with three shuttered sides that furnished constant ventilation. They enjoyed 24-hour electricity, hot water, hot plates, and miniature refrigerators in every cottage, at an all-inclusive rate of about US$30 per person per day. In French Harbour, at the Pirate Inn, occupants of the four guest rooms paid US$7.50 per day per person. Guests shared one bath without hot water and the electricity was turned off at midnight. On Guanaja, El Paradiso offered a degree of luxury somewhere between that of Cooper's Key and the Pirate Inn at about US$15.00 a day (Jackson, 1970).

A number of significant environmental repercussions stemmed from the construction of new hotels and resorts, especially those in more remote locations. These included clearing vegetation, especially mangroves; draining wetlands in order to reduce the number of insects (especially mosquitoes); building rooms, boat docks, and boat houses; constructing artificial beaches; planting ornamental plants; cutting footpaths and horse trails through the forests; and dredging coral for marinas and canals for travel inside the reefs (Davidson, 1974, p. 124). For example, during construction of Cooper's Key Resort a dredge was employed to move sand to create an artificial beach in an area that first had been cleared of mangroves (Nance, 1970, p. 42).

The great variety of marine life provided important resources for naturalists, photographers, divers, and both spear and tackle fishermen. The main tourist activities supplied by the resort hotels centered on marine life, especially saltwater game fish. At first, the Coral House in Oak Ridge, Marine Lodge at Port Royal, and Cooper's Key Resort located in Sandy Bay were predominantly fishing lodges, equipped to handle both spear and tackle fishing (Nance, 1970, p. 42). Big game fish were scarce, however, implying that big game fishing might not become a major attraction on the islands. However, bonefish in shallow lagoon waters were much more abundant, suggesting that small game fishing could become an important tourist attraction (Nance, 1970, p. 42).

Despite increased facilities and improved transportation, the Bay Islands remained a destination for the adventurous traveler during the 1960s and 1970s (Jackson, 1970). Visitors to the three principal Bay Islands were likely to use a variety of modes of transportation getting to and around the islands. They most likely flew by jet from New York, Miami, or New Orleans to San Pedro Sula in northern Honduras, where they transferred to a DC-3 for the trip to Roatán. Trips among the islands were either on four-seat single-engine planes or on the daily packet boat. There were few automobiles, trucks, and motorbikes on Roatán, and arriving tourists were transported by four-wheel-drive vehicles to resorts in Sandy Bay and French Harbour. At that time, the only automobile on Utila was an old Ford with expired Florida license plates, while motorized transport was nonexistent on Guanaja, which didn't have any roads. There were no telephones on the islands and electricity was available for only a few hours each evening in French Harbour and Guanaja. Insects, especially sandflies, mosquitoes, and ticks were serious pests and sanitation facilities usually consisted of outhouses built over the water. Only in the islands' better resorts were tourists pampered with plumbing. For most people, the islands' sanitation systems had not changed since the 1950s when Swedish adventurer, Tord Wallstrom, observed, "If you raised the cover of the W.C. in any house . . . you will look straight down into the Caribbean. The tide and the currents see to it that refuse is swiftly removed, and the water round the houses is always clean and clear" (Wallstrom, 1955).

According to Nancy Jackson, a columnist for the New York Times who visited the islands in 1970:

> The Bay Islands are as untamed and as rugged as the British seamen (some say pirates) who wrested them from the Indians and Spanish. . . . Such a vacation is not for the fellow who insists upon a wine list before dinner or the latest edition of the morning newspaper on his breakfast tray. . . . For the hardier type, the islands are an adventure. . . . The main attraction is a return to nature and the simpler life. Here, the life style recalls an era when people grew their own food, sewed their own clothes on treadle machines, shopped

at a general store and watched sunsets unobscured by skyscrapers or smog. (Jackson, 1970)

Jackson also commented on the distinctiveness of the islands and on the enduring, conflictive relationship between the islanders and the mainlanders:

> Despite their nearness to Central America and the fact that they were ceded to Honduras by Britain more than 100 years ago, the Bay Islands have no Latin flavor. The mood and menu are more early Jamaican. . . . The islanders disassociate themselves from their fellow Hondurans on the mainland. To them the mainlanders are still Spanish. . . . And they viewed the "soccer war" between Honduras and El Salvador last July as a family affair in somebody else's family.[3] . . . Bay Islanders refrain from setting foot on the mainland, preferring to seek work or pleasure in New Orleans or Tampa, where they market their shrimp. . . . The mainlanders, on the other hand rave about the natural beauties of the islands even as they call the islanders "pirates." Yet few mainlanders actually have visited the islands. (Jackson, 1970)

Finally, she notes the important changes occurring on the islands as the result of increased U.S. investment:

> Although the islands today are more English than Spanish, they may soon be more American than English as investors develop resorts to please tourists who don't fancy ticks and community showers. . . . Resorts similar to Cooper's Key are now being planned in French Harbour and Utila. . . . The developers maintain that they do not want to change the mood of the islands—merely add electricity, hot water, and wine lists. (Jackson, 1970)

The Boom in International Tourism

> Tourism is bound to come into its own, but is still in its infancy, with no more than four resorts which would attract Americans, and perhaps a dozen altogether, all of them small. I suppose some of the charm will be gone when Holiday Inn plunks a big one down on one of those spectacular beaches. (Wilensky, 1979, p. 63)

Although a modern tourist sector emerged in the islands during the 1960s, the industry grew slowly until the late 1980s, when once again improvements to the airport runway on Roatán, along with the perception of "peace" throughout Central America, contributed to a boom in tourism. The majority of factors that limited the expansion of tourism in the 1960s continued through most of the 1980s. As shown in Table 3.1, the number of tourist hotels and resorts on the islands increased only slightly between 1969 and 1985 before growing significantly through the late 1990s. Despite the initiation of a ferry service between La Ceiba on the mainland and the island villages of Utila, Oak Ridge, and French Harbour, the road system on the islands did not improve. With only a few narrow, steep, dirt roads, the movement of people and goods remained predominantly dependent on dugout canoes via the shallow intracoastal waterways until the construction of the road between

Coxen Hole, French Harbour, and Oak Ridge in the late 1970s (Wilensky, 1979, p. 62). Although a substantial boom in tourism did not take place during the 1970s, a few significant tourism developments did occur. These included the construction of a moderately large (24 units) hotel in the community of West End on the northwest shore of Roatán in 1971 and the building of at least three hotels (34 units) on Utila.

Another important event was the establishment of the Caribbean Sailing Yachts (CSY), a charter fleet company with offices on Roatán and in New Jersey, which added to the diversity of tourist experiences available in the islands. In 1979, for a cost of US$360 to US$730 per week (depending on whether it was low or high season) plus the cost of provisioning (a maximum of US$11 per day per person), it was possible to charter one of CSY's three yachts—each capable of boarding a maximum of six people. The price included fuel, snorkeling gear, linens, ice, and transportation from the Roatán airport to the marina (Wilensky, 1979, 46). In 1979, Julius Wilensky, a well-known yachtsman, was commissioned by CSY to write a *Cruising Guide to the Bay Islands* (Wilensky, 1979). In discussing the pros and cons of Bay Islands' cruising at that time, he suggested:

> The Bay Islands, in their present state of undevelopment, aren't for everyone. If you like highly sophisticated harbors with full service marinas, excellent restaurants, fine stores, elegant resorts, and formalized sightseeing, forget the Bay Islands. The best word to describe them now is primitive. But if you don't mind primitive, and if you enjoy untrammeled and unspoiled, the Bay Islands are waiting for you right now. . . . Another thing which made our cruise outstanding was some of the best swimming, snorkeling, and diving we've ever experienced. (p. 10)

Wilensky also described the incipient scuba diving opportunities on the islands that he evaluated as "limited" because of the few air stations (Wilensky, 1979, p. 43). He identified a total of four locations on Roatán where it was possible to rent equipment or refill tanks and singled out Cooper's Key Resort in Sandy Bay as having a very complete facility that included compressors, a dive boat, instructors, and scuba gear (Wilensky, 1979, p. 43).

Factors Promoting Tourism Development

The economic policy decisions made by the GOH in response to the national economic crisis of the 1980s were fundamental to the subsequent boom in tourism in the Bay Islands. In a context of declining terms of trade for its primary exports (bananas, coffee, and beef) and a continuing debt crisis, the GOH began promoting two major avenues of economic development—both of which impacted the Bay Islands: the promotion of so-called nontraditional exports (including shrimp and lobster) and the expansion of tourism. Their considerable potential for tourism development had made the Bay Islands a focal point of federal legislation since they were declared a tourism zone in 1982 (*Acuerdo Numero* 87). Particularly significant were the 1991 *Acuerdo Ministerial Numero Dos*, which established the minimum standards for any Bay Islands' development, including restrictions on coastal building and protective measures for mangroves and offshore coral and marine life, and the 1993 *Decreto 83-93*, which created a Bay Islands Commission to promote development, review all development plans, and preserve the islands' environment.

With international development assistance, Roatán's coral-fringed airstrip on the outskirts of Coxen Hole was improved to handle jet aircraft in 1988. The runway was expanded to 2,200 meters in length and 45 meters in width and a modern control tower was constructed (Gobierno de Honduras/Programa de las Naciones Unidas para el Desarrollo [GDH/PNUD], 1992a, p. 44). In July of that year the Honduran national airline, Tan Sahsa, began offering direct jet service between Roatán, the closest mainland airport (La Ceiba), several U.S. international gateways (Miami, New Orleans, and Houston), the two major Honduran cities (San Pedro Sula and Tegucigalpa), and other Central American cities. Although classified as an "international" airport, the tiny, ramshackle terminal always was quite chaotic whenever incoming flights arrived. International travelers faced incomprehensible customs and immigration procedures. Not infrequently, corrupt immigration officials demanded illegal and exorbitant visa fees from unsuspecting tourists. Tourists also had to elbow their ways through packs of island boys vying to handle their luggage. At this point, even seasoned travelers were relieved to have made hotel reservations at one of the more upscale resorts that provided minivan service from the airport. Other tourists were faced with a long, hot walk into Coxen Hole from where they could take a taxi or bus to their destination.

Even though it was now hypothetically possible to make the trip from one of the U.S. gateways to Roatán in about 5 hours, visitors often were forced to overnight in La Ceiba or San Pedro Sula. A delay of an hour or so leaving the U.S. was enough to prohibit landing on Roatán as the airfield did not have lights. This happened with sufficient frequency that Tan Sahsa had agreements to accommodate delayed travelers with several La Ceiba and San Pedro Sula hotels. In many cases, disembarking passengers found that their luggage had not arrived. Locating one's luggage and claiming it often involved several days of negotiations with unhelpful airline employees and in some instances paying "bribes" in order to ransom "kidnapped" bags. Flying on Tan Sahsa always was an adventure, but at the time there were no alternatives. Several high-ranking Honduran military officers were major owners of the airline and used their powerful influence to restrict landing rights to the national airline. Frequent customers of Tan Sahsa (who often referred to the airline as "Stay At Home Stay Alive") were not surprised when in 1994 the U.S. Federal Aviation Agency barred the airline from landing in the U.S. for major safety failures. This ruling led to the eventual bankruptcy of the airline a few years later—although not to a significant opening of the skies to international airlines. Currently, the only major international airline with landing rights on Roatán is TACA airlines, although Maya World Airways with headquarters in Guatemala flies between Guatemala City and Roatán three times per week. Apparently, Alitalia Airlines is planning to start a charter service between Italy and Roatán in the near future. It is also possible to fly American and Continental Airlines between the U.S. and San Pedro Sula and transfer to a national carrier for the final leg of the trip to Roatán.

Photo 3.1. Roatán International Airport, 1991.

Photo 3.2. Roatán International Airport, 1997.

Business decisions of TACA have included the promotion of low-fare flights directly from San Salvador. These changes have resulted in an increase in the number of Central American visitors to the islands, especially in the summer months (particularly August) and on holidays (e.g., *Semana Santa* [Holy Week])—the low season in terms of tourists from elsewhere.

In addition to airport improvements, international assistance financed the construction of the islands' first paved road—between Roatán's major population and tourist centers: Coxen Hole, French Harbour, and Oak Ridge. A spur also was built that connected the municipal center of Coxen Hole to the villages of Sandy Bay and West End, thereby facilitating the development of tourism on the northwest corner of the island. Foreign aid also contributed to the electrification of most of the islands, greatly enhancing the feasibility of expanding tourism throughout the islands.

Advertising the Bay Islands

For several decades, a growing number of travel brochures, newspapers, magazines, guidebooks, and now Internet sites have promoted the Bay Islands as an engaging vacation destination. Before that, the islands (as well as Honduras) received scant coverage in tourist-related media. The islands were not mentioned at all in Sydney Clark's travel guide, *All the Best in Central America*, published in 1946 (S. Clark, 1946). Twenty-five years later, *Your Central America Guide*, written by Henry Godfrey referred fleetingly to the islands in his brief history of Honduras and not at all in the section that recommended tourist destinations within the country (Godfrey, 1970). Similarly, a few years later, the islands were not included in Eugene Fodor's list of desirable tourist destinations along the Caribbean coastline, even though Belize, Mexico, Panama, Colombia, and Venezuela were covered (Fodor & Fisher, 1977). An exception to this lack of attention were the prophetic comments of Seldon Rodman, made in response to the inauguration of the new jet airport in San Pedro Sula in 1966 (Rodman, 1966). After noting that the airport would open up the beautiful beaches of Honduras' North Coast to tourists, he speculates, "Unless, the Bay Islands steal the whole show. As well they may" (Rodman, 1966). After describing the spectacular beauty of the islands, Rodman provides information on how to contact an agent on Guanaja for information on how to purchase one of the islands' many satellite keys, "complete with cocoa palms, beaches and the best skin diving anywhere—for as little as three thousand dollars" (Rodman, 1966, p. 164).

Even today, in an era characterized by the proliferation of travel books, Honduras and the Bay Islands receive less attention than their more tourist-dependent neighbors: Belize, Costa Rica, and Guatemala. A search of travel books available through the Internet bookstore, Amazon.Com, on August 13, 1998 revealed that of the approximately 180 travel books on individual Central American countries, only 14 books (8%) were specifically on Honduras—similar to the number of publications depicting Nicaragua, Panama, and El Salvador. At the same time, there were 46 books (26%) on Belize, 45 (26%) on Costa Rica, and 37 (21%) on Guatemala. Eliminating the travel books devoted to describing the country's archeology or offering advice to potential retirees from the U.S. and Canada, Honduras was represented by only six guide books. Of these, four were either specifically on the Bay Islands (*Diving and Snorkeling Guide to Roatan and Honduras' Bay Islands* and *Diving Bay Islands*) or included the Bay Islands in the title of the book (*Open Road's Honduras and Bay Islands Guide* and *Honduras Handbook: Including the Bay Islands and Copan*). The remainder (*Honduras: Adventures in Nature* and *Honduras: Ulysses Travel Guide*) include specific and relatively lengthy chapters on the considerable tourist potential of the islands. Moreover, the Ulysses travel guide ranks the Bay Islands as the most desirable tourist destination in the country. Quite consequential is Gollin and Mader's (1998) recent book, which portrays the latest form in which tourism to Honduras and the Bay Islands is framed and promoted (i.e., as a destination for adventure and nature tourism).

Recently, most of the larger hotels and resorts on the islands have begun to distribute attractive brochures advertising their properties—most in English. One of the first such brochures, *Honduras: Bay Islands*, was printed in 1985 by the Honduras Tourist Bureau. In addition to listing the islands' hotels and giving instructions on how to get there, the 8-page brochure includes a dozen lovely color photographs of the islands' diverse attractions. Although it appears polished at first glance, the text, written in English, contains several spelling, grammatical, and historical errors. Nevertheless, the text provides important evidence as to how the Honduras Tourist Bureau wished to represent the islands to potential foreign visitors—as an unblemished, exotic getaway, with friendly natives waiting to greet them, and located only a few hours from their homes in the U.S. The purported pirate ancestry of some islanders adds a touch of intrigue to the islands, as does the mention of black Caribs. Missing from the description of the islands' peoples, however, is any mention of the ladino population, which was significant by that time. According to the Honduras Tourist Bureau:

> To those of us who are permanently programmed into the age of technology, the islands will provide a refreshing change of pace. . . . Warmer than the Caribbean sea is the welcome you will receive from the Bay Islanders. . . . The original inhabitants were Paya Indians. . . . Today's Bay Islanders have little in common with yesterday's island natives. They are mostly English-speaking descendants of Scots-English pirates (the infamous Henry Morgan established his base of operations at Port Royal, Roatan Island), 18th century settlers from Cayman Islands and black Caribs—a mixture of Africans and Caribbean Indians. . . .

> Towns and settlements are clusters of picturesque stilt houses that line the bays and harbours. . . . For photographers, the Bay Islands are visual perfection. . . . For sun seekers and escapists, they are one of the last examples of the way the Caribbean appeared when Columbus first arrived in 1502. . . . For water sports enthusiasts there is a number of professional dive resorts who also offer swimming, snorkeling, sailing, board sailing, water skiing, and fishing. . . . Those that seek nature will find nature walks and hikes among the tropical coasts and verdant hills. . . .

Beautiful, charming and only 750 miles away from the continental U.S.A. the Bay Islands are so full of visual appeal that they will arrest the senses of the most experienced travelers. (Honduras Tourist Board, 1985)

A somewhat more realistic appraisal of the potential tourist experience on the islands was published in February 1988, a few months before the jet runway was completed on Roatán. This good-sized article entitled, "The Bay Islands of Honduras: Where scuba divers and would-be Robinson Crusoes can feel at home," appeared in the Travel Section of the *New York Times* (Allen, 1988). A related visitor's guide was also included that contained information on how to get to the islands and recommendations for the islands' three most upscale resorts (Cooper's Key Resort in Sandy Bay, Roatán, and *El Paradiso* and Bay Islands Club on Guanaja). The author heralds the Bay Islands as a new and unspoiled tourist destination, "For the venturesome traveler the Bay Islands offer untrammeled natural beauty, excellent scuba diving and other water sports, and an opportunity to skirt the beaten paths of Caribbean travel" (Allen, 1988, p. A19). At the same time, she wonders how long the islands can "escape the kind of large-scale tourist development that has both benefited and blighted so many other tropical beauty spots" (Allen, 1988, p. A19). She remarks, as well, on the disparate identity of the islands relative to the mainland, "It is as though a bit of the British West Indies cut adrift, had washed up unnoticed at the Caribbean's western edge" and notes the familiar theme of intense separateness and animosity between islanders and Spanish-speaking mainlanders (Allen, 1988, p. A19). Echoing the attitude of the islanders toward the earlier "Soccer War" between Honduras and El Salvador in 1969, the reporter observes that the ongoing Contra war along the Honduran–Nicaraguan border was thought of as "someone else's business" by the English-speaking islanders (Allen, 1988, p. A19). These themes of identity, independence, and enmity are reinforced in another *New York Times* article that appeared several months later (October 1988)—after the official inauguration of the new international airport on Roatán. Appearing in the "National" rather than the "Travel" section of the newspaper, this piece, "On Scorned Isles, They'd Have Victoria Whipped," concentrates on the islanders' individual identity from, and hostility towards, the mainland. Quoting the former Honduran-appointed governor of the islands (an islander and the owner of Cooper's Key Resort at the time), "Our people hate the Spaniards so much that there's absolutely no doubt in my mind that everybody over 50 has that Big British feeling. . . . They don't feel Honduran for a single minute. . . . I love my islands as English islands" (Gruson, 1988). Similar sentiments were voiced by island fishermen, "The day England handed us over to Honduras was the day Queen Victoria threw us to the vultures. . . . We've been in mourning ever since...Queen Victoria should be beaten with a whip. I'm an Englishman. When I die, I want them to put 'Here lies an Englishman,' on my grave" (Gruson, 1988). Especially resented were the GOH's heightened efforts to exert Honduran economic and political authority and related attempts to assimilate the islands. Particularly contentious were the appointments of mainlanders to administrative and teaching positions and the encouragement of immigration from the mainland. At that time (1988) one of the islands' senior ministers and a future mayor of Coxen Hole estimated that 50% of the of the population in the islands' two major urban centers, Coxen Hole and French Harbour, were Spanish speakers from the mainland—an increase from 10% a decade earlier (Gruson, 1988).

The years immediately following the opening of the international airport on Roatán saw the greatest proliferation of media coverage on the islands. In 1989, the Islands were featured in the July/August issue of *Aboard*, the in-flight magazine published by Tan Sahsa (Stephens, 1989). This article, "Retreat to Roatán Island," emphasized the beauty of the Island, "Roatán's spectacular halo of greens, blues, and purple emanates through its waters. Coral reefs, huge and varied in structure, produce the spectrum of colors," as well as the varied tourist activities available, "Today, more than 20 resorts, inns, and marinas cater to special travel interests such as scuba diving, snorkeling, sailing, windsurfing, and game fishing" (Stephens, 1989). At the same time, space for further tourist development also is pointed out, "Long stretches of shoreline between resorts and coastal villages remain undeveloped" (Stephens, 1989). The next year (1990), Roatán was highlighted as a prime dive tourism destination within the "Mayan World" in the central article of TACA International Airlines in-flight magazine (Rivas, 1990).

Although the islands were the subject of several subsequent articles in travel sections of major newspapers in the U.S. (e.g., Basch, 1992; Johnson, 1994b; Olson, 1994; Slater & Basch, 1997), the bulk of media attention came from the many dive magazines that proliferated in tandem with the broadening appeal of the sport. Dive magazines began lauding the Bay Islands as their number one choice for Caribbean dive vacations. In 1994, Cooper's Key Resort on Roatán was named the "Best Caribbean Dive Resort" according to *Rodale's Scuba Diving* magazine reader poll. More recently, the Bay Islands were recognized as the "Tropical Diving Capital of the Caribbean" and inducted into the *Skin Diver Travel Hall of Fame* (Wetzel, 1998).

While some articles in dive magazines treated a range of diving options on the islands others emphasized the amenities of particular dive resorts. At first, both the articles and advertisements in these magazines focused on opportunities on Roatán but later expanded coverage to include Guanaja and Utila. In the early days, the few operating dive resorts advertised themselves as if they were situated on the politically independent island nation of Roatán. Significantly, at that time the most popular T-shirts sold on the island were imprinted with the question, " Where the hell is Roatán?" As dive tourism spread from Roatán to Utila and Guanaja, resorts began to market themselves as being located in the Bay Islands, still not indicating that the Bay Islands were part of Honduras. In fact, the *Open Road* guide to Honduras still is entitled *Honduras and the Bay Islands*—suggesting that the latter is not part of the former.

Dive magazines also began marketing a new tourist diving experience—the live-aboard—as an attractive alternative to resorts and hotels (Frink, 1994). Built to handle approximately 20 divers, these vessels offer private, air-conditioned cabins, plentiful food, hot tubs, and photographic processing labs, as well as relatively unlimited diving. According to a couple from Louisiana who books accommodations on live-aboards in the Caribbean at least twice each year, "Live-aboards are

Photo 3.3. Accommodations at an upscale dive resort on Roatán.

Photo 3.4. Dive boats and dolphin pens at an upscale dive resort on Roatán.

convenient, reliable, and fun. . . . Nowadays, dive resorts are full of amateur divers who don't know what they're doing. They hold you up and are a danger to everyone. . . . Live-aboards are for 'real' divers" (personal field notes, 1997). According to the 1997 dive travel guide in *Skin Diver* magazine, "Seemingly a world away, Honduras and the Bay Islands are currently heading toward the top of the list of tempting, off the beaten trail, world-class adventure travel destinations. Discovery and adventure are available in unlimited quantities. And, aboard a modern TACA jet, you can reach Honduras in a little more than two hours from U.S. coastal gateways in Miami, Houston, and New Orleans" (Frehsee, 1997, p. 86).

The most recent addition to the diverse ways of touring the islands is via cruise ship. Ships of the Commodore Cruise lines occasionally anchor offshore near West Bay Beach and passengers are brought to the beach in small boats where they can snorkel and picnic. In May 1997, the 800-passenger, Norwegian Cruise Line/ Norwegian Star began including a 7-hour stop on Roatán as part of its regular itinerary. The week-long, *Texaribbean Cruise* sails from the Port of Houston to Calica and Cozumel in Mexico and then to Roatán where passengers can either snorkel and picnic on West Bay Beach or have a more ecotourism and cultural tourism experience, visiting the eastern part of the island. The cruise is prominently advertised by Norwegian Cruise Line on its Internet web site (http://www.ncl.com/html/).

The Internet now provides a major avenue for advertising (and communicating with) the islands, and both public and private interests take advantage of the opportunities. Currently, the Republic of Honduras Home Page (http://www.hondunet.net/) points to a major link on "National Tourism." That link provides two choices: "Our Beaches" or "Our Wildlife." Not surprisingly, the former emphasizes the Bay Islands. While the site provides general information on the history and location of the islands, it does not advertise specific hotels or other tourist services. Likewise, of the three major Honduran newspapers offering online editions, two (*El Tiempo* and *La Prensa*) include pointers to sections on tourism. In the case of *El Tiempo* (http://www.tiempo.hn) the user is faced with two choices: the Bay Islands or the archeological site of Copan. Again, only general information on the islands is provided. *La Prensa's* site (http://www.laprensahn.com) provides a much broader array of locales from which the tourist may choose: La Ceiba, Copan, Lake Yajoa, San Pedro Sula, Tegucigalpa, Tela, Trujillo, and Valle de Angeles, although the Internet visitor first sees a textual description of the Bay Islands. The above government and newspaper sites are all in Spanish. The language used to describe the islands makes clear that the Bay Islands definitely are part of Honduras. Representations of the islands include phrases such as, "a national treasure," or "*las islas perdidas* (lost islands) that have been found" after being ignored for 200 years. As noted previously, the Internet has been the most important means of informing the international public about tourist conditions on the islands in the aftermath of Hurricane Mitch.

In contrast to the official government and newspaper sites, virtually all the sites that are maintained by or for tourist businesses on the islands are in English. Many of the islands' hotels, resorts, dive shops, and real estate companies now have their own World Wide Web site or are listed in comprehensive Internet directories. Most larger establishments also have electronic mail addresses (as well as toll-free telephone numbers in the U.S.), so that it is possible to book accommodations as well as find out information about a wide range of topics of interest to potential tourists over the Internet. Even smaller businesses have been able to take advantage of the advertising potential of the Internet by working through a company in Coxen Hole that furnishes a variety of computer, Web, and business services (http://www.roatanet.com). The extent of the information available on the Internet is suggested by the results of an Internet search conducted on Monday, July 27, 1998 using the search engine Infoseek and the search term "Roatán." That search resulted in 1,881 hits.

The Growth of Tourism in the 1990s

In 1990, 2 years after the inauguration of the international airport, approximately 199,000 passengers arrived and departed from Roatán: an increase of 63% over the 122,000 passengers in 1987 (GDH/PNUD, 1992, p. 44). Of these, an estimated 15,000 were tourists, making the Bay Islands the most popular tourist destination in Honduras (Foer & Olsen, 1992). By 1993, the number of international arrivals grew to 30,000—more than the entire local population that was estimated to be about 24,000 at that time (IDB, 1994, p. 3). In 1994, the number of tourists climbed to around 40,000 and projections were that 78,000 tourists per year would visit Roatán by the end of the decade (Vega et al., 1993). Recent data from the Ministry of Tourism indicate that, by 1997, approximately 93,000 tourists visited the islands annually, significantly exceeding the estimate made in 1994 (B. Larson, personal communication, 1998).

According to profiles created by the IHT from survey data collected in the early 1990s, the typical tourist to the islands arrived by air (99%), was from the U.S. (70%), came principally for the diving (85%), stayed from 7 to 10 days (80%), was between 30 and 50 years old (83%), and earned more than US$30,000 per year in 1992 (87%). About half (49%) arrived with one companion while 43% arrived alone. The majority of visitors (66.4%) purchased inclusive tourist packages in their own countries rather than made their own arrangements (GDH/PNUD, 1992a, p. 47).

By the early 1990s, approximately 11% of the islands' labor force was employed in the service sector—most in the tourism industry. This rivaled the percentage of islanders working as fishermen (12%) and in the seafood processing plants (11%) and significantly surpassed the percentage of islanders working in agriculture (3.6%) (GDH/PNUD, 1992a, p. 69). A more recent study concluded that 80% of the islands' labor force was directly or indirectly dependent upon the tourism industry for employment, suggesting significant growth in the sector over a relatively short period (Haylock-Sanabria, Reina, & Matute, 1994, p. 245). The vast majority of islanders employed in the tourist sector were service personnel (89%) with little or no training. Only 10% of tourist workers had more than a minimal level of training. Most of these could speak English and worked in some capacity that brought them into direct contact with guests (e.g., receptionists, secretaries, restaurant hosts, and drivers). The remaining 1% of employees in the sector were managers or executives—many of these were foreigners (GDH/PNUD, 1992a, p. 47).

The number of tourist lodgings grew substantially during this period. Between 1985 and 1996 the number of Bay Islands' hotels and resorts grew almost 400% from 17 (248 units) to 80 (954 units). The internationalization of the islands' tourism industry was advanced in 1997 with the plans of Holiday Inn to build five new luxury resort hotels in Honduras, including one on Roatán ("Firmen convenio para constuir hotel," 1997). As indicated in Table 3.1, the substantial increase in accommodations was accompanied by a shift in the location of tourist facilities, including an increase in the percentage of total island accommodations available on Utila. Roatán's portion of total hotels dropped from 59% to 49% and Guanaja's share fell from 24% to 21%. Simultaneously, Utila's share of the islands' hotels grew from 18% to 30% by 1996. A similar pattern is seen in the number of units or rooms. During the period, Roatán's share of total units declined from 68% to 63% and Guanaja's dropped from 19% to 16% while Utila's portion grew from 14% to 21% of all units. By 1996, however, Roatán still had more than three times the absolute number of hotel units/rooms than did Utila and Guanaja. Table 3.2 compares and contrasts tourist facilities on Roatán, Utila, and Guanaja in terms of a number of characteristics. The islands differ not only in terms of the number of hotels but also the size of hotels as measured by the number of rooms/units.

Photo 3.5. Combination islander house, resort office, and gift shop, Roatán

Table 3.2. Characteristics of Bay Islands Hotels: 1996

	Bay Islands	Roatán	Utila	Guanaja
Number	80	39	24	17
% of total	100	49	30	21
Rooms				
Mean	12.1	15.5	8.7	8.9
SD	12.5	16.4	4.1	6.7
Median		12	8	6
Minimum	2	2	4	2
Maximum	86	86	19	23
Sum	954	603	199	152
% of total	100	63	33	16
Cost (US$)				
Mean	55.74	62.91	18.04	94.25
SD	45.18	35.33	23.9	48.88
Median		60	9	102.5
Minimum	1	15	1	20
Maximum	170	150	75	170
Sum	4125	2202	415	1508
% of total	100	53	10	37
Percent of hotels with				
Diving	48.8	59	25	59
Private bath	81.3	95	49	100
Hot water	55	79	17	53
Electricity	86.3	100	54	100
A/C	42.5	67	17	24
Fan	93.8	95	91	94
Pool	11.3	10	12.5	12
Ocean view	65	95	17	65
Restaurant	58.8	74	21	76
Bar	57.5	74	21	71
Cable TV	10	15	0	12

Source: *HONDURAS Tips* (Vol. 3, No. 4, Oct–Dec., 1996), Honduras Institute of Tourism/Mundo Maya (1996).

Roatán had on average twice as many rooms per hotel (15.5) compared to Utila (8.7) and Guanaja (8.9). Roatán also had the hotel with the largest number of rooms (86) and the greatest range in number of rooms per hotel (from 2 to 86 rooms). The largest hotel was Paradise Island, a very upscale, 15-acre resort located in French Harbour. This resort was built by the patriarch of one of the islands' elite, white families in 1989 and remains one of the most expensive resorts on Roatán (approximately US$139 per person per day in 1996). Paradise Island provides the most luxurious accommodations available on the islands. It was the islands' first, fully air-conditioned hotel with telephones, satellite televisions, refrigerators, and private balconies in every room. Composed initially of 50 rooms, the resort later was expanded to its current size of about 90 rooms. The hotel does not cater

Photo 3.6. Economy guesthouse owned by a foreigner, Roatán.

exclusively to divers but offers tourists a wide range of leisure activities. For a change of pace, divers (and nondiving guests) may choose to swim in the hotel pool, go deep-sea fishing, rent jet skis, or arrange a sightseeing tour. It was here that the 23-member U.S. Senate delegation to Central America stayed in January 1998 during their review of U.S. troops and antidrug programs in the region (Schmitt, 1998). Presumably, the U.S. Senators were unaware of the considerable environmental costs that accompanied the construction of the hotel. The owner of the hotel also owns a dredging company so it was a relatively simple and inexpensive task for him to dredge the shoreline and construct two large jetties to protect the new, white sand beach in front of his luxurious hotel. The jetties, however, cut off the natural flow of water, caused siltation, and ultimately killed much of the reef in front of the hotel (Gollin & Mader, 1998, p. 170-171).

Photo 3.7. Foreigner-owned dive boat and boat dock, Roatán.

Photo 3.8. Islander-owned restaurant and bar, Roatán.

The three major islands also differ significantly in terms of the average cost of accommodations. In 1996, the mean rental costs of a room (unit) ranged from a low of US$18.04 (median of US$9) on Utila, to US$62.91 (median of US$60) on Roatán, to US$94.25 (median of US$103) on Guanaja. Most of accommodations on Guanaja are expensive by island standards—ranging in price from US$100 to US$170 per person per night—and are located in relatively remote parts of the island, away from the population center of Bonacca Town, which is precisely where the few relatively inexpensive hotels and guesthouses are found. Roatán has the greatest range in accommodations according to price—from small guesthouses (many of which are not listed on official government hotel rosters) and cabins to moderately priced and luxurious lodgings. For some time, Utila has been thought of as the best choice for budget travelers—"the cheapest place to get dive certified in the Caribbean." In contrast to Utila, the majority of hotels and resorts on Roatán and Guanaja offer dive packages, private baths, hot water, air-conditioning, ocean views, restaurants, and bars. The reputation of Utila as a budget destination may change, however, in light of the recent construction of more upscale resorts there.

The most severe impact of Hurricane Mitch was on the island of Guanaja, which felt the power of the Category 5 hurricane for almost 2 days. Although most of the island was stripped of its vegetation and most homes and businesses were badly damaged or destroyed, the largest resorts reopened for business within a few months. The islands of Roatán and Utila suffered much less damage, although winds and waves pummeled them for several days. According to official government reports and press releases, most businesses were open in time for the 1998 Christmas season while the few remaining facilities resumed operation by early February 1999 (Egret Communications, 1999). According to the Honduran Minister of Tourism:

> Honduras was a special place to visit before Mitch—and it is just as special now. Airports, roads, resorts, hotels, and tour companies are ready to receive visitors. . . . This would be a great year to travel to Honduras. Not only will you have a rewarding experience—you will know that every dollar you spend in Honduras is helping this hardworking nation get back on its feet. (Norman Garcia, Minister of Tourism, January 1, 1999)[4]

The recent expansion of tourist construction on Utila is part of a recent onslaught of development throughout the islands enhanced by escalating foreign investment from the U.S. and elsewhere. Especially significant are the several foreigners from the U.S. who have started real estate companies on the islands, as well as the many private investors—including a few well-known international celebrities who have "purchased" island properties. Figure 3.1 summarizes the content of real estate advertisements placed in the monthly magazine, *Coconut Telegraph*, between 1992 and 1996. During that time the average number of property listings per issue increased from 1 to more than 50. At the same time, the average number of real estate agents represented in each issue grew from 2 to 13.4 and the number of locations that were advertised increased from 1 to 28. Other trends determined by

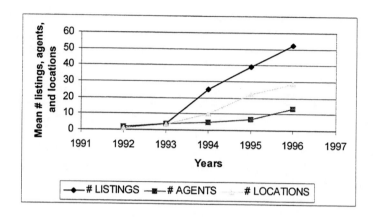

Figure 3.1. Real estate information from the *Coconut Telegraph.*

an analysis of the real estate advertisements include: 1) a decline in the number of private transactions along with an increase in transactions conducted through real estate agents; 2) significant growth in the number of parcels for sale; 3) an augmentation in the number of parcels in more remote locations away from existing communities and from the beach; and 4) a proliferation of new place names generated by development.

Associated with the growth in the number of property transactions have been considerable land speculation and exorbitant increases in the price of properties. By 1996, a 1-acre waterfront lot in most parts of Roatán sold for approximately US$200,000, while non-beachfront properties were available for about US$15,000 per acre (analysis of data in the *Coconut Telegraph*, various issues). The alleged unscrupulous dealings of foreign real estate developers have exacerbated conflicts over land tenure, led to lawsuits, and sometimes to violent confrontations. In April 1997, an Afro-Caribbean islander from Sandy Bay explained the current situation in this way:

> Basically, what's happened here is a land grab . . . [because of the lack of cadastral surveys, clear titles, etc.] land ownership is very hard to establish. . . . Islanders whose families have lived here for more than a hundred years can only show ownership [to the satisfaction of Honduran law] by going through a long, complicated, and expensive process. . . . They have to get a series of affidavits from neighbors and others saying that their family has lived on that spot of land since 1875 or whenever. . . . Since Islanders often can't legally establish ownership, especially the poorer ones without connections, they "sell" their land to these developers who've come in, who in turn sell the land to third parties—many from the States . . . the idea is to make big money today instead of a little bit of money for a long time . . . often the gullible third parties find themselves "owning" land that's already claimed by other people.

The attitude of many native and long-term residents of the islands toward the foreign developers is quite hostile. According to a longtime resident (originally from the U.S.) and one of the first individuals to open a tourist hotel on Roatán:

> The big game on Roatán these days is land. . . . John Henry Adams,[5] an international fugitive fleeing from a 26-count federal indictment handed down in Tampa, Florida, first ran to Belize, then to Roatán. He met and married an island widow, bought a Honduras passport (to avoid capture and extradition) and went into the real-estate business. Adams is the biggest real-estate operator in the Bay Islands, and he has burned a bunch of foreign visitors who did business with him. Roatán has had some pirates before, if we can believe the history books, but none of them could be compared with Adams and his Western Caribbean Properties. Incidentally, his son, Mike, is doing time in the Florida State Penitentiary. He wasn't able to get out of the country ahead of the law. Meanwhile, his father is finding true happiness— and lots of suckers—on Roatán (1997).

One of the most egregious incidents involving a land dispute occurred in April 1997. Land on Helene was "purchased' by one of the recently formed Roatán land development companies owned by a U.S. citizen and legally represented by a Honduran lawyer in San Pedro Sula. The company reportedly "bought" about 40 acres of land from a man from the U.S. who had acquired a 99-year lease to the land about 25 years ago. The company laid claim to about 100 acres of land, including beach frontage where 12 black Bay Island families had been living for almost 20 years.[6] Part of the confusion over this land deal was that it was based on a verbal contract between the islanders and the judge acting as a representative for the lawyer of the development company. In Honduras, a verbal contract is considered worthless in court. According to the president of NABIPLA, the verbal agreement was that the black islanders agreed to sell the improvements on the land— that is, their homes and their claim to the land—in exchange for land away from the beach. The first sign of problems appeared when the Judge of Civil Law appraised the homes of Bay Islanders at about US$2,500, an unrealistically low price for waterfront property in the islands. Before the deal advanced further, the Bay Islands judge arrived with a detachment of 38 soldiers from La Ceiba and burnt the homes of the 12 Bay Island families. The people who were there and who took photos had their cameras and film confiscated. One person who asked why this was being done was arrested and taken to jail. The judge's argument was that the islanders were squatting on land owned by the Roatán development company and should pay rent for the use of the space they had occupied. The islanders maintain, however, that this is not possible because neither Hondurans nor foreigners can legally have clear title to beachfront and over-the-sea properties. If the municipal government wished to rent the land to the development company, they would have to compensate the people for the improvements they had made on the land. Seeking egress for the Bay Island families, members of NABIPLA petitioned the U.N. Commission for Human Rights, Amnesty International, the Honduran Special Attorney General for Ethnic Groups (*Fiscalia de las Etnias*), and the brother of the former president of Honduras. To date, they have been unable to obtain any response concerning the case of these black Bay Islanders, not even from the municipal mayor's office in José Santos Guardiola, which technically controls the land on which the houses were built. This is not the first case of Bay Islanders' homes being destroyed in this manner, but it is the most serious and well known.

Tourism Development in Sandy Bay, West End, West Bay Beach, and Flowers Bay[7]

On Roatán, the post-1988 growth in the tourist industry was characterized by the augmented expansion of tourist facilities away from major population centers and toward the northwest coast. Primarily affected were the predominantly Afro-Caribbean communities of West End and Sandy Bay and the area of West Bay Beach (also known as Tabiyana Beach). With the notable exceptions of Cooper's Key Resort in Sandy Bay built in 1964 and Lost Lagoon in West End constructed in 1971, the northwest coast of Roatán had seen little in the way of tourist development before the late 1980s. It was only in 1993 that the first tourist lodgings opened in the immediate vicinity of West Bay Beach. As late as the early 1980s, the best and sometimes the only way to get to the community of West End—and the one hotel there—was by boat. Yet tourist potential was great, in large part because West Bay Beach, the best white sand beach on the islands, is located on the far northwestern shore and easily accessible. Tourism development in that part of the island was greatly simplified after the construction of the paved road between the airport and West End. By 1996, of the 39 hotels and resorts on Roatán listed by the IHT, 26 (67%) were found in Sandy Bay, West End, and West Bay Beach. The other major location of tourist facilities was French Harbour with eight hotels and resorts (21% of hotels on Roatán).

The communities of Sandy Bay and West End afford the opportunity to examine how similar and neighboring communities can be integrated into the tourism industry in very different ways. Tourism in the area of West Bay Beach augments the investigation of industry diversity by focusing on significant tourism growth in a locale in which no community existed previously. For purposes of contrast and to further augment the analysis of heterogeneity in the tourism sector, the community of Flowers Bay provides the chance to analyze an adjacent community that remains only minimally involved with tourism—at least directly. Flowers Bay also provides the important example of a community that is actively resisting the introduction of tourism in its prevailing form.

Table 3.3 compares and contrasts Sandy Bay, West End, and West Bay Beach on a number of important characteristics. By 1997, a total of eight tourist facilities (built between 1964 and 1996) operated in, and adjacent to, the community of Sandy Bay: 50% were classified as resorts, 25% as hotels, and 25% as cabins or rooms for rent. Accommodations ranged from 2 to 68 rooms or units in size and from US$20 to US$130 in cost. The mean number of rooms per accommodation was 18.9 rooms and average cost was US$68.63 per person per night. Four (50%) of the lodgings were owned by islanders, one (12.5%) by a ladino from the mainland, and three (37.5%) by expatriates from the U.S. The majority of hotels and resorts in Sandy

Table 3.3. Roatán, Sandy Bay, West Bay, and West End Accommodations: 1996–1997

	Roatán*	Total	Sandy Bay	West Bay	West End
Number of accommodations	39	34	8	9	17
% of total		100	18.6	20.9	60.5
Types of accommodations					
% resorts		16.2	50	55.5	3.8
% hotels		18.6	25	11.1	19.2
% cabins/rooms for rent		62.8	25	22.2	76.9
% condos/time shares		2.3	0	11.1	0
Number of rooms	603	483	151	124	208
Mean No. rooms/ accommodation	15.5	11.5	18.9	15.5	8
SD	16.4	13.5	22.3	18.7	5.2
Median	12		10	9.5	7
Minimum	2	1	2	2	1
Maximum	86	68	68	60	21
Sum	603	483	151	124	208
% of total		100	31.3	25.7	43.1
Cost (US$)					
Mean	62.91	47.78	68.63	80.83	33.73
SD	35.33	33.27	44.22	38.13	16.8
Median	60		55	75	32.5
Minimum	15	10	20	35	10
Maximum	150	150	130	150	62
Sum	2202	1911	549	485	877
% of total		100	28.7	25.4	45.9
Years built		1964–96	1964–96	1993–96	1971–96
Ownership					
% islanders		55.8	50	50	61.5
% ladinos		4.7	12.5	0	3.8
% foreigners		39.5	37.5	50	34.6
			(all U.S.)		(U.S., Italy, Aus.)
Percent of hotels with					
Diving	59	40.5	75	50	26.9
Private bath	95	85.7	100	100	76.9
Hot water	79	78.6	100	87.5	69.2
Electricity	100	100	100	100	100
A/C	67	38.1	37.5	50	34.6
Fan	95	81	75	100	76.9
Pool	10	0	0	0	0
Ocean view	95	66.7	75	87.5	57.7
Restaurant	74	50	62.5	50	46.1
Bar	74	42.9	62.8	25	42.3
Cable TV	15	2.4	0	0	2.7

Source: Analysis of survey data, April 1997. *Source: *HONDURAS Tips* (Vol 3, No. 4, Oct–Dec., 1996); Honduras Institute of Tourism/Mundo Maya.

Bay offered diving packages as part of their services as well as private baths, hot water, electricity, restaurants, and bars.

The tourism sector in Sandy Bay remains dominated by Cooper's Key Resort, which accounts for 45% of the rooms available in the community. For more than a decade it has been owned by one of the wealthy island families who also are heavily invested in the shipping and seafood processing businesses. The head of the family formally was a governor of the islands as well as a delegate to the Honduran Senate and continues to exert substantial political as well as economic power on the islands. Until recently, much of Sandy Bay was dependent on the resort not only for jobs, but also for electricity and water. The resort spatially bisects the community into "upper" and "lower" Sandy Bay. There is minimal interaction between members of the community and guests who generally remain on the resort grounds, which have been transformed into a fenced and guarded enclave that excludes the local population. Although established by an expatriate from the U.S. as a small, elite, fishing, yachting, (and later) diving resort, the current owner has transformed Cooper's Key Resort into a "Club Med" type of facility. The resort provides accommodations for more than 140 persons in about 70 cabins, and a diverse array of upscale tourism activities: yachting, sailing, kayaking, fishing, and even a dolphin show and "dolphin encounter" experience. The owner also has taken advantage of the expanding "academic" tourism market by establishing a "Marine Sciences Institute" and encouraging visits by academics who direct groups of students in various field projects. The vast majority of guests are divers from the U.S., whose primary activity is diving, who spend an average of US$150 per day per person, and, of whom, only 32% visit the Honduran mainland.

In 1980, a second tourist facility was opened in Sandy Bay by a wealthy ladino from the mainland. This moderately priced hotel containing 24 rooms continues to appeal to Spanish-speaking guests from Honduras and elsewhere in Central America. Another hotel was established 10 years later (1990) by a middle-class, black islander family—a small relatively inexpensive hotel of eight rooms. It is quite like most of the hotels in West End and has a similar clientele. In 1992, a U.S. citizen opened a relatively small and expensive new resort consisting of 14 rooms and cabins. To some extent it assumed the previous niche held by Cooper's Key Resort as a small, "elite" diving resort. A growing number of rental units (homes and rooms in private residences) are also available in Sandy Bay. In 1995 a new resort opened on the outskirts of Sandy Bay that most directly competes with Cooper's Key Resort. A couple from the U.S. with longtime ties to the U.S. military owns the resort. The latest hotel to open in Sandy Bay in 1996 was a small, five-room, moderately priced hotel. An individual from the U.S also established it.

In contrast to Sandy Bay, the tourism sector in West End is controlled by middle-class black islanders and consists of approximately 26, small-scale, relatively inexpensive accommodations for a total of 208 rooms that can accommodate at least 400 persons. In 1997, approximately 62% of hotels were owned by islanders, 4% by ladinos, and 35% by foreigners from the U.S., Italy, and Australia. These unpretentious lodgings, averaging eight rooms per facility and costing an average of US$33.73 per day per person (range from US$2 to US$50), consist of one resort, five hotels, a few cottages, and numerous rooms for rent that appeal to European, Honduran, and U.S. budget tourists, including backpackers and families. Compared to Sandy Bay, a smaller percentage of establishments in West End offer dive packages, private baths, hot water, ocean views, restaurants, and bars. To fill these voids, West End supports a growing number of dive shops, restaurants, and bars, many owned and managed by islanders. During the 1990s, the profile of tourists visiting West End has stayed remarkably similar. Approximately 50% of tourists in West End are from the U.S., 27% from Europe, and 15% from the Honduran mainland or elsewhere in Central America. They spend an average (median) of 7 days on the islands at US$25 per day. Visitors to West End engage in a much greater range of tourist activities than most of the tourists in Sandy Bay: 93% report swimming, 77% snorkeling, 46% diving, and 43% hiking. They also are much more inclined to explore the rest of Honduras and other Central American countries than tourists staying in Sandy Bay: 72% visit the Honduran mainland and 59% the other Central American countries.

The area of northwestern Roatán most recently impacted by the growth of tourism is West Bay Beach. Although the first hotel opened in 1993, by 1991 the shoreline and adjacent hillsides were covered with signs and billboards advertising the opportunity to invest in planned condominiums. Project maps detailed the boundaries of individual properties and colorful drawings depicted the finished projects. For many years, guests from Cooper's Key Resort were transported by boat to West Bay Beach for a weekly picnic on the beach, where the owner of Cooper's Key Resort and his family had considerable landholdings. In 1991, the owner constructed an unpaved (and unstabilized) road along a ridge top and through his large holdings to West Bay Beach. This road opened up the area for development and, shortly thereafter, individual parcels on either side of the road, some extending to the beach, were put up for sale. Between 1993 and 1996, nine hotels (a total of 124 rooms/units) were opened in the area, the first by a black islander from West End who already operated tourist lodgings there. To date, 50% of these constructions are owned by islanders and 50% by foreigners. It is important to note, however, that with the exception mentioned above, it is white islanders rather than black islanders who own the new properties. Approximately 55% of the new facilities can be classified as resorts, 11% as hotels, 22% as tourist cabins, and 11% as time-share condominiums. They range in size from 2 to 60 rooms. Costing an average of US$80.83 per person per night, accommodations in West Bay Beach are almost three times as expensive as those in West End and 15% higher than those in Sandy Bay. Most of the new establishments emphasize a diverse array of beach tourism activities in addition to diving. In fact, only half the new facilities offer diving packages as part of their services. The area remains somewhat isolated and guests often are required to take a boat taxi into West End for food and other services.

Adjacent to West Bay Beach, on the south side of Roatán, is the picturesque village of Flowers Bay, most of whose residents are black islanders. Despite its beautiful location at the southwestern tip of the island, the community has been relatively unaffected by the boom in tourism until recently. Accessible only by an unpaved road from Coxen Hole and by another from West End, local residents believe that their relative isolation impeded tourist development at the same pace as in West End, Sandy Bay, and elsewhere. In 1997, there were no hotels, rooms for rent, restaurants, or dive shops located in the village—although a large billboard on the outskirts of town advertised a planned condominium and housing project. While many members of the community are employed at the larger resorts in Sandy Bay and French Harbour, there are no tourism-based jobs or businesses in Flowers Bay. The most agriculturally based of the three communities, a small number of farmers have attempted to expand their production of agricultural commodities (especially beef cattle, poultry, animal products, and fresh vegetables) for sale to tourist enterprises in other communities.

Although not directly affected by tourism development within their community, the residents of Flowers Bay have had time to observe the consequences of its growth on neighboring communities and are not happy with what they've seen. According to residents, many of them have been urged by developers and private individuals to "sell" their property. Very significantly, the one grassroots organization that has emerged on the islands to resist the current pattern and trends in the industry's growth, NABIPLA, was started by individuals from Flowers Bay in 1991. A featured article in the first newsletter of the organization, *Bay Islanders' Echo: The Way We See Things*, admonished islanders, "Don't Sell Out the Bay Islands" (NABIPLA, 1995). In their words:

> In 1991 a cloud emerged over these beautiful exotic islands which we expected to have poured out blessings of equal financial opportunities for every islander: However when the cloud began to release its first showers our expectations were drowned by a flood of social, political and economic misery, that devastated our integrity. The victims of this scenario were the *NATIVE BAY ISLANDERS*; and the catalyst was the increasing number of real estate companies which are purchasing vast amounts of land from the poor at low prices and reselling at high rates. These companies are converting their shareholders into billionaires while the *BAY ISLANDERS* are dreaming of the mighty green dollar. This will deny you and your children and generations to come a chance of ever owning a piece of property on these islands. . . .

Developers have also begun to destroy our islands by cutting our mangrove, dredging our harbours and deforesting our land. **Is this progress or regress? Is this the Bay Island you want your children, and their future generations to grow up in?** Let's protect, conserve, and confront these problems together. This is important to you, and you are important to us. Don't worry about the jolly green giant (DOLLAR) he'll be here soon enough! Our children must grow up in a clean environment and enjoy the natural beauty of our birthright. Please don't sell out the Bay Islands to those that don't care about them and us. History has taught us that progress and development comes with a price, are we willing to pay this price by allowing developers to destroy our livelihood and our birthright? (NABIPLA, 1995)

Conclusions

While discussing the changes in travel writing that occurred between the World War I and World War II, Paul Fussell distinguishes *tourists* from two other types of persons who take trips—*explorers* and *travelers* (Fussell, 1980, pp. 37-50). He says that the explorer seeks the undiscovered, the traveler attempts to learn that which can be known by study and experience, and the tourist seeks that which already has been discovered by business and shaped by mass publicity. Fussell recognizes that the age of exploration is long past and asserts that travel is no longer possible in the modern world. Therefore, today all who make journeys are tourists. For Fussell it is mislabeling to refer to a *travel agent* or a *travel agency* because those terms refer to a manner of times gone by. Fussell expands his typology to include the *antitourist*—someone who attempts to avoid any of the accouterments of the stereotypical tourist and seeks out places that are perceived to be more remote and authentic than those visited by the standard tourist. The antitourist imagines himself to be a traveler. Fussell's classification is useful in differentiating the various types of persons who have visited the Bay Islands over the ages: the explorers such as Christopher Columbus; the travelers including ethnologists and archeologists such as Mitchell-Hedges and Duncan Strong; and finally the tourists and antitourists, who make up the majority of the current crop of visitors to the islands.

Although useful, Fussell's typology lacks a class for the scoundrels, the renegades, the fugitives, the mercenaries, or the malcontents—and there have been many such individuals who have journeyed to the Bay Islands. Although the islands may no longer evoke the image and sense of mystery that drew explorers and travelers (as conceptualized by Fussell), many islanders would say that the scoundrels keep coming—nowadays in the guise of unscrupulous real estate developers. However, it is not correct to say that it is foreign investors alone who have catalyzed the boom in tourism—and accompanying benefits and costs. Rather, the decisions of many local, national, and international actors have interacted to provoke the momentous growth of tourism and its associated consequences. These include the political and economic policy decisions of the Honduran government, the recommendations of consultants hired by international development organizations, the decisions of international aid agencies to help fund critical infrastructural improvements, the representations of the islands by the media, and the attempts by island elite and the middle class to take advantage of the outstanding emerging opportunities.

Today, the islands lure visitors not so much because of their thrilling history but because of their beauty—both above and below the sea—and the possibility of adventure that they present. Although the Bay Islands' reputation as a premier dive destination is its biggest attraction, present-day tourists and antitourists can choose from a broad list of activities including snorkeling, fishing, yachting, sailing, cruising, or just lying on the beach. A number of hotels, resorts, rental properties, cabins, guest houses, rooms for rent, and live-aboards provide tourists with a wide range of choices and price ranges. The person who wishes to participate in a mass tourism experience can choose to enjoy the facilities at places like Paradise Island, while the antitourist may prefer to swim, sunbathe, and sleep on a hammock overlooking the beach at one of the small, simple guest houses in West End. The adventure, nature, or ecotourist, on the other hand, may pick a place like Cooper's Key or one of the newer dive resorts on Guanaja or Utila and explore the fascinating reef and underwater ship wrecks three times per day or night. Couples longing for a romantic getaway may favor one of the newer small hotels or airy cabins in Sandy Bay and West End. And if one truly enjoys the islands there is the ability to invest in one of the islands' increasing number of time-share condominiums and permanent residences.

The benefits stemming from the growth of tourism have been substantial: a growing amount of hard currency has entered the national and local economies; a number of Bay Islanders have grown wealthy (or wealthier) through their investments in the expanding industry; an increasing number of islanders and mainlanders have found employment; and an escalating number of foreign visitors have enjoyed the beauty and adventure the islands afford. Although the benefits have been great, the costs of tourism also have been significant. Increased social conflict evident in the heightened number of land disputes is only one of those costs. Serious environmental destruction stemming from the largely unregulated expansion of the industry as well as from the escalating human population is another critical problem. The islands encompass various groups—by divisions of ethnicity, nationality, class, and gender—and consequential concerns about the relative costs/risks and benefits of the expanding industry on the islands' diverse peoples also have been raised.

Notes

[1] Philip Ashton was captured in Port Rossaway by the pirate, Ned Low, on June 15, 1722 (Neider, 1952).

[2] This and other tourist businesses are referred to by pseudonyms.

[3] The so-called "Soccer War" was fought between El Salvador and Honduras for 5 days in July 1969. During the war, all communication and transportation to and from the islands stopped and the Bay Islands were cut off completely from the outside world. With island boats prohibited from trading with the mainland, the stores quickly ran out of staple foods. Because islanders did not want their sons to be conscripted into the Honduran Army (and forced to fight in the "Spaniards' War") they put their sons on boats and took them out to sea for the duration. Nance pointed to the war as a potent reminder of Honduran political instability and as a major deterrent to tourism development (Nance, 1970, p. 88).

[4] It is important to point out that the rosy picture of the tourism situation in the Bay Islands and in Honduras more generally is being painted by the government and the owners of tourism businesses with vested interests in luring international travelers to Honduras.

[5]A pseudonym.

[6]Ever since black islanders came to the Bay Islands, they have built their homes on stilts over the water. There are a number of theories as to why they have done this—to avoid sand fleas, because it is cooler over the water, tradition, or because white islanders had already claimed all the land. Whatever the reason, these islanders are in a dilemma with respect to land titles. All water is considered "national"—belonging to the state—so sites over the water cannot be legally titled. Also, all land within 40 feet of the ocean is national or municipal land that cannot be titled because it is part of the "royal road" (*camino real*) along the beach. So, for example, a pier constructed on the beach and the family coconut trees planted near the shore cannot be titled either. Should people living on national land decide to sell, all they can sell are the improvements, not the land itself. After living on the land for 10 years or more, however, the land is considered theirs and they cannot be summarily evicted, according to the Honduran Constitution. If they cannot sell the land, no one else can legally sell it either. However, illegal sales and fencing of *camino real* beach land have been reported on both the Atlantic and Pacific coasts of Honduras as well as in the Bay Islands (Griffin, 1998b).

[7]Information in this section is based on ethnographic and survey data collected between 1991 and 1997, rather than on information supplied by the IHT, because IHT data generally do not include data on small-scale accommodations (e.g., rooms for rent and cabins). For purposes of this chapter, tourist accommodations are classified into five types: 1) hotels defined to include lodgings that rent rooms as well as provide some meals; 2) resorts classified as hotels that also provide additional tourist activities such as diving, fishing, boating, etc.; 3) rooms for rent or guest houses that include rooms situated within a private residence; 4) cabins, which include stand-alone structures built to provide lodgings for tourists; and 5) time-share condominiums.

Chapter 4

Tourism, Demography, and Environment

> We were seafaring people of English and Scottish stock. . . . We started the
> fishing industry and got that going, then we started the shipping business and
> got that going, and then we started with the diving and got that going a little
> bit . . . and then the Hondurans started coming. (Former mayor of Coxen
> Hole and patriarch of one of the wealthy white islander families, quoted in
> Basch, 1992)

Until recently, their relative isolation, poor communications capacity, lack of
infrastructure, scant tourist facilities, and relatively low human population density
protected the Bay Islands from many of the adverse social and environmental costs
of tourism that characterize much of the eastern Caribbean. Beginning in the
1960s, a small tourist industry composed primarily of divers and recreational
sailors took pleasure in the splendid reef, clear waters, secluded harbors, and
tranquil beaches. At the same time, according to most social, economic, education,
and health measures, the Bay Islanders maintained a quality of life that significantly
surpassed that of Honduran ladinos living on the mainland. A recent assessment by
the United Nations Development Programme (UNDP) concluded that the residents
of the Bay Islands continue to enjoy the highest standard of living in the country.
However, these positive circumstances may be changing in the context of the
unchecked growth of the tourism industry. By 1990, the Bay Islands were the most
popular tourist destination in Honduras. By 1997, approximately 93,000 tourists
visited the islands—significantly exceeding the projected estimates that had been
made just a few years earlier. Although accurate population data for the islands do
not exist, this figure probably represents from two to about three times the
number of current residents. Economic models predict that within 20 years
tourists will spend from US$51 to US$73 million per year in the Bay Islands
depending on the rate at which tourism grows (Vega et al., 1993, p. 19).

Expansion of the industry has provoked the immigration of thousands of desperately poor ladinos from the mainland who seek a better life on the islands through
employment in the growing tourism sector. Recent estimates concur that ladinos
comprise at least 50% of island residents. In addition to tourists and ladino mainlanders, the islands' population currently is being augmented by an unknown but

growing number of part-time and permanent foreign residents. Until recently, Bay Island and other Honduran interests dominated the tourist industry on the islands. More recently, however, these initial promoters have been joined by a number of foreign real estate developers and other well-capitalized investors whose aims include converting previously undeveloped portions of coastal and upland areas into large-scale resorts and upscale housing subdivisions. As discussed in the previous chapter, their efforts have provoked widespread land speculation, an upward spiral in land prices, and intensified social conflicts—not only over land but also over access to, and use of, the islands' limited freshwater and marine resources. Although a small number of expatriates and retirees from the U.S., Great Britain, and elsewhere have started businesses and/or made the islands their permanent or vacation home for several decades, the recent arrival of large-scale foreign developers markedly increased the number of foreign residents as well as exacerbated conflicts over environmental resources.

This chapter links the boom in the tourism sector with its human demographic and environmental consequences within the context of ongoing conservation efforts. It begins with discussions of the legal and regulatory framework affecting the islands' environment and natural resources along with major conservation efforts. It goes on to introduce the perspectives of the islands' residents on the major environmental and other problems they currently confront. Within this background, it summarizes current patterns in human demography and settlement. It discusses critical demographic changes emanating from the significant increase in the human population due to the migration of ladinos from the Honduran mainland and the skyrocketing increase in the number of international tourists. It then reviews the impact of tourism development and these demographic changes on the islands' environment and resources, especially the effects on critical habitats, wildlife, forests, reefs, fresh/seawater, and other marine resources.

Legislative and Regulatory Framework

The 1997 Honduran Presidential Executive Order (*Acuerdo Ejecutive Número 005-97*) created the Bay Islands National Marine Park and integrated the park into the National System of Protected Areas. The order was justified on the basis of several legal, regulatory, and environmental considerations (Government of Honduras [GOH], 1997). According to Articles 172 and 340 of the Honduran Constitution and Article 35 of the General Environmental Law, the Honduran State is responsible for conserving the country's biological, hydrological, historical, and cultural resources and for contributing to sustainable development in surrounding communities. Article 41 of the General Environmental Law specifically stipulates that the GOH is responsible for the protection of the coastal and marine ecosystems of the Bay Islands. The presidential decree recognizes that the islands' terrestrial and marine ecosystems currently are at risk. It identifies a number of particular environmental problems currently plaguing the islands, including: deforestation, erosion, related increases in sedimentation, and the associated degradation of coastal and marine ecosystems. It highlights the loss of approximately 249 hectares of mangroves since 1989, primarily attributed to urban growth, inappropriate land use (linked primarily to erosion emanating from the conversion of upland forest to pastures), and the construction of tourist-related infrastructure and facilities. Also noted is the absence of public drinking water, sewerage, and solid-waste disposal systems. The order points out that due to these deficiencies most human-generated waste is directly deposited into the sea and causes serious environmental decline in coastal and marine areas. The decree also indicates that overexploitation by the islands' extensive fishing fleet has significantly reduced fishing yields—thereby negatively affecting one of the principal economic activities of the Bay Islands. Significantly missing from the GOH decree is any mention of the repercussions of increasing human populations on the islands' environment and natural resources.

According to the presidential order, the recently created marine park has several objectives (GOH, 1997). The most important is "to promote economic development through the rational exploitation of renewable and nonrenewable resources, especially through the least destructive means, tourism and recreation." Another stated goal is to maintain an "ecological equilibrium" that protects the genetic resources and biological diversity of the islands, while a third objective is to establish a system of protected areas aimed at conserving the islands' marine and coastal resources. The order proposes to manage human activities within the park through the passage and enforcement of environmental legislation, the installation of control buoys, the implementation of use restrictions, and the monitoring of environmental conditions. Zonation also is proposed as a means of delimiting various use and protected areas. These include multiple use zones, economic development zones, zones in which fishing is restricted, and protected zones in which no economic activities are allowed. To facilitate these goals, broader public support is to be promoted through the involvement of community users in the planning, implementation, and management processes. The park will be administered through a United Administration (*Unidad Administrativa*) that includes representatives of the island municipalities and designated individuals from the Department of Protected Areas and Wildlife of the Honduran Forestry Development Corporation (*Direccion de Areas Protegidas y Vida Silvestre de la Corporación Hondurena de Desarrollo Forestal* [DAPVS/AFE-COHDEFOR]), the Commission for Integrated Coastal Zone Management (*Comisión de Manejo Integral Costero* [COMICO]), and the Ministry of Natural Resources and Environment (*Secretaria de Recursos Naturales y Ambiente* [SERNA]). Finally, sustainable financing of the park is to come from the implementation of a cost recuperation system that generates income through measures such as admission and user fees.

The problems and prescriptions presented in the ambitious presidential decree are not original but reflect perceptions of environmental difficulties and potential solutions that have been proposed for almost two decades by various international donors as well as by the GOH itself (e.g., J. R. Clark & Smith, 1988; Dulin, 1979; GDH/ PNUD, 1992a, 1992b; Halcrow and Partners, 1983; IDB, 1992, 1994, 1996; Secretaria de Estado en los Despachos de Recursos Naturales y Ambiente/Proyecto Manejo Ambiental Islas de la Bahia [SEDA/PMAIB], 1997; Sorensen, 1993; Vega et al., 1993).

Major regulatory authority for conserving the environment of the Bay Islands was first conferred on the Honduran Ministry of Culture and Tourism (SECTUR) in 1982 when the GOH declared the Bay Islands a tourist zone. A second important ministerial decree for environmental regulations on the Bay Islands was Agreement Two (*Acuerdo Dos*), which adopted the master plan contained in an environmental study of Roatán completed in 1983 (Halcrow and Partners, 1983). This decree, issued by the Ministry of Government and Justice in February 1991, established general norms for development on the islands, including specific regulations governing authorizations for development projects, zoning, and protection of natural resources. It requires the following: approval of all applications to undertake development projects, with approval first required from the municipality and then by the IHT; establishment of a specific zoning plan to govern development of any structures within 140 meters of the beach; a grace period of 1.5 years from declaration of the law for industrial factories to begin treating their waste products; and protection of the reef and its ecological communities from the discharges of wastes from ships on the open sea and from dredging and construction projects. In addition, Agreement Two specifically prohibits the collection of black coral, the use of harpoons, the use of toxic substances in the reef, the felling of mangroves, the exploitation of the reef for minerals, and water lots (the construction of buildings in shallow water over the ocean).

A subsequent presidential decree established the Commission for Development of the Bay Islands (the Commission) in May 1993 whose purpose is to "encourage development programs and projects for the Bay Islands that maintain the integrity of the environment" ("Plans for Sustainable Development," 1993). This nonprofit foundation has legal status, its own financial resources, and is composed of individuals from both the government and private sectors. Members of the Executive Council include the president of Honduras, who also is the president of the Commission; the Minister of Government and Justice; the Director of Tourism; the governor of the Bay Islands; and the mayors of the four island municipalities. One of the first tasks of the Executive Board was to choose eight representatives (and eight alternatives) from the private sector. These included the owners of the largest resorts and other prominent business people as well as one member each from the islands' two major nongovernmental organizations, the Bay Islands Conservation Association (BICA) and the now defunct Bay Islands Development Promotion Association (APRODIB). Of these members, half plus one must be Hondurans with 5 or more years of residency in the Bay Islands. Like the 1997 presidential decree that established the Bay Islands National Marine Park, these regulatory means attempt to reconcile economic development with environmental conservation. Particularly noticeable in the structure of the Commission is that regulatory power remains in the hands of government officials and the island elite.

As a means of addressing possible environmental costs stemming from its various economic and fiscal incentives, the GOH passed the General Environmental Law in June 1993, which founded the Ministry of the Environment (*Secretaria de Estado* en el Despacho de Ambiente [SEDA]) and established the legal process for obtaining an Environmental License. Under this legislation, all projects and/or economic activities likely to degrade or contaminate the environment must present an environmental impact study approved by SEDA prior to receiving any concession or project permit from a government agency. Moreover, the execution of any project without first obtaining an Environmental License constitutes an environmental crime. In the Bay Islands, as in the rest of Honduras, SEDA as a ministry-level office was given significant power to oversee the environmental feasibility of tourism-related projects. One of SEDA's important roles in the islands was to execute the US$23.9 million Bay Islands Environmental Management Project funded by the IDB that is discussed later in this chapter.

Over the years, concern over achieving a balance between economic growth and environmental integrity on the islands led to the development of several plans to address simultaneously initiatives to expand tourism and conserve the environment. Some of these studies focused primarily on marine ecosystems (e.g., J. R. Clark & Smith, 1988) while others were more concerned with watershed management and forest protection (e.g., Dulin, 1979). Until the early 1990s, the most thorough environmental study was the Environmental Control Plan for Roatán (Halcrow and Partners, 1983), which provided the basis for Agreement Two.

Major Conservation Efforts: The Bay Islands Environmental Management Project

In addition to the Bay Islands National Marine Park, certain areas or all of the Bay Islands are part of several other international, national, and municipal conservation initiatives. These include the Meso-American Biological Corridor, the most recent reincarnation of the Path of the Panther (*Paseo Pantera*) project sponsored by the Wildlife Conservation Society (WCS) with significant funding from USAID and the Global Environmental Fund of the World Bank. This remarkably ambitious endeavor is based on the recognition that Central America is not composed of seven separate tropical ecosystems belonging to seven sovereign republics. Rather, it's a single ecological system whose germplasm, mammals, and migratory birds do not recognize political boundaries. In 1994 at the Presidential Summit of the Americas in Miami, all seven Central American countries agreed in principle to create a single Meso-American Biological Corridor composed of a network of national and transborder nature reserves and protected areas combined with environmentally benign forest plantations. The Meso-American Biological Corridor has been gaining fame, not as a 2,000-mile-long nature preserve, but as an integrating concept into which a variety of environmental projects can fit. The U.S. and European governments, private foundations, and international development banks have committed some US$600 million. The World Bank is the single largest donor with US$160 million. The projects range from managing forests, to preserving indigenous land rights, to strengthening national environmental laws. In the Bay Islands WCS efforts have focused on developing a management plan for the Sandy Bay-West End Marine Reserve, which will be discussed later in this chapter.

Another regional agreement aimed specifically at protecting the Meso-American Caribbean Reef, the largest coral reef system in the Atlantic, was signed in July 1998 by the presidents of Belize, Guatemala, Mexico, and Honduras. Supported, in part, by the World Wildlife Fund, the agreement creates an "action plan" that sets forth a series of local, national, and regional initiatives to preserve the region's extensive reef system that stretches from the coast of Cancun, Mexico to the Bay Islands. The Meso-American Caribbean Reef has been designated as a World Heritage Site by the United Nations Educational, Scientific, and Cultural Organization (UNESCO) and recognized as one of the "Global 200" sites of critical importance to global biodiversity. To date, no specific projects have been earmarked for the Bay Islands.

The Bay Islands' most comprehensive, ambitious, and well-funded environmental conservation effort to date is in the process of being implemented—an environmental management plan to guide development and conserve the islands' natural resources financed by the IDB. In late 1994, after several years of conducting feasibility studies through the UNDP, the IDB approved financing the Bay Islands Environmental Management Project with a loan of US$19.1 million from the IDB supplement with US$4.8 million from Honduras. The project was fully funded and operational as of April 1996. According to project documents, the IDB is to work with SEDA and island NGOs, including APRODIB and BICA. The general objective of the challenging project is "to maintain and improve the quality of the environment on the Bay Islands as a basis for sustainable economic development" (IDB, 1994) and "must benefit the 24,000 people who live on the islands," according to the project's former executive director. Among the stated objectives are protecting coastal and marine ecosystems through a system of integrated management; strengthening local capacity for planning, management, and administration; and improving the standard of living of the inhabitants through improvements in water supply and construction of basic sanitation. Similar to the 1997 presidential degree, the IDB project does not address directly the social or environmental problems emanating from escalating human populations. To date, little if any evidence of project implementation or success is detectable. Despite the participatory rhetoric written into project documents, interviews with local people in the communities of Sandy Bay, West End, and Flowers Bay during the summer of 1995 and 1997 revealed that few residents (apart from a small group of wealthier business owners) were well informed about the project or had been consulted in any way. Some residents were badly misinformed, believing that the US$23.9 million would be distributed in cash among island residents.

In 1996, the executive director of the IDB project resigned over major differences of opinion with the leadership of SEDA and the GOH over how the project should be managed. Especially contentious was the "decentralized" approach that had originally been agreed upon and the growing reluctance of the GOH to transfer the needed administrative autonomy to the Roatán project unit—an aversion that persists until today. Not long afterwards, the two members of the Roatán project unit were fired by the GOH, thereby dissolving the unit. The IDB traditionally takes an "at arms length" approach to supervision and monitoring once a project has been approved. The bulk of the responsibility for project execution rests with the government, at least in principle. Responsibility within the IDB to monitor project execution lies with the local offices, in the Bay Islands case, the IDB office in the Honduran capital of Tegucigalpa. The loss of the IDB project's executive director in Tegucigalpa and the field staff on Roatán seriously impeded the implementation of the project (senior IDB staff member, personal communication, 1997).

The decision by the GOH in December 1996 to "restructure" its ministries, ostensibly as part of efforts to cut government expenditures, added to anxiety over the ultimate implementation and fruition of the IDB project in the Bay Islands. As part of this restructuring, SEDA was "reorganized" and downgraded from its ministry level. Although, it is not clear what the implications of this reorganization will be for the eventual success of the IDB project, in 1997 a senior staff officer of the Regional Water and Sanitation Network of Central America characterized the project as "dragging its collective heals." Serious reservations have been expressed by staff of a major bilateral development assistance agency who are concerned that the sanitation investments may rely on inappropriate technology and levels of discharge that will be potentially damaging to reefs. An evaluation of the project in late 1997 by a senior IDB staff member is telling:

> My concern is that the upper reaches of the Bank may be under the impression that all is well since, after all, the loan was approved. In reality, Honduras has started paying commission fees on a loan with diminishing prospects of ever seeing any environmental and social benefits. This weighs heavily on the minds of those of us who made a case for the project two years ago. (Senior IDB staff member, personal communication, 1997)

In this context, it is difficult to be optimistic about the ultimate success of the IDB project as it now stands.

Residents' Views on Environmental and Other Island Problems

The many feasibility studies conducted while preparing the IDB loan proposal included very limited surveys of the local population in which they were able to express their views regarding the major problems that existed on the islands. As reported by residents and in order of seriousness these included: 1) drugs and alcoholism; 2) garbage; 3) deforestation and burning of forests; 4) insufficient potable water; 5) the lack of a sewage system; and 6) inferior education limited to instruction in Spanish (GDH/PNUD, 1992a, p. 72). Although local residents registered many of the same environmental concerns that were noted in the GOH and donor-sponsored studies, the residents' concerns encompassed social and cultural as well as environmental matters. Most serious, from their point of view, were problems stemming from drug and alcohol use. On the basis of interviews with community leaders, one feasibility study concluded:

> . . . it is likely that 9 out of 10 juveniles have had contact with drugs . . . and drugs affect the entire population without regard to race, religion, or social

status . . . moreover, there is no treatment center on the islands. (GDH/PNUD, 1992a, p. 72)

Indeed, problems related to drug use have become so serious that communities, such as Sandy Bay, have antidrug marches and regular meetings to discuss ways of dealing with their mounting use and the related violence and crime. Escalating crime affects not only local residents but tourists as well. After spending several months in early 1998 in Sandy Bay, a staff member of an international environmental organization commented:

> Things don't seem to be improving. The government and law enforcement is as weak as ever while crime is becoming more common and serious. There were a number of assaults (with firearms) on tourists while I was there in the spring and several murders as well. (Staff member, personal communication, 1998).

Concerned over the high drug and crime rate, the municipality of Guanaja recently began implementing a series of measures to control the entry of visitors—actions largely aimed at ladino immigrants from the mainland. As of June 1998, all persons traveling to Guanaja must carry their identity cards and a police statement indicating whether or not the person ever has committed a crime. In addition, only persons who already have a job arranged are allowed on the island; others are turned away. In justifying the measures, the mayor of Guanaja said, "There are a lot of drugs, they are selling crack like candy and nobody is doing anything" (Week in Review, 1998). Aiming these measures at arriving immigrants from the Honduran mainland implies the perception that rising drug-related problems stem from the influx of Honduran ladinos. In fact, many islanders are very direct in ascribing blame to mainlanders. According to an elderly Afro-Caribbean Islander woman from West End:

> We've got Euro-trash [backpacker tourists from Europe] and we've got Spaniards. . . . They're trash too. . . . They don't want to work . . . well some of them work, especially the women . . . but the men . . . they bring drugs, they sell drugs, some to the tourists but as much to our kids. (Personal communication, 1997)

The major problem identified by residents as "inferior education limited to instruction in Spanish" has been introduced in previous chapters. It refers to islanders' concerns over loss of ethnic identity and culture as well as their diminished capacity to take advantage of the economic opportunities in the tourist sector that are available to fluent speakers of English.

The conservation strategy completed for the 1992 USAID and *Paseo Pantera* Project of the WCS included four "participatory-planning" workshops, two on Roatán, one on Utila, and one on Guanaja. The workshops provided local residents some opportunity to discuss issues of land use and conservation, ongoing efforts and future plans for environmental education, and the proposal for a national marine park developed by the UNDP (Vega et al., 1993, p. 20). The extent to which these workshops were "participatory" is open to question because participation was by invitation only and attendees tended to identify themselves predominantly as owners of tourism or other businesses or as government officials. Although a number of environmental problems were identified during these workshops the majority centered on those affecting land-based ecosystems related to poor agricultural practices in general, cattle ranching in particular, wildfires, and deforestation. It is not surprising that workshop participants did not emphasize the destructive environmental consequences of dredging, construction, water use, and other activities directly stemming from the tourism industry—the workshops were dominated by those with a stake in the expanding industry. For members of the workshops, the dominant environmental problems were ascribed to:

> . . . excessive population growth caused principally by the migration of Hondurans from the mainland . . . [who] favor migratory agriculture and development of dense housing complexes . . . recently, the process of watershed destruction was greatly accelerated due to a growing number of hillside farms, a characteristic practice of immigrants from the mainland. (Vega et al., 1993)

Not surprisingly the "suggested solutions" favored "controlling" migration from the mainland in order to minimize its negative impact (Vega et al., 1993, p. 191). Generally, islanders, much more than the GOH, explicitly link population growth to environmental destruction on the islands. The reluctance of the GOH to confront immigration and population issues is understandable given that increasing the numbers of ladinos on the islands increases the presence and control of the GOH while simultaneously diminishing the power of most islanders.

Population Growth in the Bay Islands

Figure 4.1 shows the pattern of population growth in the Bay Islands from 1834 to 1996. It clearly demonstrates a significant increase in the rate of growth during the last two decades. Between the mid-1800s and the early 1960s, the population of the islands grew at about 3.5% per year—about the same annual rate of growth as on the mainland. From 1961 through 1974 the annual population growth rate increased to about 3.6% annually. However, between 1974 and 1988, the annual rate of growth increased substantially to approximately 4.5% and then skyrocketed to at least 5% between 1988 and 1996. The annual rate of increase on the Bay Islands is more significant in light of the decreasing overall rate of growth that occurred on the mainland during the same period: from 3.4% between 1970 and 1980, to 3.3% from 1980 to 1990, and finally to 3.1% between 1990 and 1996 (Stonich, 1993; United Nations, 1998, p. 135). In 1991, about 24,000 people lived on the Bay Islands, 16,000 (66.25%) on Roatán, 6,000 (24.7%) on Guanaja, and 2,200 (9.1%) on Utila (GDH/PNUD, 1992a, p. 65).

Between 1988 and 1996, the population of Coxen Hole increased 60% (from 3,901 to 6,200), while French Harbour grew 55% (from 2,451 to 3,800), and the population of Oak Ridge almost doubled (96%—from 1,304 to 2,560) (SEDA/PMAIB, 1997, p. 12). Some recent estimates conclude that the resident population on all the

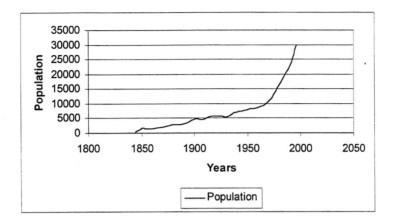

Figure 4.1. Bay Islands population: 1834–1996. Source: Davidson (1974), SECPLAN (1989), SEDA/PMBIA (1997), Waddell (1959), Watt (1973).

islands may be 50,000 (e.g., Pettrie, 1996). The islands are undergoing a high rate of urbanization. Currently an estimated 81% of the islands' residents live in urban areas while only 15% live in rural areas. The percentage of urban dwellers on the Bay Islands is almost twice that on the mainland (44%) (World Resources Institute, United Nations Environment Programme, United Nations Development Bank, & The World Bank, 1996, p. 151). Annual rates of population increase on the islands since 1990 are approximately the same as those of mainland urban areas such as San Pedro Sula and Tegucigalpa (4.5%) and far surpass those of rural areas of Honduras (1.8%) (World Resources Institute et al., 1996, p. 151). A very high rate of rural to urban migration has characterized Honduras for the last several decades, as a growing number of impoverished rural families have found it increasingly impossible to eke out a living on their meager farm holdings (Stonich, 1993). The equivalent rates of urban growth on the mainland and on the Bay Islands suggest that poor Hondurans on the mainland believe that the economic opportunities on the islands are equal to those in mainland urban centers. Mainlanders also are responding to the lure of high wages, which often are nearly twice the rates paid on the mainland.

The accelerated migration of ladinos has shifted the ethnic composition and distribution of human settlements on the islands. According to data from various national censuses of population, the percentage of ladinos on the Bay Islands grew from 7% in 1970, to 12% in 1981, before reaching 16% by 1988. Although no official population census has been done by the GOH since 1988, community-level population censuses conducted as part of this study reveal a significant increase in the percentage of ladino residents—approaching 50% in some communities. These findings are consistent with recent estimates for all the islands made by officials of municipal and national government agencies. Especially affected are communities that are well integrated into the tourism sector. Immigrants have established residence in (or on the outskirts of) communities such as Sandy Bay and West End where tourism-related employment is available and which until recently were overwhelmingly composed of Afro-Caribbean, black Bay Islanders. Between 1982 and 1993 the population of Sandy Bay doubled—increasing from about 600 to 1,200 inhabitants. During the same time, the population of West End grew 45%, from approximately 275 to 350 persons. In contrast, Flowers Bay, where the tourism industry had not developed, experienced a population decline of 29% (from 671 to 477 residents) during the same period (computed from data in Halcrow and Partners, 1983, and community population censuses conducted in 1993). Estimates made in 1998 as part of the Sandy Bay-West End Marine Reserve management project assert that the population of the Sandy Bay, West End, West Bay Beach area is between 4,000 and 5,000 persons—indicating a doubling of the population in the last 5 years.

Ladinos also have settled in scattered hamlets in upland areas where they grow some food crops and hunt wild game as well as travel to tourist, fishery, or industrial centers to work. In addition, immigrants founded two large ladino enclaves that began as squatter settlements, "El Swampo" (The Swamp) on the outskirts of Coxen Hole and "Los Fuertes" (The Fort) outside of French Harbour. Some black islander communities, such as Flowers Bay on Roatán, have done all they can to prohibit ladino immigrants from settling in their villages, while similar efforts have been made on Guanaja where white islanders hold considerable political and economic power.

Measuring the Impact of Tourists

Two measures of the impact of tourists usually applied at the national level are the tourist intensity ratio (TIR) and the tourist density ratio (TDR). The TIR is the percentage of tourists to local residents in a given year, and the TDR is the ratio of tourists to land area. Table 4.1 compares the Caribbean, Mexico, and Central America according to TIR and TDR in 1995. In terms of TIR, it indicates that, within the Caribbean region, TIRs varied dramatically from a high of 1331.6% in the British Virgin Islands to a low of 2.0% in Haiti. It also demonstrates that the Caribbean region had a much higher average TIR (323.5%) than did Mexico (22.3%) or Central America (16.6%). In 1995, Belize had the highest TIR of all the Central American countries (60.4%) and Honduras the lowest (3.6%). Similarly, in terms of the TDR, the highest ratios were found in the Caribbean, with some Caribbean island nations have TDRs in excess of 1,000 tourists per square kilometer. Mexico and Central America had far lower TDRs, 10.3 and 6.6 persons per square kilometer, respectively. Honduras had the lowest TDR of all the places considered. These aggregate data suggest that tourists have relatively little impact in Honduras. However, when the Honduran data are spatially disaggregated a very different picture appears (Table 4.2). The Bay Islands comprise only 0.2% of the land area in Honduras, yet in 1991 they were the destination of more than 10% of foreign visitors. By 1997, tourists to the Bay Islands comprised 20% of all foreigners who visited Honduras during the year. Between 1974 and 1997, the TIR rose from 7.6% to 301%, and the TDR increased from 4 to 360 tourists per square kilometer. Most

Table 4.1. Tourist Impacts in the Caribbean, Mexico, and Central America: 1995

	Population (thousands)	Tourists (thousands)	Area (km²)	TIR (%)	TDR (tour./km²)
Caribbean	**35,743**	**13,142**	**233,899**	**323.5**	**826.1**
Anguilla	8	39	96	487.5	406.3
Antigua and Baruda	66	212	442	321.2	479.6
Aruba	70	619	193	884.3	3,207.3
Bahamas	278	1,598	13,878	574.8	115.1
Barbados	264	442	430	167.4	1,027.9
Bermuda	63	388	53	615.9	7,320.8
British Virgin Islands	19	253	151	1,331.6	1,675.5
Cayman Islands	31	361	264	1,164.5	1,367.4
Cuba	10,964	742	110,861	6.8	6.7
Dominica	71	60	751	84.5	79.9
Dominican Republic	7,915	1,746	48,734	22.1	35.8
Grenada	92	108	344	117.4	314.0
Guadeloupe	424	640	1,705	150.9	375.4
Haiti	7,180	145	27,750	2.0	5.2
Jamaica	2,530	1,019	10,990	40.3	92.7
Martinique	380	457	1,102	120.3	414.7
Montserrat	11	18	102	163.6	176.5
Puerto Rico	3,701	3,131	8,875	84.6	352.8
Saint Kitts & Nevis	41	79	261	192.7	302.7
Saint Lucia	145	232	622	160.0	373.0
St. Vincent & the Grenadines	111	60	388	54.1	154.6
Trinidad & Tobago	1,260	260	5,130	20.6	50.7
Turks and Caicos	14	79	430	564.3	183.7
U.S. Virgin Islands	105	454	347	432.4	1,308.4
Mexico	**90,487**	**20,162**	**1,958,201**	**22.3**	**10.3**
Central America	**32,956**	**2,555**	**521,331**	**16.6**	**6.6**
Belize	217	131	22,696	60.4	5.8
Costa Rica	3,333	785	51,100	23.6	15.4
El Salvador	5,662	235	21,041	4.2	11.2
Guatemala	10,621	563	108,889	5.3	5.2
Honduras	5,953	215	112,088	3.6	1.9
Nicaragua	4,539	281	130,000	6.2	2.2
Panama	2,631	345	75,517	13.1	4.6

TIR = number of international tourist arrivals/total population) × 100. TDR = number of international tourist arrivals/area in square kilometers.
Source: Population and surface area data from United Nations (1998, Table 3, p. 135; Table 5, pp. 155–156); tourist arrivals from World Tourism Organization (1997, p. 52).

of the increase occurred after 1988, when the jet runway was completed on Roatán, opening up the islands to direct international flights. In 1997, the TIR for the Bay Islands approached the mean TIR for the Caribbean region and surpassed

Table 4.2. Tourist Impacts in the Bay Islands: 1974–1997

Year	Population	Tourists	Area (km²)	TIR (%)	TDR (tour./km²)
1974	13,194	1,000	258	7.6	4
1988	21,553	15,000	258	69.5	58
1992	23,850	30,000	258	125.8	116
1994	26,300	40,000	258	152.1	155
1997	30,883	93,000	258	301	360

Source: Calculated from data in SECPLAN (1989), Sorensen (1993), and Stonich et al. (1995).

those of 15 of the 24 Caribbean nations covered in the analysis, including major international tourist destinations such as Barbados and Jamaica. The significantly lower TDRs for the Bay Islands compared to most Caribbean destinations is both encouraging and frightening, as these data suggest the extent to which the number of tourists to the Bay Islands may grow in the upcoming years. They also highlight the crucial need to develop the infrastructure necessary to meet the potential growing demand in an environmentally sound manner that maintains the natural features tourists expect to encounter.

Separating the data for the Bay Islands from the national-level data reveals one of the major limitations in measuring tourist impacts at the national level. It also points out that while tourists may have little impact on Honduras overall, they have exceptionally high impact on the Bay Islands. In addition, between 1988 and 1997 the total number of tourists to the islands increased by 520%. This was significantly higher than the percentage increase in the number of island residents (including ladino immigrants), which rose approximately 44% during the same period. By the mid-1990s, the combined effects of the escalating number of international tourists and ladino immigrants elevated the human population to a level at which the island's freshwater supply, as well as food and other natural resources, was threatened, and many local communities' abilities to maintain human health services and other vital services were overwhelmed (Stonich, 1998). In the words of a 30-year resident of the islands originally from the U.S.:

> Roatán, which used to be one of the most beautiful, unspoiled, pristine islands in the entire Caribbean . . . is going down the tubes and it might be too late even now, to save it. . . . Too many people in too small a space is a recipe for big trouble, and Roatán has big trouble. . . . The need for building sites, roads, and firewood has resulted in most of the trees being cut down. The loss of trees and other ground cover has destroyed the potable water aquifer. The water table has dropped like a rock. Wells that used to provide an abundance of fresh water for 10,000 people are now—faced with the demands of two or three times that number—either dry or contaminated by surface or sub-surface infusion. . . . Smart people buy their drinking water in plastic bottles. (Personal communication, 1997)

These concerns raise the significant question of whether it is population growth per se that is the root cause of the environmental degradation occurring on the islands. An essentially demographic explanation, however, is an oversimplification of reality because the majority of population growth is from tourists and ladino immigrants and is directly associated to the expansion of the tourism industry. Part of this expansion has included significant infrastructural development in certain domains (especially airport improvement and road construction) and simultaneously the serious lack of infrastructural development in other critical areas (especially drinking water, sewerage, and solid waste disposal systems). While it is clear that escalating numbers of tourists and immigrants put more pressure on the islands' environment and natural resources, development efforts have aimed at augmenting the number of tourist arrivals—regardless of the environmental and human costs. A more fundamental basis of environmental degradation in the Bay Islands is the rapid, largely uncontrolled, expansion of the tourist industry.

Land Use and Land Cover

The most recent assessment of land use and land cover on the Bay Islands was done as part of the 1992 conservation study conducted for USAID and WCS mentioned above (Vega et al., 1993). Using aerial photographs supplemented with field visits, 10 principal categories of land cover and land use, in addition to inland bodies of water and urbanized areas, were determined for each of the largest islands as well as for the Bay Islands as a whole (Table 4.3). For the entire archipelago these included primary forest (1.9%), secondary forest (34.9%), mixed forest (0.7%), coniferous forests (3.9%), mangroves (7.6), wetlands (9.9%), brush (2.9%), pastures (3.4%), permanent agriculture (1.4%), annual agriculture (0.2%), water (0.1%), and urban (3.2%). Human activities have affected all areas of the islands. Almost all of the islands were cleared at some time, and less than 2% of the islands remain as primary forest. Even in these areas, the most desirable trees have been harvested. Until recently mangrove and wetland areas have not been significantly altered by human intervention. Now, however, some mangrove areas have begun to be cut and filled in order to construct hotels and other buildings for tourism near the coasts. The two most common types of land use on the Bay Islands are pastures and secondary forest, which in combination with brush lands suggests that the majority of the islands have been cleared recently, most likely over the past 15 years (Vega et al., 1993, p. 36).

According to the USAID/WSC-funded study, pastures are the least desirable land cover on the islands. Pastures and extensive grazing have very low productivity and the greatest land use conflict is the existence of pastures in areas appropriate only for management of natural forests or for complete protection. The pastures degrade rapidly from overgrazing, leading to soil compaction and soil erosion. In addition, creation and maintenance of pastures often result in uncontrolled fires that spread to nearby forests and destroy much of the habitat of native species (Vega et al., 1993, p. 36).

Table 4.3. Land Use and Land Cover on the Bay Islands

Category

Island	Primary Forest	Secondary Forest	Mixed Forest	Coniferous Forest	Mangroves	Wetlands	Brush	Pastures	Permanent Crops	Annual Crops	Urban	Water	Total
Roatán	321	5,429	29	60	643	6	442	4,842	107	10	553	0	12,441
%	2.6	43.6	0.2	0.5	5.2	0.1	3.6	38.9	0.9	0.1	4.4	0	100
Guanaja	76	1,296	128	856	283	11	137	2,673	105	44	109	0	5,718
%	1.3	22.7	2.2	15	5	0.2	2.4	46.7	1.8	0.8	1.9	0	100
Utila	0	802	0	0	741	2,304	0	206	69	0	85	13	4,220
%	0	19	0	0	17.6	54.6	0	4.9	1.6	0	2	0.3	100
Barbareta	60	390	0	0	19	0	23	6	16	0	1	0	514
%	11.7	75.7	0	0	3.7	0	4.4	1.2	3	0	0.2	0	100
Helene	0	222	0	0	95	0	8	61	22	4	11	0	424
%	0	52.5	0	0	22.5	0	1.9	14.4	5.3	0.8	2.6	0	100
Morat	0	22	0	0	0	0	20	12	5	0	0	0	59
%	0	36.7	0	0	0	0	33.7	20.4	8.8	0.2	0	0	100
Total	457	8,161	157	916	1,781	2,320	630	7,800	325	57	758	13	23,376
%	1.9	34.9	0.7	3.9	7.6	9.9	2.7	33.4	1.4	0.2	3.2	0.1	100

Area in hectares (upper row) and percent (lower row).

Primary forest: This unit is defined as broadleaf forests with little or no intervention, such as extraction of some valuable species using artisan techniques.

Secondary forest: This unit is composed of young forest that is more than 4 meters in height in areas that have been substantially disturbed.

Mixed forest: This forest is characterized as being a mixture with equal proportions of broadleaved and coniferous vegetation.

Coniferous forest: This forest is characterized by being composed primarily of conifreous trees, the dominant species is Caribbean pine (*Pinus caribaea*).

Mangroves: These are flat areas along beaches and coasts that are flooded or subject to flooding. Red mangrove (*Rhizophora mangle*) is the dominant species.

Wetlands: These areas generally are flooded or are subject to seasonal flooding and are composed of grasses, cattails, ferns, and palms.

Brush: These areas are categorized as having herbaceous or bushy vegetation with secondary growth that does not exceed 4 meters in height.

Pastures: These are areas that have been seeded in grasses used by cattle or contain natural grasses that can include trees or bushes.

Permanent crops: These areas are permanently dedicated to agriculture and include species such as coconut, plantain, fruit trees, or general cover crops.

Annual crops: These areas significantly expose the soil, require annual cleaning, and are used for annual crops, especially for basic grains (corn and beans).

Source: Vega et al. (1993, pp. 37–43).

Environmental Conditions

The Bay Islands' fragile ecosystems in combination with the demands of an escalating human population and a largely unfettered tourist industry have resulted in unprecedented environmental decline. Problems emanate from habitat destruction, deforestation, erosion, and sediment discharge due to site clearing and pasture expansion; the lack of sewerage, solid waste, and treatment facilities; and the absence of hydro-geological studies that result in the haphazard digging of an escalating number of wells. Consequences include contamination of fresh and seawater; increased salinity in underground aquifers; a declining supply of potable water; and degradation of coastal zones including mangrove destruction, beach degradation, and coral reef damage (Vega et al., 1993).

The principal forces of habitat destruction on the Bay Islands include deforestation, inappropriate agricultural practices, highway building, and unsound tourist-related construction. Habitat destruction also results in fragmentation. When a habitat is fragmented, crucial resources for many species may be in short supply in some areas during some times of the year, the amount of vegetative cover declines, and continuous corridors become fewer. Small individual fragments are usually inadequate to maintain viable populations of many species with low populations, leading to the extinction or local extirpation of species. When interactions between different species are permanently altered, a persistent loss of biodiversity occurs in the remaining forest islands.

More than 70% of the island of Roatán has been cleared recently. Deforestation has been caused primarily by the expansion of pasture by wealthier islanders and the spread of hillside agriculture by the increasing number of poor ladino immigrants from the mainland. A practice reported as early as the late 1970s was loaning land to immigrant farmers for a single cropping season, with the condition that the immigrants clear the plot and plant pasture grasses afterwards (Dulin, 1979). This is a common practice on the mainland as well (Stonich, 1993). This method allows the landowner to expand pasture at a relatively low cost. In addition, with land titles generally uncertain, the creation of pastures or other improvements provides added guarantees of land ownership to islanders. Simultaneously, immigrant farmers benefit from immediate access to land for a crop essential to household livelihoods. According to most environmental assessments, this system provides short-term but unsustainable economic benefits because much of the land used for pasture is appropriate only for forestry (e.g., Vega et al., 1993, p. 61). The total pasture area (4,842 hectares or 38.9% of land area) significantly exceeds the appropriate level for the agroecological conditions on Roatán, which was judged to be 1,30 hectares (Vega et al., 1993, p. 43). Extensive grazing and expanding pastures into marginal areas has led to soil compaction, erosion, and sedimentation.

Accelerating destruction of the islands' forests, especially on Roatán, was construction of highways. Previously, transport around the islands was via water, a means of transportation that made the steep, upland areas relatively inaccessible. The construction of Roatán's main highway from Coxen Hole to Oak Ridge during the 1970s contributed to a rapid alteration of Roatán's vegetative cover. The road was constructed along the central part of the island, almost on the watershed divide, and facilitated access to fragile areas in the previously remote headwaters of most of the islands' watersheds.

Eliminating the forests in the upper part of Roatán's watersheds has altered the natural hydro-period to the extent that all but one of Roatán's streams dry up during the dry season, especially during April and May. In addition, wells are affected by the rapid runoff over the denuded lands and diminishing underground aquifers are apparent from the increasing number of dry wells. The presence of trees in such areas would promote a slow percolation, which would recharge the aquifers (Vega et al., 1993, p. 43).

On Roatán, both nonpoint and point-specific erosion generate sediment deposits in coastal areas. Serious nonpoint sources of sediments include degraded watersheds in which a variety of erosion processes result in excessive sediments in the streams during the rainy season. The USAID/WCS report identifies major point-specific sources of sediment discharge that are attributable to the actions of powerful public and private stakeholders (Vega et al., 1993). All are related to infrastructure development necessary for tourism—including construction of the road to the airport, the extension of the main highway from French Harbour to

Photo 4.1. Erosion and gully due to unstabilized road contruction, Roatán.

Punta Pimienta, and the private road leading to West Bay Beach. Clearing for hotel construction also has resulted in serious problems of sediment discharge, particularly during the rainy season when heavy rains increase runoff to the beach and destroy areas of corals, mangroves, and seagrass. One of the most serious sources of sediment is the unstabilized, unpaved road from West End to West Bay Beach, the most popular bathing beach on Roatán, as discussed in Chapter 3. The owner of Cooper's Key Resort, who also owns much of the property adjacent to West Bay Beach, constructed the road. The road was built to improve access to this area of tropical forest and premier beach property in order to promote the sale of land and the development of coastal subdivisions. An owner of one of the small hotels on West Bay Beach christened the thick red discharge frequently flowing from the road down the steep hillside through his property and onto reefs and seagrass beds as "Red Clay Creek."

One of the feasibility studies carried out in preparation of the IDB loan concludes that as much as 90% of the reef at West End is dead or dying (GDH/PNUD, 1992b). This destruction is due to increased sedimentation, eutrophication, chemical contamination, degradation in adjacent environments, direct physical destruction (e.g., through harmful anchoring and diving practices), contamination from solid wastes, and inappropriate fishing practices (GDH/PNUD, 1992b). Although local dive masters, local NGOs, and others dispute this estimate as excessively high, they agree that the health of the reef has deteriorated and a significant percentage is dead—perhaps as much as 50%.

Human Environmental Health

The lowering of the water table and seawater intrusion that occur as water is extracted from the ground by an increasing number of wells has led to a high salt content in the water supply of many communities. Residents who can afford to do so now buy commercial bottled water for drinking. Beginning in 1993, water processed and bottled in the North Coast industrial city of San Pedro Sula was transported to the Bay Islands by boat and sold through a local franchise. By 1995, the islands' two largest grocery stores began selling their own bottled water. There are also reports that some part-time residents transport their drinking water from the U.S.

Serious declines in the quality and quantity of potable water are the most critical environmental health risks that have emerged on the islands and have provoked widespread user conflicts. Groundwater, supplemented seasonally by rainwater, provides the major source of potable water on all the islands. A 1994 study that included a survey of island residents found that 84% of respondents obtained drinking water from private wells while the remainder purchased water from a municipal collection tank (Haylock-Sanabria et al., 1994). With increasing frequency, water shortages have resulted in rationing and/or an irregular supply both to domestic and commercial users. It is not unusual for residents to be without water for several hours per day, sometimes for much longer.

Photo 4.2. "Traditional" method of sewage disposal on Roatán.

Photo 4.3. Common current method of sewage disposal on Roatán.

Photo 4.4. Polluted drainage area, Roatán.

An additional water-related problem is the absence of a sewerage treatment system. This results in an undetermined but large amount of untreated raw sewage being piped directly into the sea. About 22% of island residents have no household sewerage disposal system whatsoever, an estimated 28% of households use latrines that empty directly into the sea, and about 40% of households have some type of septic system (GDH/PNUD, 1992a, p. 55). Even where latrines and septic fields or tanks exist, they frequently leak contaminated water into soil and groundwater. The recent growth of the cattle population, in part to meet rising tourist demand, especially on Roatán, further contributes to the contamination of groundwater and it is common to see cattle grazing in fenced pastures close to wells. In response to shortages, anyone who is able digs a well (often several) with little forethought or knowledge of suitable location or depth. To help alleviate resulting problems,

APRODIB, with funding from international donor agencies, promoted the building and use of composting latrines, the creation of hydro-geological maps, and the digging of new (more appropriately located and chlorinated) community wells. To date, however, local municipal agencies seem to be operating with little coordination and success. The lack of an adequate island-wide solid waste collection and disposal system provides a further source of contamination of the existing water supply as well as prime breeding sites for mosquitoes and other pests. Current conditions have escalated the incidence of water-borne diseases including cholera, dysentery, and hepatitis, as well as facilitated the transmission of water-related diseases such as malaria and dengue fever, which thrive in unsanitary conditions. Diminished access to potable water, increased salinity in the remaining supply, and increased contamination of fresh water, brackish, and seawater are among the most significant problems and contentious issues on the islands and are likely to affect the continued growth and future sustainability of the tourist industry.

Endangered Species

It is not only the islands' human population that is in jeopardy. Although the abundant wildlife of the Bay Islands offers an opportunity to diversify the islands' tourism industry, both terrestrial and marine species are being seriously affected by human activities. Overexploitation is responsible for the near extinction of the queen conch (*Strombus gigas*), lobster (*Panulirus argus*), and black coral (*Antipathes* sp). Swamp crabs (*Cardisoma guanhumi*) also are threatened due to commercial overexploitation and habitat destruction. The terrestrial species most sought for commercial purposes are the Roatán parrot (for the international pet market, especially in the U.S. and Grand Cayman) and the iguana (for sale of their meat and eggs). Eighteen island species are classified as being either endangered or threatened with extinction due to destruction and fragmentation of habitats, hunting, fishing, and capture for the pet trade. A total of five species and one subspecies—three reptiles, two birds, and one mammal—have been classified as threatened. Their populations are reduced to the extent that they could disappear over the next decade if hunting and capture remain unchecked. Threatened species include the Roatán parrot (*Amazona xantholora*), chachalaca (*Ortalis vetula*), iguana (*Iguana iguana*), grey lizard (*Ctenosaura bakery*), black lizard (*Ctenosaura similis*), and the white tailed deer (*Odocoileus virginianus*). Eleven species and one subspecies are categorized as endangered, either locally or worldwide, including three marine invertebrates and nine vertebrates. They include the rosy boa (*Boa constrictor*), coral snake (*Micrurus ruatanus*), American crocodile (*Crocodylus acutus*), jicotea turtle (*Chrysems ornata*), green sea turtle (*Chelonia mydas*), hawksbill turtle (*Eretmochelys imbricata*), carey turtle (*Caretta caretta*), ridley turtle (*Lepidochelys olivaces*), leatherback turtle (*Dermochelys coriaces*), queen conch (*Strombus gigas*), ocean lobster (*Panulirus argus*), and black coral (*Antipathes* spp.) (Vega et al., 1993, p. 59). Two of the 18 species and two of the subspecies are endemic to the Bay Islands: the Roatán parrot, the coral snake, the rosy boa, and the chachalaca (Vega et al., 1993, p. 58). In addition to endangered and threatened species, at least four species are locally extinct: the manatee (*Trichechus manatus*), the brown booby (*Sula leucogaster*), the red-footed booby (*Sula sula*), and the Caribbean monk seal (*Monachus tropicalis*), which also is globally extinct (Vega et al., 1993, pp. 60–61).

Protected Areas

Honduras has established a number of protected areas based on the model used by the International Union for the Conservation of Nature (IUCN). Additional populations of flora and fauna have been granted special protected status. According to a recent study done for the Island Resources Foundation, the Bay Islands encompass three of the 11 marine parks and reserves in Honduras: the Sandy Bay-West End Marine Reserve on Roatán, the Turtle Harbor Reserve on Utila, and the marine park on Guanaja (Mascia, 1998). All three were established by municipal ordinance and are managed through BICA.

Vega et al. (1993, p. 81–84) recommended that 12 protected areas be designated on the Bay Islands in order to preserve the islands' biodiversity and freshwater supply as well as to benefit the tourism industry. Five areas on Roatán were suggested, including the Sandy Bay Marine Reserve (which subsequently was expanded to become the Sandy Bay-West End Marine reserve) and the West End forest. On Utila, four areas were designated and on Guanaja two areas. The study also recommended that the entire area around the Bay Islands be declared a marine-protected area. This recommendation differed from the proposal prepared by the GOH and UNDP advisors. While the former recommended that the entire area be a marine-protected area encompassing smaller marine parks, the latter advocated that the entire area around the Bay Islands be considered a national marine park with small, internal zones of special management. The latter recommendation is in line with the presidential decree that established the Bay Islands National Marine Park in 1997.

Despite a growing number of municipal ordinances and enhanced national recognition, attempts to manage conservation areas on the Bay Islands historically have met with little success. For example, one of the first areas to be protected was the Guanaja Forestry Reserve established in 1961. Vega et al. (1993, p. 63) report that at the time of their study in 1992 few residents were aware that these forests had been protected. Moreover, a management plan had never been drafted, personnel had never been assigned, and no research had ever been conducted. Likewise, on Roatán, the Port Royal Wildlife Refuge was established in 1979 via Acta No. 20 of the Municipality of José Santos Guardiola. Thirteen years later, in 1992, no management plan had been prepared for this protected area. According to the secretary of BICA:

> Sure we've had two marine parks here since the 1980s . . . but as far as we're concerned they're just paper parks—no rules, no park rangers, not even a painted sign to tell people where they are. (Secretary of BICA quoted in Gordon, 1993, p. 78)

Sandy Bay-West End Marine Reserve

The Sandy Bay-West End Marine Reserve (SBWEMR) was the first marine reserve in Honduras and is the best known and well-funded protected area on the islands. The reserve encompasses a wide range of inshore, Caribbean habitats as well as a diverse marine biota attractive to the growing tourist population (Figure 4.2). In 1989, the 4.2-km area from Lawson Rock on the east to Gibson Bight on the west was designated as the Sandy Bay Marine Reserve by the municipality of Roatán. In 1993, the reserve was extended to about 13 km with the addition of the West End Marine Reserve that included the West End and West Bay Beach areas where the sharp rise in tourism and tourist-related construction put added strain on the coastal and marine environments. From the shoreline outward, the reserve includes all waters within the farthest limits of the outer reef (Luttinger, 1997).

The Sandy Bay Marine Reserve was started by the actions of a few people from the community, including a dive master and a local school teacher, who sought initial funding from the owner of the largest resort within the proposed reserve. According to one of the principal founders:

> After 25 years, divers [from the above resort] and spear fishers had negatively affected the reef near the resort and Sandy Bay. We wouldn't think anything of anchoring on the coral or spearfishing for our supper. But then we noticed a decline in the reef, in the number of species, and in the number of fish overall. We applied to the municipality to establish the Sandy Bay reserve. The municipality approved the reserve. We also tried to have the GOH Congress declare the reserve . . . but the GOH has yet to declare it. With the reserve established in Sandy Bay, increased pressure was put on the surrounding area of West End. Members of West End wanted their own reserve. (Founding member of the Sandy Bay Marine Reserve, personal communication, 1997)

The SBWEMR is managed through BICA through a 12-member board of directors, most of whom are BICA members and who are associated with tourist businesses that are dependent on the health of the marine resources that lie within the reserve. All financial contributions to the reserve and all expenses are conveyed through the BICA office in Roatán. In 1995, the SBWEMR had eight salaried positions (a director; six marine guards, a bookkeeper/secretary) and one volunteer position (a cleaning person). The reserve operated on a budget of about US$2,200 per month based on voluntary contributions from local businesses. A total of about 30 businesses located within the reserve contributed an average (median) of approximately US$6 per month. Before the expansion of the reserve in 1993, the owner of Cooper's Key Resort, the largest resort in the reserve, contributed about 98% of the reserve's total operating budget (Seidl, 1996, pp. 43–45). Since then the contributions by local businesses have become more evenly distributed, although the total operating budget has fallen dramatically.

Reserve policies stress regulation, surveillance, and enforcement. Regulations include the prohibition of anchors, spearfishing, destruction and collection of coral, harvesting of marine life (especially conch and lobster), and fishing with nets within the reserve. Although net fishing is disallowed, line fishing is permitted. Also included is a ban on construction of new marinas and piers within the reserve, as well as the disposal of solid waste. Yachts and sail vessels moored within the reserve are required to have holding tanks for sewage. The reserve, in

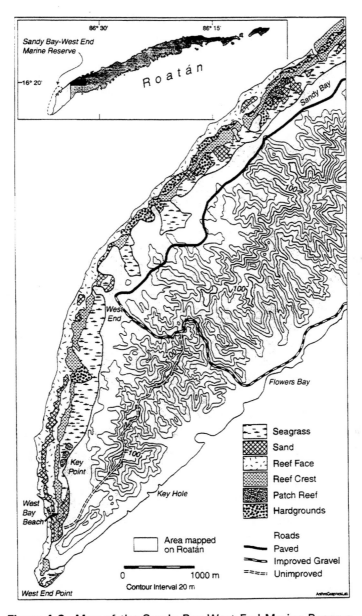

Figure 4.2. Map of the Sandy Bay-West End Marine Reserve.

cooperation with the U.S.-based National Marine Sanctuaries Program and Reef Relief, coordinates private efforts among local dive shops to implement a mooring buoy program.

Recognizing that access to the economic resources within the reserve is diminished by its regulations, the reserve implemented a limited job-training program. It paid 95% of the cost of an open water certification cost to encourage local divers and spear fishermen to train as dive guides/dive masters. Unfortunately, many trained individuals could not find employment as dive masters, because most dive masters are foreigners—from the U.S., Europe, Australia, South Africa, and elsewhere. A few of the affected individuals were hired as guards and a few others were trained to work as waiters and in other low-end jobs in the tourist industry. At first, reserve guards hired from within the ranks of the community were placed in the awkward position of carrying out surveillance on their neighbors. More recently, guards have been recruited from the local police and/or from the swelling number of immigrant ladinos looking for work (SBWEMR board member, personal communication, 1997).

Reserve policies are implemented through a management plan that stresses monitoring and enforcement, which account for 93% of total reserve expenses. This includes salaries for guards, maintenance of boats and motors, and gasoline. The remaining 7% of the budget is allocated for administration and cleanup (Luttinger, 1997; Seidl, 1996, p. 49). When possible, two boats and four guards are on duty 24 hours a day. They patrol the reserve in order to keep people from dredging, harming turtle hatcheries and seagrass, cutting mangroves, and collecting coral, lobster, and conch. Guards also monitor diving and fishing activities. The reef guards have included former spear fishermen as well as members of the police who have the authority to arrest poachers and other offenders on the spot. Poachers, usually local residents who have been caught spearfishing or with illegal catches of lobster and conch, are assigned to do community service, fined, or jailed ("Underwater Wilds," 1994).

Recently, changes within the reserve have notably affected its capacity to carry out activities. One of the most serious is a significant decline in funding, which stems from the decision of the owner of the large resort, who provided the bulk of the operating funds, to recant his monthly contribution. Subsequently, other local businesses rescinded or reduced their contributions. According to a recent article touting the success of the reserve, the large resort owner's decision was based on a disagreement over management of the reserve—implying some sort of philosophical difference over policy (Luttinger, 1997). However, according to a member of the board of directors of the reserve, the decision emanated from a severe conflict between reserve members and the owner, who built a spacious, luxurious home and marina within the reserve in clear violation of reserve regulations (field interviews, 1997). The construction also required permits under the national environmental legislation discussed earlier in this chapter. Construction of the large complex included dredging a large channel. Clearing the channel not only destroyed segments of the reef and shoreline but also impeded public access along the beach—although the owner did construct a feeble bridge over the channel. A local environmentalist and founding member of the reserve put it this way:

> There was a big local controversy over [the resort owner's] decision to build
> the marina . . . every NGO opposed his plan . . . while we [the NGO leaders]
> were visiting the proposed site and reviewing the plans, the construction

materials were being brought in . . . every NGO opposed the plan but [he] went ahead . . . he got a permit from Tegucigalpa . . . it was strange . . . since then there has been a big decline in financial support for the reserve [from the owner]. (Bay Island environmentalist and founding member of the reserve, personal communication, 1998)

When asked how the owner had gotten permission to dredge the channel and build the marina in light of the number of regulations and laws prohibiting such construction, a resident of West End responded:

He [the owner of the large resort] don't need permission to do anything . . . around here, if people want to do something they ask him for permission. (West End resident, personal communication, 1997)

This same resort owner is responsible for the construction of the unstabilized road to West Bay Beach that has led to serious erosion affecting the beach, seagrass beds, and reef, discussed earlier in this chapter. Among other activities carried out by this powerful individual within the reserve that have provoked environmental controversies are the capture of wild dolphins, dolphin performances in the guise of educational programs, and associated swim and dive with the dolphin encounters. The last activity is particularly contentious to community members who are regularly harassed by the dive boat crew should they be swimming or snorkeling in the area being used by the dolphins and tourist divers. In addition, dive masters in the employ of this individual reportedly feed the reef fish daily so that the recreational divers are assured of observing abundant fish in addition to dolphins. This influential owner's most recent controversial project was the intentional sinking of an old ship off the resort so that his guests could have easy access to a "shipwreck dive site." Unfortunately, the ship was sunk in a fragile portion of the reef that is home to hundreds of eels (field interviews, 1997).

The injustice that powerful individuals flagrantly engage in extremely destructive projects explicitly prohibited by reserve regulations while they are arrested, fined, and jailed for minor poaching activities has not escaped the notice of poorer members of the communities bordering the reserve. The middle-class owners of the small businesses within the reserve (islanders, ladinos, and foreigners) also resent the fact that powerful island elite with money and influence can get away with environmentally destructive projects while they must adhere to the rules and regulations.

Local conflicts surrounding the reserve escalated in April 1997 when a ladino guard, who had worked for the reserve for only a short time, shot and killed a 17-year-old black islander in Sandy Bay who allegedly had a history of poaching from the reserve. According to reports from local residents, the boy and his friends apparently got into an argument with the reserve guard, who fired his 9-millimeter Uzi and shot the boy, who died the next day. Reserve guards are not supposed to carry guns and the killing created quite a contentious situation that intensified well beyond the community. The incident was reported by NABIPLA to CONPAH, to which NABIPLA belongs. On May 24, 1997, the case was included in a CONPAH report documenting recent human rights violations against indigenous peoples in Honduras that was sent to the Honduran National Commissioner on Human Rights (*Comisionado Nacional de Derechos Humanos* [CONADH]) and posted on the World Wide Web (http://www.ibw.con.ni/~cgenica/asesinat.htm). CONPAH demanded an investigation of the killing by local authorities and the arrest of the guard, who was referred to as an "agent of the police of the marine park (*un agente de policia del Parque Marino*)." The report connected the killing of the teenager, purportedly an active member of NABIPLA, to the eviction of the 12 islander families from their homes on the island of Helene that occurred a month earlier (this incident was described in Chapter 3). In July 1997, both incidents were incorporated by CONPAH into a letter sent to the Honduran President, Carlos Roberto Reina. This letter was modified into an NGO sign-on letter and transmitted to the Center for International Policy in Washington, DC and to the South and Meso-American Indian Rights Center (SAIIC) in Oakland, CA. It then became an "Urgent Action" entitled, "Threat of Violence in Honduras Over Land Rights," which was sent via the Internet to members of several indigenous and human rights' list servers. According to the cover letter, the purpose was, " to have Honduran and international organizations sign on and support these indigenous land struggles" (http://bioc02.uthscsa.edu/natnet/archive/n1/9707/0032.html). The letter further stipulated that, ". . . Black leaders are still under threat for their ongoing efforts to ensure the basic right to land for their peoples."

It was in this antagonistic context that BICA announced ambitious efforts to design and implement management plans for the Sandy Bay-West End Marine Reserve on Roatán and the Turtle Harbour Wildlife Refuge on Utila in late 1997. *Fundacíon Vida* (a national NGO supported in large part by USAID) provided financing for the 3-year project through funding by USAID and technical support from WCS. According to a BICA press release, the project's main objective is:

> . . . to promote the conservation of the Bay Islands natural and marine resources in both protected areas. This will be achieved through the design and implementation of management plans for both areas, daily patrols by boat and on land, reef monitoring programs to identify problems and seek solutions. The installation of sediment traps . . . will minimize negative impacts in our marine environment. . . . We aim to educate our people about the importance of our fragile resources and the need to protect, conserve, and manage in a sustainable manner. Our ecotourism program will help us educate our local and international tourist. Generating at the same time revenues that will help us cover operative costs. (Bay Islands Conservation Association [BICA], 1997)

A summary of the draft management plan was distributed to the public and government officials on Roatán in July 1998 to solicit comments regarding the most controversial parts of the plan. The capacity of this draft plan to bring about community-based management will be assessed in Chapter 6. Staff of WCS hope to receive approval from AHE-COHDEFOR and SERNA by the end of 1998. In light of the current economic climate and substantial controversies surrounding the reserve, BICA and its supporters are faced with a formidable challenge.

Conclusions

It is conspicuous that, over the years, an increasing amount of money has gone to fund an escalating number of consultants, environmental assessments, and management plans for the Bay Islands. It remains to be seen if any will come to fruition or, if they do, the effects they will have on the human residents as well as on the environment and natural resources of the islands. In any case, recent initiatives are steeped in so-called participatory approaches that urge or demand that community-based conservation and development be central to the efforts. For example, both the 1992 USAID/WCS conservation strategy and the IDB environmental management project proposal encourage a great deal of community involvement and local control.

The 1992 USAID/WCS study concluded with a series of nine principal recommendations that remain relevant today:

1. The maximization of agricultural lands through the cultivation of appropriate annual, semipermanent, and permanent crops.

2. The modernization or termination of livestock grazing.

3. The promotion of forestry production in appropriate areas.

4. The reforestation and control of runoff in critical areas.

5. The stabilization of denuded areas associated with the construction of highways.

6. The consolidation of the system of protected areas.

7. The establishment and enforcement of regulations prohibiting illegal hunting, fishing, and capture of wild species and the introduction of exotic species.

8. The devolution of national authority for wildlife and wildlands management to a specific Bay Islands park authority that could develop co-management agreements with local NGOs and municipalities.

9. The promotion of public participation in the development and implementation of the environmental management plan, not only through environmental education but also through the local population's participation in the economic benefits of tourism (Vega et al., 1993).

The following chapters concentrate on opportunities and obstacles to realizing the above objectives—particularly those related to linkages between the distribution of the economic benefits of tourism, risk, public participation, and conservation.

Chapter 5

The Impacts of Tourism on Community, Ethnicity, Class, and Gender

While the environmental consequences of tourism on the Bay Islands have gotten considerable notice, the repercussions on the islands' diverse peoples have received little attention. Many crucial questions barely have been raised. Should one of the major goals of tourism development be to ensure that the islands' residents (longtime inhabitants as well as recent arrivals) have the means to a reasonable livelihood and the continued viability of their cultures? If so, what are the effects of the growth of tourism on the relative prosperity and well-being traditionally enjoyed by many of the islands' peoples? Further, if segments of the islands' population are paying the price of tourism (while others reap the benefits) how can they be expected to support the mounting number of proposed environmental protection and conservation efforts? Without the participation and cooperation of the majority of inhabitants, how can the islands' environmental resources, crucial for a viable tourism industry, be sustained? This chapter addresses this lacunae. It explores the human consequences of the expanding tourism industry by divisions of community, nationality, ethnicity, class, and gender. It demonstrates the relative benefits and costs arising from current patterns of tourism at the local level. Analysis focuses on the communities of Sandy Bay, West End, and Flowers Bay, which vary significantly in terms of their integration into the tourist sector. The boom in tourism on the Bay Islands that began in the late 1980s occurred first in the area along the coast that stretches from Sandy Bay to West End, before it expanded to the adjacent area of West Bay Beach. This tourism "hot spot" still accounts for the majority of tourist-related businesses on Roatán island, as discussed in Chapter 3. This chapter examines the profound linkages between the tourist industry, household economic strategies, and patterns in consumption, diet, nutrition, and health.

Community, Ethnicity, Class, and Gender[1]

West End and Flowers Bay were among the first communities on the western shore of Roatán to be founded by Afro-Caribbean colonists from the Cayman Islands

Photo 5.1. Islander community on the western shore of Roatán.

between 1844 and 1852. These immigrants desired sea frontage properties that were unavailable to them in the more populated centers, such as Coxen Hole and French Harbour, which were dominated by white settlers (Davidson, 1974, p. 79). The locale around Sandy Bay and Anthony's Cay was the site of at least three British land titles during the 1740s. However, permanent settlement of the area by Afro-Caribbeans occurred during the second wave of island settlement between 1860 and 1890 when Sandy Bay was founded in 1865. It was 70 years before Anthony's Cay was settled in 1935 (Davidson, 1974, p. 58; Watt, 1973, pp. 108, 302–305).

Ian Watt, who did research around 1970 on the settlement history of Roatán, summarized a few of the relevant characteristics of West End, Flowers Bay, and Sandy Bay at that time. The two communities of West End and Flowers Bay were of similar size (from 100 to 200 people). The residents were predominantly Creole (black, Afro-Caribbean) and they made their living through subsistence farming and fishing (Watt, 1973, p. 108). Settlement was linear with house dwellings built parallel to the shore. Sandy Bay also was inhabited predominantly by black islanders and had approximately the same number of inhabitants as West End and Flowers Bay. It was distinguished from the other two communities, however, by the presence of Cooper's Key Resort that provided employment to local villagers who also depended economically on fishing and farming. In contrast to West End and Flowers Bay, many residents of Sandy Bay lived on hillsides away from the shore, apparently to escape insect pests and the seasonally high waves that occurred during winter storms (Davidson, 1974, p. 103).

As part of this study, population censuses of the three communities were conducted in 1993. Sandy Bay had 190 occupied housing units and a total population of approximately 1,200. It was more than three times as large as West End (which had 65 occupied housing units and a population of about 350 persons) and about twice as large as Flowers Bay (with 106 occupied housing units and 477 residents). Flowers Bay had the highest percentage of residents who classified themselves as islanders (90%) compared to 65% in West End and 52% in Sandy Bay. In Sandy Bay and West End, the percentage of ladinos significantly exceeded that counted in earlier national population censuses.

Although the Bay Islands usually are classified as part of the "English-speaking Caribbean," the percentage of women and men householders who speak Spanish (89%) exceeds those who speak English (66%). Eighty-four percent of islanders who speak Creole and English as their primary language also speak Spanish, while only 33% of Spanish-speaking ladinos also speak English. This is especially so for relatively recent migrants from the mainland—those who have been on the island for 5 years or less. This intensified "Hispanicization" of the islands is also intimated

Photo 5.2. Baptist church on Roatán.

by islander householders who report that while 84% of them speak Spanish, only 50% of their parents did.

The three communities are similar in the relative distribution of Catholics and Protestants with more than 88% of all residents belonging to one of several Protestant denominations (including most commonly the Church of God, Methodist, Baptist, or Seventh Day Adventist). Although there is a statistically significant relationship between ethnicity (i.e., islander and ladino) and religion, this association is by no means absolute. Although most Catholics are ladinos, the majority of ladinos (64%) also belong to one of the Protestant churches.

In terms of literacy and education, women appear to have somewhat higher literacy rates than men (97% of women versus 87% of men reported that they could read) while school attendance was similar (mean number of years: 5.7). Differences in school attendance between islanders and ladinos, however, are statistically significant ($p \leq 0.05$) with islander women attending school for 6.1 years in contrast to ladino women (4.9 years). Similarly, islander men attended school for 5.3 years in contrast to ladino men (4.4 years). These data begin to delineate community and ethnic patterns that are helpful in assessing the extent to which various island groups have the capacity to take advantage of new economic opportunities provided by the growth of the tourism industry. The islanders, virtually all of whom are bilingual, literate, and with more education, have certain advantages over their predominately monolingual and less literate ladino counterparts. National censuses suggest a recent increase in illiteracy throughout the islands due in part to the migration of large numbers of illiterate ladinos from the mainland. In 1988 an estimated 11.3% of islander residents were classified as illiterate; by 1992 that percentage had grown to 16.2%, still only half the national average of 32% (GDH/PNUD, 1992a, p. 61). Increasing illiteracy throughout the islands portends badly in terms of island residents' future capacity to take advantage of better jobs in the tourist sector.

Household Structure and Demography

Table 5.1 compares the communities and ethnic groups on the basis of several variables pertaining to demography and household structure. Of these, the age of the householder and the number of people living in the household (household size) were best able to discriminate among the population by ethnicity. The mean (and median) ages of islander women and men were significantly higher than those of ladinos, as were the average (mean and median) number of years each respective group had lived in the community. By community, householders from Flowers Bay had the highest mean (and median) age and had lived in their community for the greatest number of years. They were followed by householders from West End and finally from Sandy Bay. In summary, islanders tend to be older than ladinos, with the eldest population (composed almost entirely of islanders) living in Flowers Bay. The average size of ladino households was significantly larger (by more than two persons) than that of islanders. Differences in household size among communities were also significant: ranging from a high of 6.5 persons

Table 5.1. Comparison of Demography and Household Structure by Community, Ethnicity, and Gender

	Total	Community			Ethnicity	
		West End	Sandy Bay	Flowers Bay	Islanders	Ladinos
Women Head (N)	141	36	53	52	97	44
Age (years)	42.8 ± 17	42.3 ± 16	39.6 ± 16	46.5 ± 16	45.9 ± 17	$36 \pm 13***$
Length of time in community (years)	24.6 ± 11	28.2 ± 23	20 ± 17	29.4 ± 19	31.5 ± 19	$13.7 \pm 12***$
Median	20	24	16	27	27	10
Fertility[a]	4.8 ± 3.2	4.1 ± 2.8	5.2 ± 3.2	5 ± 3.5	4.9 ± 3.3	4.8 ± 3
Men Head (N)	93	28	38	27	64	29
Age (years)	47.9 ± 16	47.7 ± 16	43.8 ± 15	53.6 ± 15	49.7 ± 17	43.9 ± 14
Length of time in community (years)	23.9 ± 21	13.7 ± 11	16.9 ± 17	40.1 ± 21	36.8 ± 20	$9.1 \pm 8***$
Median	15	10	13	49	33	6
Household Structure						
Household size[b]	5.3 ± 3	4.8 ± 2	6.5 ± 3.5	$4.5 \pm 2.5***$	4.8 ± 2.4	$6.5 \pm 3.7**$
Median	5	5	7	4	5	7
No. of children living in house	2.2 ± 2	2.1 ± 1.5	3.0 ± 2.3	$1.4 \pm 1.5***$	1.8 ± 1.7	$3 \pm 2.2***$
Median	2	2	3	1	2	3
Dependency ratio[c]	0.8 ± 0.8	0.9 ± 0.8	0.98 ± 0.8	$0.5 \pm 0.6**$	0.7 ± 0.7	$0.98 \pm 0.8*$
% women headed[d]	29%	25%	36%	25%	31%	25%

[a]The total number of births to each woman householder.
[b]The number of people living in the household.
[c]The ratio of economically "productive" to economically "nonproductive" household members. Calculated as the number of children ±13 years of age + the number of adults ≥65 years of age/number of adults 14–64 years of age.
[d]The percentage of households headed by women.
*$p \leq 0.05$; **$p \leq 0.01$; ***$p \leq 0.001$.

(median of 7) in Sandy Bay, to 4.8 persons (median of 5) in West End, to 4.5 persons (median of 4) in Flowers Bay.

The diversity in the size of islander and ladino households is not due to differences in fertility in the two groups but rather to variation in the age structure of households (i.e., the younger average age of ladino households). The fertility rates of islander and ladino women were quite similar and varied only slightly among communities. This was true for all women, for women who were 45 years of age or older (who had completed their childbearing years), and for younger women (i.e, less than 45 years old). The communities and ethnic groups did vary significantly in terms of the mean number of children living in the household, with households in Sandy Bay and those with ladinos as heads having a mean of 3.1 children who were less than 13 years old. Not surprisingly, the dependency ratios for these two groups also exceeded those for West End, Flowers Bay, and islanders, respectively.

Ethnic groups and communities vary as well in the percentage of nuclear and extended families, and in the percentage of households headed by women. The relatively high percentage of women-headed households (29% of all households, 36% in Sandy Bay, and 31% among islanders) exceeds by approximately 10% the estimated percentage of women-headed households at the national level and among rural households on the mainland (Stonich, 1993). In large part, the relatively high rate of women-headed households is due to the prolonged absences of

Photo 5.3. Islander children, Roatán.

Photo 5.4. Ladino children, Roatán.

islander men who work as fishermen, on cruise ships, or in the merchant marine. In summary, households in Sandy Bay and those of ladinos tend to be larger, younger, and with more dependent children than households in West End and those with islanders as household heads. Further, the community of Sandy Bay and the population of islanders generally have a higher percentage of households headed by women than do the other groups.

The Household Economy

Analysis of the economic options utilized by islander and ladino households reveals substantial reliance on the tourism industry. Seventy-six percent of all women householders and 69% of all men householders earn income from work that is directly or indirectly related to tourism.[2] This dependence is greater for ladinos (83% for women and 76% for men) than for islanders (69% for women and 64% for men), and for women (74%) than for men (68%). Household economic dependence on the tourism sector is greatest in Sandy Bay (88% of women and 81% of men), somewhat less in West End (67% of women and 69% of men), and least in Flowers Bay (37% of women and 67% of men). Approximately 80% of the women and 70% of the men who reside in West End and Sandy Bay also work in their home communities while only 40% of the women and 39% of the men who live in Flowers Bay also work there. Despite the absence of tourist facilities in Flowers Bay, residents rely on income earned at hotels, restaurants in Coxen Hole and French Harbour (the municipal center and adjacent town that are accessible by frequent bus service), in the booming construction business, and from the sale of fish, farm, and processed food products to tourist enterprises. Moreover, 13% of households in Flowers Bay reported that in 1993 their primary source of cash to meet household needs was through the sale of land to nonlocals for the construction of tourist-related ventures or private residences.

Several variables describing household economic strategies are compared in Table 5.2. In total, these data suggest that, despite overall reliance on the tourism sector and some overlap between the patterns of ladinos and poor islanders, household economic strategies vary significantly by ethnicity. In general, ladinos are much more exclusively dependent than islanders on monetized income earned through

Photo 5.5. Traditional islander house, fishing dory, and new house construction, Roatán.

Table 5.2. Comparison of Household Economy by Community, Ethnicity, and Gender

	Total	Community			Ethnicity	
		West End	Sandy Bay	Flowers Bay	Islanders	Ladinos
Women's income[a]	41.2 ± 96	81.7 ± 184	32 ± 33	23.7 ± 34	47.8 ± 114	26.9 ± 25
Median	23.4	25.4	25.4	16.9	23.4	25.4
≥US$100/week[b]	7%	18%	4%	2%	8%	2%
Men's income[c]	93.6 ± 143	121 ± 169	93.2 ± 152	58.1 ± 61	117 ± 172	51.5 ± 35
Median	50.8	70	50.8	33.9	55.1	46.6
≥US$100/week[d]	20%	25%	18%	20%	27%	8%
Monetary income diversity (MID)[e]	1.9 ± 1.1	1.8 ± 0.1	1.6 ± 0.9	2.3 ± 1.2***	2.1 ± 1.1	1.5 ± 0.8***
Median	2	2	1	2	2	1
No. animals[f]	1.5 ± 2.8	1.9 ± 1.6	0.9 ± 1.1	1.9 ± 4.3	1.7 ± 3.3	0.98 ± 1.3***
Median	1	2	0	1	1	0
No. poultry[g]	2.8 ± 9.1	0.39 ± 0.84	0.47 ± 0.78	8.9 ± 14.2*	3.9 ± 10.9***	0.50 ± 0.96***
Median	0	0	0	0	0	0
Nonmonetary income diversity (NID)[h]	3.3 ± 2.0	3.2 ± 2.1	3.1 ± 2.1	3.6 ± 1.9	3.7 ± 1.9	2.6 ± 2.1**
Median	3	3	3	4	4	2
Sources of NID[i]						
With land or farm[j]	43%	50%	30%	52%	50%	30%**
With gardens	36%	42%	28%	41%	46%	14%***
With fruit trees	66%	77%	60%	67%	72%	54%*
Who hunt	1%	14%	15%	26%	22%	11%
Who fish	52%	43%	58%	50%	64%	25%***
Gather wild plants	27%	11%	42%	21%	25%	30%
Own animals	58%	69%	49%	60%	64%	46%*
Own poultry	34%	22%	32%	44%	37%	27%

[a]Cash income (US$) earned by women householder during previous week. [b]Percentage of women householders who earned US$100 or more during the previous week. [c]Cash income (US$) earned by men householder during previous week. [d]Percentage of male householders who earned US$100 or more during the previous week. [e]A rank scale calculated on the basis of 13 sources of monetary income delineated in the text. [f]Total number of horses, burros, beef cattle, bulls, hogs, pigs, goats, and milk cows owned. [g]Total number of roosters, hens, chickens, ducks, turkeys and other poultry owned. [h]A rank scale calculated on the eight sources of nonmonetary income. The individual items are described in the text. [i]Sources of nonmonetary income used to calculate NID. Percentage of households in each category that engage in that activity.
*$p \leq 0.05$; **$p \leq 0.01$; ***$p \leq 0.001$.

wages paid while employed by tourist-related businesses. In contrast, islanders participate in a much more diverse array of monetized and nonmonetized income-generating activities. In addition, both islanders and ladinos sometimes receive payment for work in the form of food, housing, and transportation.[3] Islanders are much more apt to have access to nonmonetized sources of income, the products from which can be consumed domestically or sold. They are more likely to have land used for farming, house gardens, and fruit trees, to fish (as well as to own a boat and to sell fish), to hunt, and to raise large animals (cattle, cows, hogs, and pigs) and poultry. Only in gathering wild plants for food and medicine does the percentage of ladino households exceed slightly that of islanders. As shown in Table 5.2, the nonmonetary income diversity index of islander households significantly surpasses that of ladinos.[4]

While differences among communities in household nonmonetary economic diversity were not statistically significant, households in Flowers Bay took part in the greatest number of nonmonetary activities. These households are particularly distinguished by their high participation in agricultural activities, especially raising poultry, and by their expanding participation in the beef cattle industry. Flowers Bay had both the highest percentage of households that raised poultry and the highest mean number of poultry owned. Sixteen percent of all households in the three communities raised beef cattle, with ownership fairly evenly distributed between islanders (14%) and ladinos (18%), most of whom owned only one or two head. The community of West End had the greatest percentage of households that owned cattle (33% of households). Two islander families in Flower's Bay owned the largest herds (16 and 25 head). In both cases, these households had expanded their herds in the last 5 years to meet the rising demand brought about by the growth of tourism. On the one hand, this may be interpreted positively as a link between the tourism and agricultural sectors. On the other, the unfettered development of the cattle industry on the island is already apparent in expanding deforested areas and eroded pastures located on steep hillsides. In any case, augmented agricultural production in Flowers Bay is another indication of the extent to which the community is integrated into the tourism industry even though tourist facilities have not yet been built there. It also is an example of how agriculture in the community is being transformed from being primarily subsistence to commercially based as households take advantage of expanding opportunities.[5]

In addition to a greater assortment of nonmonetary economic options, islanders also have access to a wider range of sources of cash to meet daily expenses. Householders were asked to report on all the ways in which they obtained money for daily needs. Responses were placed in 13 different categories and a composite score (monetary income diversity index) was calculated for each household on the basis of whether or not they obtained cash from each category. This rank scale measured the degree of diversity in the individual household's sources of cash to meet daily expenses. Possible scores ranged from 0 to 13. Categories included: income earned by woman householder; income earned by male householder; income/remittances from daughters; income/remittances from sons; sale of land; rental property; remittances from ex-spouse; savings and investments; retirement

Photo 5.6. Traditional islander house with porch and wooden stilts, Roatán

pension; and remittances from father of children. As shown in Table 5.2, the mean (and median) monetary income diversity score for islanders was significantly greater than that for ladinos. In terms of ethnicity, the most important differences were the extent to which each group depended on remittances from family members other than the woman and man householders. For islanders, 33% reported remittances from daughters, 36% from sons, and 21% from other family members. In contrast, ladino households reported remittances of only 11%, 14%, and 11% from those respective groups. In addition, no ladino households received income from the sale of land or home, rental property, an ex-spouse, inheritance, savings, or retirement pension. Similar to nonmonetary economic diversity, residents of Flowers Bay obtained cash for daily expenses from the most diverse sources, while inhabitants of Sandy Bay acquired money from the least number of sources. To a great extent, differences among communities are due to the relative distribution of islanders and ladinos living in the communities.

Table 5.2 reveals differences in the economic options by gender as well as by ethnicity and community. While almost 50% of women householders had engaged in some activity to earn cash during the previous year, the mean weekly income of islander women was almost twice as high as that of ladino women. This occurred despite ladino women working in excess of 3 hours a day more than islander women. The high standard deviation of the mean income for islanders, however,

Photo 5.7. Ladino ghetto on lagoon, Roatán.

implies a significant range in islanders' incomes. Simultaneously, the median
income of islander women was slightly less than that of ladino women. Together,
these data demonstrate that the weekly incomes of the majority of islander and
ladino women were similar and suggests a dualistic monetary income distribution
in which a relatively small number of islander women encompass the high end. In
fact, of the 7% of women who earned US$100 per week or more, only one was a
ladino (an attorney). All islander women in the high-end income category had their
own business (hotel, restaurant, store) or sold food items (prepared baked goods or
animal products) from their homes. For the entire sample of islander women, the
greatest proportion (40%) earned income from the sale of items produced or raised
at home: animals (pigs and chickens), eggs, milk coconut oil, bread, and fish. Other
sources of income included working as maids (19%), waitresses or cooks (3%),
owning their own businesses (16%), and from rental properties (cabins and rooms in
their homes). For ladino women, the majority worked as maids (48%) or as waitresses (25%), with only a small percentage (10%) earning income from petty com-
modity production and sale. The daily needs of ladino women were met primarily by
wages they earned themselves (70%) while islander women relied more heavily on
financial contributions from other family members (spouses and children).

Almost all ladino men (93%) and the majority of islander men (78%) had engaged
in some activity to earn cash during the previous year and 31% of men reported
having some kind of secondary occupation. In many ways analysis of the weekly

Photo 5.8. Ladino house on hillside, Roatán.

incomes of islander and ladino men parallels that of women. Similarly, the mean weekly income of islander men was more than twice as high as that of ladinos. Likewise, the high standard deviation of the mean income of islander men, along with the discrepancy between the mean and the median income, implies a considerable range in islanders' incomes and a dualistic income distribution in which a small number of islanders earn significantly more than both ladinos and most islanders. In contrast to women, however, the mean (and median) weekly incomes of islander and ladino men were approximately twice those of islander and ladino women, respectively. In addition, a greater percentage of men (20%) had weekly incomes of US$100 or more. Analogous to women workers, only two ladino men were in this highest earning group: both owned tourist-related businesses in West End. Islander men with the highest weekly incomes worked as fishing boat captains, seamen or stewards on cruise ships or fishing boats, or as dive masters; owned their own businesses (almost all tourist related); or earned rental incomes. The primary kind of work of the entire sample of islander men included: waiter/ store clerk (20%); various construction jobs (14%); groundskeepers ("machete work") (14%); raising and selling agricultural products (10%); management of hotels/restaurants/rental properties (10%); fishing (8%); seamen (6%); dive master (4%); or driver (3%). The greatest proportion of ladinos were groundskeepers (20%), followed by construction workers (16%); security guards (8%), petty commodity sellers (seashells and prehistoric artifacts) (8%); waiters/store clerks (4%); dive masters and dive boat crew members (4%); and taxi drivers (4%).

Although the percentage of households with male householders absent for 1 month or more within the past year was approximately equal regardless of community or ethnic group (mean of 27% of all households), islander men were absent for a significantly longer period of time (mean of 7.9 months, median of 9 months) than were ladino men (mean of 3.4 months, median of 3 months). Most islander men were employed as seamen or other crew on fishing vessels and/or cruise ships where they earned incomes ranging from US$500 to US$1000 per month. In contrast, most ladino men spent their time away from the community working (or looking for work) as laborers in the largest island towns of Coxen Hole and French Harbour or, more frequently, on the mainland (especially in the coastal city of La Ceiba). Generally, ladinos temporarily migrated in search of work during the rainy season on the islands (October through February), the off-season for tourism, when jobs in the tourist sector are fewest and when violent storms from the north prohibit fishing. It is the season, as well, when 51% of residents (49% of islanders and 55% of ladinos) report periods of family food shortages. If ladinos are fortunate and find employment on the islands they can earn approximately US$6 per day as laborers (US$36/week or US$144/month). Wages are much lower on the mainland (as are prices), with the daily wage at about US$1 in 1993. Assuming a 6-day work week and the prevailing daily wage, the maximum ladinos could earn on the mainland was about US$24 per month—far less than islanders working on ships. In general, the income earned by islanders and ladinos temporarily working outside their communities fulfills very different functions. For ladinos, it helps meet basic subsistence needs when jobs related to tourism are unavailable. For islanders, it often provides the means to take advantage of the emerging opportunities in the tourism industry. For example, the small (but expanding) resort, "Coconut Palms Plantation Resort," owned and managed by an extended islander family from West End, opened in 1990. Money to start the enterprise came, in large part, from the savings of the owner who worked for more than a decade as a steward on cruise ships in the Caribbean. With supplementary funding from other family members working in the U.S., the owners began the business. In 1990, the enterprise included five double cabins, a separate dining building, and a small house for the owners and their family. It also included a dive shop operated on a concessionary basis with a non-Honduran. By 1993 the business had expanded to include three additional (and more luxurious cabins), a greatly enlarged dive shop, a boutique, and a large two-story house for the owners. Currently, the owners and their grown children all work, full- or part-time, at the hotel. Similar to their counterparts elsewhere in the Caribbean, Bay Islanders (predominantly men) have been working at sea in various capacities for generations (Davidson, 1974). In this sample, 89% of male islander householders had worked off the islands for more than 3 months. Of these, 80% had worked on ships and in ship building in the U.S., Canada, and elsewhere throughout the world, many for far longer than 3 months. These relatively well-paid jobs have provided the means by which the Bay Islanders have managed to maintain a relatively high standard of living, well above that of their Honduran ladino counterparts on the mainland.

Well-Being as Indicated by Household Consumption

Variations in well-being between islander and ladino households are shown by the higher weekly income and by the wider range of both monetary and nonmonetary economic options available to islanders, and suggest that the well-being of, at least some, islanders is greater than that of ladinos. Patterns in household consumption (measures of material wealth and access to market goods) provide additional evidence. Table 5.3 summarizes the variation by community and ethnicity on three variables related to household consumption: material style of life (MSL) index; house size; and weekly food expenditures. It shows that, in terms of indices of material wealth (MSL and house size), islander households significantly surpass ladinos. The results also disclose a greater range in household wealth among islanders, intimating greater socioeconomic differentiation. In addition, Table 5.3 reveals a rank ordering of communities in terms of wealth: from the most affluent (West End), to the less wealthy (Flowers Bay), to the least prosperous (Sandy Bay). As with ethnicity, increasing wealth in a community is associated with greater variation in wealth among members of that community.

High food prices throughout the islands were among the primary concerns mentioned by ladino and islander families alike. Cash disbursements to meet household food needs were the principal expenses of most families. According to a government study, the price of a market basket (*canasta basica*) of food for a family of five on the islands was about US$52.00 per week (GDH/PNUD, 1992a, p. 64). This amount is twice the median weekly income of women in Sandy Bay, West End, and Flowers Bay, and approximately equals the median income of men in the communities. The price of the typical market basket at the supermarket in Coxen Hole was 14% higher than at the supermarket in French Harbour and 95% higher than at supermarkets on the mainland (GDH/PNUD, 1992a, p. 64). A comparative study of food prices in the small stores in West End showed that prices there averaged 21% higher than in Coxen Hole.

Island residents and tourists alike are dependent on food imported from the U.S. through distribution channels controlled by island elite. Seventy percent of all products on supermarket shelves are imported from the U.S. This is attributable to several factors: a long-term tradition of purchasing and importing goods from the U.S.; the maintenance of excellent marine transportation links with the U.S.; the virtual absence of island food production; and increased demand emanating from growing numbers of tourists. Generally U.S. products sell for about 30% above their U.S. retail price due to a 20% import duty plus sales taxes (Pettrie, 1996).

The seafood shipping companies have a virtual monopoly on the import and distribution of U.S. food products. Approximately 90% of the food imported by the islands is purchased directly from Florida grocery wholesalers by the Bay Islands shipping companies. The companies ship their seafood products (primarily shrimp, lobster, and conch) directly to the ports of Tampa and Miami, where they are exchanged for U.S. goods and shipped back to the Bay Islands. Because the owners of the shipping companies also are the proprietors of the islands' biggest super-

Table 5.3. Comparison of Well-Being as Indicated by Household Consumption

	Total	Community			Ethnicity	
		West End	Sandy Bay	Flowers Bay	Islanders	Ladinos
Material style of life (MSL)[a]	7.6 ± 3.1	9.0 ± 3.7	6.9 ± 2.7	7.5 ± 2.6**	8.4 ± 2.9	6.0 ± 2.7***
Median	7	10	6	7	9	6
House size[b]	3.1 ± 1.5	3.5 ± 2.1	2.8 ± 1.2	3.2 ± 1.3*	3.6 ± 1.6	2.7 ± 1.3*
Cash expenditures on market foods[c]	42.7 ± 37	61.9 ± 61	39.2 ± 25	32.9 ± 15**	42.4 ± 42	43.6 ± 25
Median	33.9	42.4	33.9	33.9	33.9	33.9
Per capita cash expenditures on market foods[d]	10.3 ± 9.3	14.1 ± 11	8.7 ± 9.5**	9.4 ± 6.8	10.6 ± 9.3	9.8 ± 9.3
Median	7.1	10.2	5.1	8.2	8.5	6.4

[a]A rank scale of ownership of or access to 15 common household items (radio, table, wooden chairs, plastic or aluminum chairs, upholstered chairs, sofa, sewing machine, wardrobe, bicycle, refrigerator, china cabinet, tape player/stereo, television, truck/car, microwave).
[b]Number of rooms in house.
[c]US$/household during the previous week.
[d]US$/person/household over the previous week.
*$p \leq 0.05$; **$p \leq 0.01$; ***$p \leq 0.001$.

markets and some of the largest hotels, they effectively control the islands' food distribution network. Other hotels and smaller stores are dependent on this distribution system (Pettrie, 1996).

Interpretation of household weekly food expenditures is less straightforward than for other consumer goods. With the exception of the community of West End, which demonstrates significantly higher values in terms of a number of measures of wealth, median weekly outlays are remarkably similar across ethnic and community groups (approximately US$34 per week). This also is true of mean weekly expenses across ethnic groups. This amount is 35% below the government estimate of US$52 per week necessary to meet the needs of a family of five. This significant difference insinuates the critical importance of food procured from other sources. The similarity in household weekly food expenditures across ethnic and community lines can be explained, in part, by the islanders' greater access to domestically produced food through farming, fishing, hunting, house gardens, and fruit trees. In addition, a relatively high percentage of islanders (21%) report receiving food in exchange for work. With these options, islanders can spend less than they would otherwise need to spend for food. Without these options, ladinos have little choice but to expend earned income on food. At the same time, the range in weekly food disbursements by islanders is considerably greater than by ladinos, again insinuating greater socioeconomic differentiation among islanders. There is greater variation in mean weekly food expenditures by community than by ethnicity, with households in Flowers Bay spending the least per week on food. In part, this is accounted for by the larger commitment to subsistence production in that community. Another important factor in determining weekly food expenditures is the number of people living in the household. As shown in Table 5.3, the median per capita expenditure by islanders is US$2.10 greater than that of ladinos. By community, residents of Sandy Bay (with the highest percentage of ladino households) spend the least per person for food, approximately US$5.10 per week. In sum, analysis of patterns in household consumption (measures of material wealth and access to market goods) supports the results of the investigation of household economic production. It indicates that, in terms of economic production and consumption, islander households as a group have more options and are wealthier than ladinos; an intersecting set of poorer islanders and ladinos with similar household economic strategies and patterns of consumption exists; and a relatively small group (almost all islanders) of relatively high-income and high-consumer households has emerged.

Patterns in Nutritional Status

The significant demographic, economic, social, and ecological changes related to the growth of tourism in the Bay Islands insinuate associated changes in nutritional status and environmental health for various island groups. The higher purchasing power of islander households and their greater access to home-produced foods (from farms, farm animals, house gardens, fruit trees, wild foods, and seafood) have implications for domestic food consumption and nutritional status.

While median and mean weekly expenditures on food are remarkably similar across ethnic groups, mean/median per capita expenditures by islanders are about twice those of ladinos. The demographic characteristics of ladino households (significantly younger, with larger households, more dependent children, and higher dependency ratios) further jeopardize their livelihood.

Although islanders and ladinos report comparable patterns of food shortages (49% of islanders and 55% of ladinos report the existence of such periods with a similar mean duration of 2.8 months [median = 2 months]), anthropometric evaluation of islander and ladino children less than 60 months of age (see Appendix for details) suggests that islanders are significantly better able to cope with such shortfalls. Figure 5.1 compares the distribution of height-for-age Z-scores (a measure of chronic undernutrition or growth stunting) of the entire sample population to that of the standard reference population.[6] It shows that the prevalence for growth stunting (i.e., height-for-age Z-score < –2.0) is 8.4% of the sample population. The weight-for-age Z-score reveals a much lower rate of seasonal undernutrition (1%). Although the corresponding mean values of age, weight, and height did not vary significantly between the islander and ladino children in the sample, undernutrition is significantly more prevalent among ladino children in the sample than among islander children. The average height-for-age Z-score of ladino children was –0.25 ± 1.57 compared to 0.8 ± 1.65 for islander children ($T = 3.02, p \leq 0.003$). This pattern is shown graphically in Figure 5.2, which plots the distribution of height-for-age Z-scores for islander and ladino children against that of the standard reference population. It demonstrates quite dramatically that all the cases of chronic undernutrition (stunting) are found among ladino children, approximately 15% of ladino children. Analysis of weight-for-age Z-scores also reveals seasonal undernutrition only among ladino children but at a much lower rate (2% of ladino

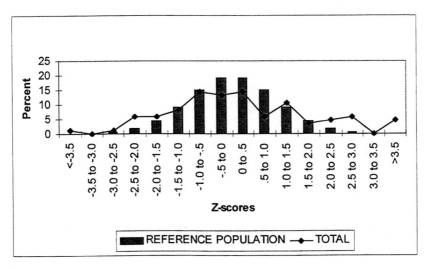

Figure 5.1. Z-score distribution of height-for-age (total sample population). Computed from anthropometric data (see Appendix).

children). Weight-for-height Z-scores are relatively higher for ladino children due to their diminutive stature (Trowbridge et al., 1987). While these data are only suggestive, because of the small number of children in the sample, they indicate that the nutritional status of ladino children is significantly lower than that of islanders, although substantially better than that of children living on the mainland where an estimated 40% of children are chronically undernourished.[7]

Well-Being as Suggested by Environmental Health

Serious declines in the quality and quantity of potable water are the most critical environmental health risks that have emerged on the islands and have provoked widespread user conflicts. Declining water quality and increasing water scarcity do not affect island residents and tourists equally, and certain groups face the associated risks disproportionately. Table 5.4 compares access to the various sources of drinking water in rural and urban areas of Honduras and in the three Bay Islands' communities included in the study. It shows that patterns in access to a water supply system for rural and urban areas of Honduras are similar to those in Latin America and the Caribbean as a whole. Approximately 90% of urban households and 55% of rural households have access to either a house connection or a public faucet, while 10% of urban and 47% of rural households are without access. The data for the three communities disaggregated by ethnicity and nationality, however, reveal patterns distinct from the national-level data. The recent foreign residents of the communities get their water from diverse sources: 40% from private wells connected directly to their homes and 20% each from municipal water piped to their homes, bottled water, or some combination of these. In addition, virtually all foreign residents treat their water in some way, either with a chlorine, ultraviolet,

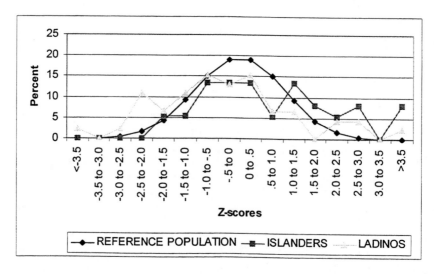

Figure 5.2. Z-score distribution of height-for-age (islanders and ladinos). Computed from anthropometric data (see Appendix).

Table 5.4. Source of Water Supply: Honduras and Bay Islands: 1993

	Honduras		Bay Islands		
Source of Water (% of Households)	Urban	Rural	Islanders (N = 97)	Ladinos (N = 44)	Foreign Residents (N = 5)
Municipal well piped to house	82%	40.20%	57%	38%	20%
Private well piped to house	n.a.	n.a.	6%	2%	40%
Public faucet (easy access)	7.50%	13.30%	8%	33%	0%
Public seep (spring)	n.a.	n.a.	0%	7%	0%
Bottled water	n.a.	n.a.	3%	0%	20%
Combination of sources	n.a.	n.a.	21%	0%	20%
Without a water supply	9.60%	46.50%	0%	0%	0%
Treatment (chlorine and/or UV/membrane filter)	3%	n.a.	11%	0%	100%
Treatment (boiling)	n.a.	n.a.	33%	9%	20%

Source: For Honduras, Pan American Health Organization (PAHO) (1994); for Bay Islands, analysis of survey data.

or membrane filtration system or by boiling. In marked contrast to foreign residents, recent ladino immigrants are most likely to get their water supply from municipal wells piped to their residences (38%) or from a public faucet (33%). Ladinos are also the only group without regular access to a water supply system: 7% of ladino households collect water from two seeps (referred to as "springs" by local residents). Only 9% of ladino households treat their water—all by boiling. The most diverse pattern of access and treatment is found among islander households: 57% rely on municipal water connected to their homes; 6% have private wells with direct connections; 8% depend on public faucets; 3% on bottled water; and 21% on some combination of sources. A small percentage (11%) treat their water with chlorine and a further 33% by boiling.

Similar differences in patterns of utilization of excreta disposal facilities are revealed in Table 5.5. The small group of relatively affluent foreign residents has greatest access to a functioning toilet (80%) as well as septic fields/tanks (60%). Ladinos have least access to such facilities (only 16% have functioning toilets and only 14% septic fields/tanks) and are most likely to live in houses with nonfunctioning toilets/latrines or no disposal facilities at all. The pattern for islanders is intermediate between foreign residents and ladinos: 50% with a functioning toilet, 35% with a functioning latrine, 15% with a nonfunctioning toilet/latrine, and 36% with a septic tank/field.

Drinking Water Quality

It is extremely simple to summarize the analyses of the 200 samples of drinking water and of brackish and seawater collected from shoreline sites adjacent to human habitation/beaches. All untreated sources of drinking water tested positive for the presence of total coliforms and *E. coli*. Private wells, public wells, "springs," rainwater cisterns—all were contaminated. Even the "purified" bottled water that had been shipped to the islands from the processing plant in San Pedro Sula and distributed through the new franchise on Roatán was contaminated. It is impossible to measure the decline in water quality over time or to correlate deterioration to increases in tourism because, as far as is known, no widespread community testing of potable water had been done previously. However, anecdotal evidence does exist. Local residents report that they are more frequently ill now with diarrheal diseases than in the past.

Uncontaminated water was found rarely and only when it had undergone some treatment (e.g., chlorine, membrane filters, and/or ultraviolet [UV] systems). Such systems, especially the use of UV and filtration systems, were found only in the homes of the affluent island elite and foreign residents and in one high-priced dive resort. Many of the middle-class owners of the moderately priced hotels are fearful of jeopardizing the health of their guests and are taking steps to try to ensure them a safe water supply through the purchase of "pure" bottled water. While analyses question how "safe" such water really is, even uncontaminated water often becomes contaminated in the process of being served to guests (e.g., through the addition of unpurified ice, by being poured into wet pitchers that have been washed in contaminated water, etc.). Presently, it appears that the only divisions of the island population that are assured a safe water supply are the relatively affluent foreign residents, the small number of elite families, and the foreign guests in a number of upscale hotels that have their own water purification systems.

Brackish and Seawater Quality

Contamination of seawater also is of growing concern, although most often voiced in terms of its potential effects on recreational divers and the tourism industry rather than on the health of local residents. Table 5.6 summarizes the results of fecal coliform analyses of seawater from dive sites and along the shoreline of

Table 5.5. Source of Excreta Disposal Facility: Honduras and Bay Islands: 1993

Excreta Disposal (% of Households)	Honduras		Bay Islands		
	Urban	Rural	Islanders (N = 97)	Ladinos (N = 44)	Foreign Residents (N = 5)
Functioning toilet	53%	n.a.	50%	16%	80%
Functioning latrine	38%	45%	35%	32%	20%
Nonfunctioning toilet or latrine	n.a.	n.a.	15%	34%	0%
None/other	9%	55%	0%	18%	0%
Septic tank/septic field	n.a.	n.a.	36%	14%	0%
Sewerage connection	39.50%	5.70%	0%	0%	0%

Source: For Honduras, PAHO (1994); for Bay Islands, analysis of survey data.

bathing beaches near West Bay Beach, from the urban center of French Harbour, and from the communities of Sandy Bay, West End, and Flowers Bay. The grading system (good, acceptable, and unacceptable) is based on criterion of the World Health Organization for bacterial water quality (World Health Organization/United Nations Environment Program [WHO/UNEP], 1977). These classes are related to respective rates of swimming-associated gastroenteritides and skin symptoms. The density of fecal coliforms near recreational areas of the major urban center of French Harbour increased from about 500 (within the acceptable range) to more than 1,000 organisms per 100 milliliters (unacceptable) between 1991 and 1993. By 1993, unacceptable levels also occurred near drainage areas in the small community of Flowers Bay. Although precise densities are unspecified, unacceptable levels of total coliform and fecal coliform have also been reported for surface water and seawater collected near the other major Roatán urban centers of Coxen Hole and Oak Ridge (IDB, 1994). While "good" and "acceptable" levels of contamination currently exist at most dive sites, West Bay Beach, and most shoreline locations, unregulated development, escalating populations, and the absence of water supply and waste disposal systems likely will cause higher levels of contamination in the future.

Water Quality and Environmental Health

Current conditions have escalated the incidence of water-borne diseases, including cholera, dysentery, and hepatitis, as well as facilitated the transmission of water-related diseases such as malaria and dengue fever, which thrive in unsanitary conditions (IDB, 1994). Table 5.7 compares the relative percentage of outpatient visits by major diagnoses in Honduras and at St. Luke's Cornerstone Medical Mission located in Sandy Bay. As the only free nongovernmental medical clinic on Roatán, St. Luke's was the primary source of medical care for the poorest segment of the population living in Sandy Bay and in nearby communities. The disproportionate use of the clinic by the poor is indicated by the relatively high number of ladinos who make use of the clinic. While about 48% of the nontourist population of Sandy Bay classify themselves as ladino, ladinos make up 70% of nontourist patients to St. Luke's Mission clinic. As shown in Table 5.7, water-borne, water-washed, and water-related infections and diseases are the major causes of patient visits to the clinic for both islanders and ladinos of all age groups. Acute respiratory infections, diarrhea, and parasites are the most common causes of clinic visits by both groups. Ladinos and islanders vary most in the incidence of malaria, which accounts for about 14% of ladino visits but only 7% of islander visits. This difference likely is due to higher levels of prevalence among ladino immigrants, most of whom come from the northern part of Honduras where more than 70% of the total number of malaria cases in the country are diagnosed. Not surprisingly, barotrauma (recompression sickness) and otitis (ear infections) are the major reasons for clinic visits by tourist divers, although tourists have rates of diarrhea and skin infections comparable to those of local people. The degree to which tourists are affected by malaria is unknown, as the tourists' average stay on the islands (6.5 days) is usually too short for the disease symptoms to appear.

Table 5.6. Fecal Coliform Analyses of Seawater Sites: 1991–1993

Site of Sample	Total fecal coliforms (c.f.u./100 ml)				
	AOA[a] (1991)	AOA (1992)	AOA (1993)	Study	Grade 1993[b]
Dive sites	4 to 8	2 to 4	2 to 4	n.a.	good
Bathing beaches (West End/West Bay)	n.a.	n.a.	n.a.	50 to 200	good/acceptable
French Harbour (center)	600	>1,000	>1,000	>1,000	unacceptable
French Harbour (dock/recreational boating area near large dive resort)	400	>1,000	>1,000	n.a.	unacceptable
Sand Bay (shoreline adjacent to dolphin pens, large resort)	30 to 40	8 to 24	0	50 to 200	good/acceptable
Sandy Bay (shoreline adjacent to community)	n.a.	n.a.	n.a.	200 to 500	acceptable
West End (shoreline adjacent to dive resort)	n.a.	n.a.	n.a.	30 to 50	good
West End (shoreline adjacent to community)	n.a.	n.a.	n.a.	50 to 300	good/acceptable
Flowers Bay (shoreline adjacent to community)	n.a.	n.a	n.a.	300>1,000	acceptable/unacceptable

[a]Aquarium of the Americas.

[b]This grading system is based on the criterion of the World Health Organization for bacterial beach water quality using the upper median levels of bacteria counts obtained from five consecutive samples: <100 per 100 ml = good; 100 to <1,000 per 100 ml = acceptable; >1,000 per 100 ml = unacceptable (WHO/UNEP, 1977). These classes are related to respective swimming-associated gastroenterides and skin symptom rates of 1–7 per 1,000 swimmers, 7–16 per 1,000 swimmers, and >17 per 1,000 swimmers (Cheung, Hung, Chang, & Kleevens, 1991).

Source: AOA (1991); AOA (1992); AOA (1993); analyses of study samples.

Table 5.7. Outpatient Visits by Diagnosis: Honduras (1988) and St. Luke's Mission, Sandy Bay, Bay Islands (1994)

Diagnosis	Honduras	St. Luke's Mission (% of all cases)[a]					
		Total	Islanders	Ladinos	Tourists	> 1 Year[b]	1–5 Years
Acute respiratory infections (ARI)	13.9%	12.8%	15.4%	16.0%	1.2%	43.1%	29.0%
Diarrhea	16.5%	4.7%	4.8%	4.2%	5.4%	15.6%	6.6%
Parasites	n.a.	7.3%	6.8%	9.8%	2.1%	5.5%	16.7%
Malaria	n.a.	9.7%	6.6%	13.8%	3.5%	1.8%	8.0%
Skin infections	3.0%	4.0%	4.8%	3.3%	4.7%	3.7%	6.1%
Otitis	n.a.	4.7%	2.9%	3.3%	9.5%	7.3%	3.7%
Baratrauma	n.a.	7.5%	0.4%	0.9%	28.8%	0.0%	0.0%

[a]All patient records for 1994 were analyzed. Of the total of 2,509 patient records, 23% were islanders, 53% were ladinos, and 24% were tourists. In addition, 5% of patients were children less than 1 year of age and 18% were children between the ages of 1 and 5 years.
[b]According to the Pan American Health Organization (PAHO, 1994), in 1990 the leading causes of death for children under 1 year of age in Honduras were intestinal infections, which accounted for 41% of all deaths, and acute respiratory infections, which accounted for 18% of all deaths.
Source: For Honduras, PAHO (1994); for St. Luke's Mission, analysis of patient records.

Winners, Losers, and Enhanced Social Conflict

The costs and benefits of tourism development on Roatán are very similar to those reported for Tortuguero, Costa Rica. As in Costa Rica, the Honduran government has been more interested in increasing foreign exchange through tourist dollars and in national integration than in successfully integrating local communities into the tourism industry. The consequences of tourism have included increased social differentiation and a growing gap between rich and poor; the assignment of the majority of ladinos and islanders to low-status, low-paid, temporary jobs; reduced access for local people to the natural resources on which they depend for their livelihoods; escalating prices for food, manufactured goods, and housing; land speculation and spiraling land costs; increased outside ownership of local resources; and deterioration of the biophysical environment. According to measures of economic production, income, wealth, consumption, and nutrition considered in this chapter, Afro-Caribbean islanders range in wealth from well off to very poor. Ladinos, on average, tend to be significantly poorer and to be at higher nutritional and environmental health risk than islanders. The most striking result of the anthropometric studies of children was that undernutrition was found only among ladino children—albeit at rates lower than on the mainland.

Those who have benefited from tourism by taking advantage of emerging opportunities have been those with sufficient incomes to invest in tourist-related enterprises—generally those elite and middle-class islanders who were wealthier to begin with. Even poorer islanders are in a better position than recently arriving ladinos to benefit from expanding opportunities in tourism because they tend to be better educated, bilingual, and part of more complex social and economic networks that sustain them through the off-season in tourism employment. In Sandy Bay, ladinos are consigned the lowest paying, lowest status jobs, generally those that do not require they speak English (to the predominately English-speaking clientele). The position of ladino women is even more precarious, given that they hold the jobs with the least status, earn only half that of ladino men, and must confront the double demands of domestic and wage work. On the other hand, islanders, who speak English, tend to be employed in higher paying service positions such as dive masters, waiters, hotel clerks, and so forth—jobs which require that they communicate frequently with English-speaking guests. Top managerial positions in the larger hotels, however, tend to be filled by nonislanders, frequently by foreigners. While in West End, the modest hotels and other tourist businesses (small dive shops and restaurants) tend to be owned by middle-class island residents, most are islanders (with the exception of a few foreigners and ladinos). As in Sandy Bay, recent ladino immigrants from the mainland are consigned to the lowest paying, seasonal jobs in the tourist sector. They live, hidden from the eyes of most tourists, in a shabby ghetto of small wooden structures built on stilts, above a lagoon filled with human waste and other garbage. For such families, and similar ones in Sandy Bay, reduced access to communal fishing, hunting, and gathering resources, through private development or the establishment of protected areas, diminishes their economic options further. There is little question why they and their poorer islander counterparts are suspicious of any efforts to designate areas of the islands as marine or nature reserves.

The majority of island residents (76% of all households sampled, 68% of islander households, and 88% of ladino households) favor tourism development throughout the Bay Islands as well as in their own communities. However, a growing number of residents are becoming skeptical about the relative benefits emanating from the tourist industry. While 75% of households reported that they believed tourism will benefit the islands economically, only 39% reported that they thought they would benefit from tourism personally. Their concerns were conveyed very well by a 34-year-old islander fisherman from West End who said, "For some people it's [tourism] good, for some [it's] bad . . . only some people profit . . . but the higher prices affect everyone." Standing on the beach in front of her family's large blue wooden house and looking into the future, an elderly islander woman whose family has lived on the islands since the 1850s pointed up to the hills and said, "In 20 years, that's where we'll [local people] all be . . . some foreigner will own this place [beach front and adjacent property]." Many recent ladino immigrants also express disappointment in "Paradise" as did this 31-year-old mother of four who said:

> We came here because we had no land and there was no work in Belfate [on the mainland] . . . the photographs [of the Bay Islands] look like paradise . . . but there's not enough work here either . . . no good work . . . we make [earn wages] more here when we find work but things cost twice as much.

For poor ladino and islander families, inadequate benefits from employment in the tourism sector have combined with reduced access to what had been publicly available fishing, hunting, and gathering resources through protected areas such as the Sandy Bay-West End Marine Reserve. In the words of a 35-year-old ladino immigrant to West End:

> I do plantation work [yard work], my wife works as a maid at Palm View Cabins, and my kids sell fish when they can catch them. It's difficult and sometimes only the little ones eat. Sometimes at night I go out and fish on the reef or hunt iguana in the hills. They tell us not to [take fish and shellfish from the reef and hunt iguana] but my kids have to eat.

Many poorer island residents (both islanders and ladinos) are indignant about being urged to end or reduce their fishing and hunting activities by wealthier inhabitants. Less affluent residents are well aware that it is these more powerful stakeholders who are the owners of commercial fishing fleets, shipping companies, hotels, resorts, supermarkets, and other businesses. Poorer residents also are aware that it is the islands' elite, as well as foreign developers, who are principally responsible for overfishing shrimp and lobster and who are engaged in a real estate and hotel building spree (despite the shortage of fresh water and the absence of sewerage and other solid waste disposal systems), unsound road building, mangrove destruction, extensive dredging of the reef, and other environmentally destructive activities. Many poor local people feel that their own temperance will be of no benefit unless everyone can be made to restrict his or her fishing effort or other environmentally destructive activity. "I'll stop hunting iguanas when they [island elite, Honduran elite, and foreign investors] stop dredging for new marinas and hotels and over-fishing," said a 72-year-old Afro-Caribbean islander whose family had lived on the islands for several generations. The gap in wealth between resort owners, whose guests make the most use of the reef, and local subsistence users, only strengthens the stance of poorer residents who feel they should not bear the burden of environmental conservation. It is not surprising that the Sandy Bay-West End Marine Reserve is having difficulty restricting use despite the fact that it now is part of the Honduran protected area system.

Notes

[1]For purposes of this chapter, ethnic classifications are based on residents' own self-identification as ladinos or islanders. The communities considered are composed of primarily of black, Afro-Caribbean islanders and ladinos rather than "white," Anglo-Caribbean islanders.

[2]This group includes those who work directly with tourists such as hotel and restaurant workers as well as indirectly, including construction and maintenance workers, in support of the tourist industry. It also contains participants in both the formal and informal economic sectors.

[3]As part of the household surveys, householders were asked if during the last month they had received payment for work other than in cash. Twenty-one percent

of islanders and 4% of ladinos responded positively to receiving payment in food; 2% of islanders and 13% of ladinos worked in exchange for housing; and 4% of ladinos received payment in the form of transportation.

[4]A composite measure of the degree of diversity in nonmonetary economic options included in an individual household's economic strategy was computed (nonmonetary income diversity index). All eight nonmonetary sources of income described in the body of this chapter were included. Individual household scores were computed on the basis of whether or not each nonmonetary activity was practiced by that household. Households were given 1 point for each activity practiced. Thus, scores could range from 0 (no nonmonetary activities) to a maximum of 8 (all nonmonetary activities).

[5]This is not to imply that this transition is either good or bad. Many times during its history the Bay Islands have been economically dependent on the export of agricultural commodities.

[6]In the sample of 168 children ≤60 months of age, the mean age was 36.4 ± 19.99 months, height was 93.4 ± 15.2 cm, and weight was 14.7 ± 4.6 kg. To evaluate children's nutritional status, all anthropometric variables were standardized as Z-scores relative to published norms. Height-for-age, weight-for-age, and weight-for-height were standardized using *ANTHRO: Software for Calculating Pediatric Anthropometry* (Version 1.01, 10 December 1990), developed by the U.S. Department of Health and Human Services. For the entire sample, the corresponding mean height-for-age Z-score was 0.21 ± 1.7; weight-for-age Z-score (a measure of seasonal undernutrition) was 0.31 ± 1.38; and weight-for-height Z-score was 0.29 ± 1.15. For an explanation of the use of Z-scores as a measure of growth and undernutrition see Krok (1988).

[7]Very few national-level nutritional surveys are available. These have found very high levels of undernutrition and growth stunting among families living in rural areas. According to the 1986 national nutritional study of all first graders in Honduras, the Bay Islands municipalities of Roatán, Guanaja, Oak Ridge, and Utila had the lowest prevalence of undernutrition in the nation—approximately 11% of first graders were more than 2 standard deviations below the average height for age ratios of the reference population, in contrast to 40% of children nationwide (*Secretaria de Educación Publica. Dirección General de Educacion Primaria. Servicio de Alimentacion Escolar de Honduras/Instituto de Nutricion de Centro America y Panama* [SAEH/INCAP], 1987).

Chapter 6

Contending Coalitions Surrounding Tourism and Conservation

> The economic development aspect of this project [*Paseo Pantera*] is baloney. We're a conservation organization: We want to save turtles. If that other stuff comes along, that's fine, but we only put that in the proposal for the funders [primarily USAID]. (U.S. conservationist referring to the *Paseo Pantera* project, quoted by Royte, 1992)

> I tend to agree of having to confront political and economic realities in the Bay Islands. And it may take a more direct approach from the international community, including ourselves. (Senior IDB staff member discussing implementation of the IDB management project for the Bay Islands, personal communication, 1997)

> . . . NABIPLA agrees with the world's environmental movement, but we need to fight the battle from the root. NABIPLA believes that our children are the number 1 endangered species. (NABIPLA, 1995, p. 3)

The remarks by the U.S. conservation specialist and the IDB official divulge two major obstacles to achieving integrated, community-based conservation and equitable tourism development in the Bay Islands. The unguarded comment by the environmentalist associated with the *Paseo Pantera* project (the precursor of the Meso-American Biological Corridor) discloses the underlying values and motives of the international environmental organizations that designed and managed the project—the preservation of turtles. In addition to revealing that environmental goals are paramount, the remark also exposes the insincerity of these organizations in terms of their commitment to achieving the economic development aspects of the project. In contrast, the statement by the IDB official was made in order to explain the lag in implementing the local management aspect of the IDB project. It attributes delays in implementation in part to the failure to directly confront the social, economic, and political realities on the islands.

These two comments represent extremely different but equally critical factors that impede integrated, community-based conservation and development initiatives in the Bay Islands: the first based on underlying ideology, values, and goals and the second on disregarding the structure of island society, especially relations of

145

power. This chapter examines these and other major obstacles (as well as incentives) to community participation in tourism and conservation efforts in the Bay Islands. It begins with a discussion of the fundamental contradictions between recent tourism development and conservation initiatives. It continues with the identification of the important local, national, and international interest groups (stakeholders) including the government of Honduras and its various agencies, NGOs, international donors, and conservation organizations. It examines the associated social, ethnic, cultural, and economic conflicts among interest groups over tourism and natural resources. Particularly important is an examination of the relative power of these interest groups and the formation of contending coalitions around power relations. It discloses current trends in community-based conservation and tourism in the islands by assessing the management plan for the Sandy Bay-West End Marine Reserve. This discussion includes the feasibility of NABIPLA, as an ethnically based grassroots organization, to enhance local participation in tourism development and conservation efforts. The chapter culminates with a series of recommendations designed to move toward effective community-based tourism development and conservation on the Bay Islands and elsewhere.

Linking Development, Conservation, and Community

The U.N. Conference on the Environment and Development (also known as UNCED or the Rio Summit) that took place in Rio de Janeiro in 1992 catalyzed a global agenda around the connections between development and the environment. In fact, the development–conservation nexus was recognized by the international community as early as the 1970s. The Rio Summit marked the 20th anniversary of the U.N. Conference on the Human Environment, which convened in Stockholm in 1972 to consider how human activities alter the global environment. The recommendations of subsequent international councils, such as the United Nations World Commission on Environment and Development that published the influential *Bruntland Report* in 1987, and the numerous environmental initiatives that followed, testify to the expanding global awareness that complex interconnections exist between development processes and the state of the environment. While a great deal of the discussion at these international meetings emphasized global and national policies, the environmental initiatives that ensued also included limited efforts to integrate environmental conservation (especially biological diversity) with the maintenance of people's livelihoods at the local level. For example, the *World Conservation Strategy* in 1980 stressed the importance of linking protected area management with the economic activities of local communities (United Nations Environment Programme, International Union for Conservation of Nature and Natural Resources, World Wildlife Fund, Food and Agriculture Organization of the United Nations, & UNESCO, 1980). Two years later, the World Congress on National Parks in Bali, Indonesia called for greater support for communities located adjacent to parks through such measures as education, revenue sharing, participation in decisions, appropriate development schemes such as ecotourism, and access to crucial resources (McNeely & Miller, 1984). Shortly thereafter, in 1985, the WWF confronted the messy and problematic challenge of integrating conservation and development by initiating the Wildlands and Human Needs Program. Originally encompassing about 20 integrated conservation and development projects (ICDPs), the program attempted "to improve the quality of life of rural people through practical field projects that integrated the management of natural resources with grassroots economic development" (Larson, Freudenberger, & Wyckoff-Baird, 1997, p. 5).According to a recent review of their decade-long experience implementing ICDPs,WWF concluded:

> All international conservation organizations now seek in varying degrees to
> address local needs while conserving biodiversity and ecological
> processes. . . . In the mid-1980s, ICDPs were a radical divergence from the
> norm.Today, such projects constitute over half of WWF's funding. (Larson et
> al., 1997, pp. 5-6)

Based on their experience, the WWF divided ICDPs into two generations.The first generation, designed in the early 1980s, attempted to reduce conflicts between people and protected areas by compensating local residents for the loss of natural resources, sometimes with cash but more frequently with health clinics, schools, and other social services. Unfortunately, many of the early ICDPs became large, multifaceted, and inevitably unmanageable. Similar to the large integrated rural development projects of the 1970s, large ICDPs became impossible to manage effectively due to their unrealistic goals and timetables and excessive dependence on outside funding and expertise (Larson et al., 1997, p. 7). Despite their name, first-generation ICDPs were not very integrated at all. Instead, conservation organizations and their partners implemented alternative income-generating activities in communities adjoining protected areas on the assumption that the new sources of livelihood would replace those judged to be harmful to the environment. People in local communities rarely had an opportunity to express their needs and remained alienated from the management of protected resources as well as many of the development interventions (Larson et al., 1997, p. 7).

Based on lessons learned from these initial efforts, conservation organizations significantly refined and modified the second-generation ICDPs that were developed in the early 1990s. One significant change is that recent projects focus more on land outside of protected areas—where much of the world's biodiversity exists. In addition, whereas first-generation ICDPs tended to see local people as the source of environmental and conservation problems, second-generation ICDPs perceived local people as having the rights and the responsibilities for resource management. Commonly referred to as community-based conservation projects, second-generation ICDPs tend to be more community driven, focused on improving community skills in resource planning and management, and aimed at achieving collaborative management arrangements between communities and governments. Supporters contend that these kinds of projects are more likely to succeed, because they are designed and implemented with more community involvement and more directly link conservation and development activities (Larson et al., 1997, p. 7).

Several issues regarding the present generation of ICDPs were raised in Chapter 1—primarily centered around conceptualizations of community, participation, representation, and accountability. Various additional concerns have been raised about ICDPs, including the need to provide adequate funding over longer time frames; to ensure more explicit linkages between conservation and development initiatives; to incorporate monitoring and evaluation programs throughout the lifetime of projects; to build on local knowledge; and to promote active participation of community stakeholders (Brown & Wyckoff-Baird, 1992; Wells et al., 1992). Several recent reviews of ICDPs have raised other serious questions about the approach. Critics caution that ICDPs, increasingly funded by development agencies like USAID, have become too focused on rural development, tend to be located in areas that are not biologically important, or are too fragile or small to support resource extraction by local communities (Larson et al., 1997, p. 9). In part to address such criticisms, current efforts by WWF and others, such as the Atlantic Reef Conservation Project mentioned in Chapter 4, tend to focus on the ecoregion or landscape level rather than on smaller spatial areas such as communities. These diverse criticisms disclose the ongoing conflicts about the relative primacy of the human and environmental goals of ICDPs.

It is difficult but feasible to place development and conservation efforts in the Bay Islands within the framework outlined above. First, in contrast to ICDPs, the vast majority of tourism development in the Bay Islands has either ignored or attempted to circumvent environmental laws and regulations and conservation initiatives rather than to integrate conservation goals into tourism development schemes. Second, the conservation efforts either already implemented, or in process, on the islands virtually overlook development objectives for less powerful residents of the islands. Meager attempts to train local people to be park guards, dive masters, or jewelry makers are inadequate in terms of compensating local residents for diminished access to natural resources and are at the root of growing enmity toward such efforts. In some respects, conservation efforts on the islands correspond most closely to first-generation ICDPs. They tend to see local people as the problem and attempt, albeit feebly, to compensate them for losses to livelihoods. In contrast to the strategies of ICDPs, the best known local-level conservation effort, the Sandy Bay-West End Marine Reserve (SBWEMR), is dominated by an overwhelming emphasis on regulations and enforcement. As regards the Bay Islands, three major "lessons learned" by the WWF are most relevant:

- In densely settled areas, strict enforcement of protected area regulations cannot by itself prevent the illegal use of resources . . . strict enforcement is costly both in financial and political terms.
- Compensation does not necessarily change peoples' attitudes and behaviors.
- Changing peoples' resource use patterns is a complex undertaking and requires a sophisticated understanding of the political, economic, and social context of their lives (Larson et al., 1997, p. 6).

Social Categories, Interest Groups, and Stakeholders[1]

Chapter 1 raised several essential questions that are crucial to achieving successful community-based conservation and development initiatives. These included: What is meant by community? Who participates? What constitutes participation? Chapter 1 also pointed out that while there may be no consensus about the meaning of "community," one essential aspect of communities is their heterogeneity. Ample evidence from anthropological and other studies has demonstrated that even the smallest settlement in the most technologically simple society is internally divided not simply by age, kinship, and gender but also by economic, political, and social inequalities. In contemporary villages, urban neighborhoods, and larger sociopolitical units, the internal horizontal and vertical divisions are much more complex. Even in communities where outsiders may see uniform shared poverty, insiders will perceive and experience economic inequality and formal or informal differences in political power and access to external power-holding groups. Socioeconomic inequalities and the leadership that may emanate from such inequalities are inherently neither good nor bad for development and conservation projects. Local leaders with more than average wealth, power, and education may be able to mobilize the minds and actions of their co-residents better than anyone else or, to the contrary, they (or those who emerge precisely because a new project has come into being) may be able to capture its benefits for themselves and their allies. Socioeconomic heterogeneity (inequality, diversity of interests, latent as well as overt social structures within even the smallest settlements, the complexity of local cultures, etc.) has immediate implications for successful community participation—especially for pointing to the need for thorough socio-cultural analysis that identifies relevant, multilevel stakeholders. Sound stakeholder analysis can identify the subgroups within the population affected by the pro-posed development and/or conservation project, help determine overlapping relations of power among these groups, and make clear the extent to which existing community institutions are representative of all or particular interest groups (Schwartz et al., 1996).

Stakeholders may be defined as groups or categories of people who directly and demonstrably gain or lose rights and/or resources through development and conservation processes. They may include government agencies, NGOs, donor organizations, and corporations as well as various categories of the local popula-tion. Relevant groups or individual stakeholders may be determined by a number of criteria (e.g., by class, ethnicity, nationality, gender, age, race, occupation, etc.). In addition, identification of stakeholders should include an assessment of their relative power or kinds of power. Although missing in much stakeholder analysis, a political ecological or political economic analysis is crucial in relating stake-holders to degrees of power over natural resources and other people. Such rankings are essential to ensure that less powerful stakeholders receive the benefits (and do not pay all the costs) of development and conservation policies and projects.

Determining the relevant stakeholders in a particular context is neither easy nor simple. To identify stakeholders, subgroups, power relations among stakeholders, and contending coalitions among stakeholders, there is no alternative to sociocul-tural field research prior to initiating a project. Although there are reliable and rapid participatory appraisal methodologies in the social sciences, they are effective in good part because the practitioners usually have knowledge of earlier, in-depth anthropological studies of the sociocultural region under study (Chambers, 1994c; van Willigen & Finan, 1991). The cost of slighting sociocultural studies can be high. A comprehensive analysis of ex post evaluation findings and World Bank and USAID analyses indicated that "the average economic rate of return for rural development projects which have incorporated sociocultural analysis was more than double that for projects which had been poorly appraised from a sociocultural viewpoint" (Cernea, 1992). Sociocultural analyses are complex, always site specific, and take time (although financial costs are relatively low or moderate). Without sociocultural analyses, stakeholder analysis is apt to be shallow and pro forma. Moreover, subsequent "community participation" in development and conservation projects is likely to be mere rhetoric, and without community participation, projects are apt to be inefficient, inequitable, not cost beneficial, and short-lived.

Thorough sociocultural and stakeholder analyses from a political ecological perspective comprise the core of this book. The results encompass much of Chapters 4 and 5, which disclose the costs and benefits of tourism development and conservation efforts on island residents by divisions of community, class, ethnicity, nationality, and gender. These categories delineate many of the relevant stakeholder groups on the Bay Islands and inform many of the significant differences among them. Among the important findings and conclusions are:

- increased socioeconomic differentiation among stakeholders as a result of tourism developments;
- the assignment of the majority of ladinos and islanders to low-status, low-paid, temporary jobs;
- differential food security;
- increased outside ownership of local resources;
- reduced access for local people to the natural resources on which they depend for their livelihoods;
- differential access to increasingly scarce water resources;
- differential environmental health risks.

The remainder of this section examines pertinent stakeholders more explicitly, including their motives, goals, and aspirations. It pays special attention to coalitions between and among extra-local and local stakeholders. Table 6.1 identifies the relevant stakeholders with interests in tourism development and conservation efforts in the Bay Islands, as well as major coalitions that have emerged among these interest groups.

International Stakeholders

A variety of international social actors have a stake in the Bay Islands. The most important of these include multilateral donors such as the IDB, bilateral development agencies such as USAID, and international environmental NGOs including the Wildlife Conservation Society. Recently, the Center for International Policy, and the South and Meso-American Indian Rights Center have become interested in the

Table 6.1. Stakeholders and Coalitions Surrounding Tourism and Conservation

	Coalition 1	Coalition 2	Coalition 3
International Stakeholders			
Multilateral donors and development agencies			
UNDP	I		
Inter-American Development Bank (IDB)	X		
USAID	X		
NGOs			
WCS, Gainesville, FL	X		
CIP, Washington, DC		I	
SAIIC, Oakland, CA		I	
International tourism industry			
National Stakeholders			
GOH (various agencies)	X		
National Commissioner for Human Rights		I	
National elite	I		
NGOs			
CONPAH		X	
Fundación Vida	X		
Bay Islands/Local Stakeholders			
Local governments: the municipalities	I		I
Commission Pro Tourism Development of the Bay Islands (Commission)	X		
NGOs			
BICA	X		
NABIPLA		X	
APRODIB	X		
Communities			
West End		I	
Sandy Bay		I	
Flowers Bay		X	
West Bay Beach		I	
Other communities		?	
Ethnic groups			
"White" islanders	X		
Afro-Caribbean, black islanders		X	
Ladinos			
Socioeconomic groups			
The wealthy	X		
The middle class	I	I	
The poor		X	
Gender groups			
Women			
Men			
Nationalities			
Hondurans			
Foreigners	I		X

X = strong linkage; I = emerging/weak/indirect linkage; ? = unknown.

islands because of human rights abuses against black Bay Islanders brought to their attention by NAPIPLA. Other international agencies such as the UNDP have played key roles in promoting environmental management and conservation efforts on the islands. For example, the UNDP in collaboration with the GOH financed and managed the many feasibility studies conducted in the preparation of the loan proposal submitted to the IDB.

- **Inter-American Development Bank (IDB).** The IDB Environmental Management Project for the Bay Islands was discussed at length in Chapter 4. Several goals of the IDB project (e.g., protecting coastal and marine ecosystems, establishing a cadastral system, improving the water supply, and constructing a sanitation system) enhance the islands' capacity to promote and maintain tourism. However, the project has experienced significant delays in implementation due in large part to disagreements with the GOH over decentralizing authority over management of the project to the Bay Islands' department and four municipalities.
- **United States Agency for International Development (USAID).** The major part played by USAID in supporting U.S. foreign policy in Central America for the last 40 years is well known. Currently, USAID assistance is a trickle of what it was in the 1980s; however, much of what is disbursed in Honduras (and elsewhere) is through NGOs. In the case of the Bay Islands, U.S. assistance for conservation projects is channeled primarily through WCS and *Fundación Vida*.
- **Nongovernmental Organizations**
  - **Wildlife Conservation Society (WCS), Gainesville, FL.** WCS efforts in Central America were described in Chapter 4. Those that specifically involve the Bay Islands include the design of a management plan for the Sandy Bay-West End Marine Reserve, part of the *Paseo Pantera*/Meso-American Biological Corridor project. This project is funded largely by USAID through the Honduran national NGO, *Fundación Vida*. As suggested in the introduction to this chapter, the overriding goal of WCS appears to be externally imposed environmental preservation rather than community-based economic development and conservation. A review of the draft summary management plan for the Sandy Bay-West End Marine Reserve makes this very clear as will be discussed later in this chapter (WCS, 1998).
  - **Center for International Policy (CIP), Washington, DC.** CIP was founded in 1975. It works extensively with the Arias Foundation to promote the demilitarization of Central America. Its efforts in promoting human rights aim at analyzing and spotlighting the causes of human rights abuses as well as advocating policies to reduce violations (http://www.us.net/cip). CIP became involved in the Bay Islands in connection with the murder and displacement of black Bay Islanders.
  - **South and Meso-American Indian Rights Center (SAIIC), Oakland, CA.** The goal of SAIIC is to link indigenous peoples and their supporters throughout the continent. It was established in 1983 in Bolivia during a conference of native peoples and has grown into an organization that promotes continent global network. Its major goals are to promote human rights, protect the

natural environment, and fight for the rights of indigenous peoples. It supports a variety of programs in the following areas: human rights and environmental activism; information resources; women's projects; technical assistance to indigenous communities and organizations; and cultural exchanges (http://www.nativeweb.org/saiic). Along with CIP, SAIIC distributed electronically an "Urgent Agent" regarding the killing of a black islander teenager in Sandy Bay by a marine reserve guard and the dispossession of 12 black islander families from Helene in 1997.

- **International Tourism Industry.** Although foreign investment in the Bay Islands has increased significantly in recent years, this investment has come from private investors and developers rather than from large, transnational tourism firms. The exceptions are Taca International Airlines, which has regularly scheduled service to Roatán, and Norwegian Cruise Lines, which includes a 1-day stopover on Roatán as part of its *Texarribean* Cruise. This may be changing, however, as suggested by the recent announcements by Holiday Inn to build a luxury resort on Roatán and by Alitalia Airlines to begin a charter service between Italy and Roatán.

National Stakeholders

A number of national-level, public and private sector groups have interests in the Bay Islands. These include the government of Honduras through several agencies, Honduran elite, and environmental organizations. In the last few years, the autonomous National Commissioner for Human Rights (CONADH) has been drawn into conflicts on the islands through the appeals of the Confederation of Autochthonous Peoples of Honduras (CONPAH) acting on behalf of NABIPLA.

- **Government of Honduras (GOH).** The most powerful national-level stakeholder on the islands is the government of Honduras through several agencies, some of which have conflicting interests and overlapping jurisdictions.
  - One of the most important goals of the GOH is to increase foreign exchange through enhanced tourism revenues. As discussed at length elsewhere, the GOH currently is engaged in several efforts to promote tourism development including the recent establishment of a ministry-level office of tourism. To ensure funding of the new ministry, a 4% tax recently has been levied on tour operators, rent-a-car companies, and hotels. Funds from this new tax will go toward marketing Honduras' tourism industry in major foreign markets. This tax is similar to the 3% tax passed in Costa Rica several years ago, which may be repealed in the near future. The GOH also accelerated revision of Article 107 of the Honduran Constitution to allow foreign ownership of coastal and frontier properties—despite the escalating protests of Honduras' indigenous peoples.
  - As the most popular tourist destination within Honduras, the GOH is aware of the need to integrate the Bay Islands into the Honduran economy, polity, society, and culture more firmly than ever before. To facilitate this, government presence is exercised through the appointment of ladinos as municipal administrators, teachers, customs and immigration officials, and local police

(associated with the Honduran military). In addition, despite the requests of the Bay Islanders to control migration, the GOH has allowed the unfettered migration of ladino mainlanders to the islands. This has shifted the balance of population on the islands in favor of ladinos. Migration to the islands is a complex matter. While population growth is one of the factors that has contributed to environmental destruction on the islands, the Bay Islands are part of Honduras and government restrictions on migration to the islands would prohibit freedom of movement throughout the country by Honduran citizens—a dubious precedent. Moreover, Honduras is the third poorest country in Latin America and gravely needs additional employment options for its desperately poor citizens. The Bay Islands are perceived to be a locus of such opportunities. On what basis can the GOH prevent its citizens from seeking ways to improve the quality of their lives?

- The designation of the Bay Islands National Marine Park may also be an attempt by the GOH to enhance control over the islands. In part because of pressure from international donors, the GOH passed the Law of Municipalities (*la Ley de Municipialdades*) (*Decreto 134*) in October 1990. This law decentralized government authority and responsibility for economic development, protection, and management of natural resources, and public services, to departments and municipalities. The law specifically refers to the promotion of tourism as a responsibility of municipalities. In the case of the Bay Islands, the Law of Municipalities presented a challenge to government efforts to control the islands' development, services, and resources. According to the law, responsibility for these activities was passed to local, departmental, and municipal governments. The struggle between local and national government control has been at the heart of the struggle to realize the IDB Environmental Management Plan. According to Honduran legal specialists, once a region is declared a protected area by the Honduran Congress, responsibility and authority reverts to the national government. Thus, the creation of the Bay Islands National Marine Park may be an attempt by the GOH to reassert national control over the islands. The complex zonation plan included as part of the park designation and executed almost entirely without input from the local level suggests this may be the case.

- The GOH is not a monolithic block. Several government agencies and departments have some jurisdiction and responsibilities in the Bay Islands, including: the Secretary of Tourism, the Ministry of Natural Resources (SERMA), the Honduran Forestry Development Corporation (COHDEFOR), and the Ministry of Public Works and Transportation (SECOPT). Certain agencies such as the COHDEFOR and the recently created SERMA have engaged in jurisdictional disputes throughout Honduras, which have hampered effective management and protection of natural resources.

- **National Elite**. To date, investment in island tourism by Honduran elite from the mainland has been minimal, although a small number have invested in hotels and resorts in various places on the islands, including Oak Ridge and West End. This is in marked contrast to island elite, who are major stakeholders in the islands' tourism industry.

- **National Commissioner for Human Rights (CONADH).** A presidential decree in 1992 created the office of the human rights ombudsman, the National Commissioner for Human Rights. This autonomous agency has jurisdiction over all public agencies as well as private agencies running public services. CONADH is empowered with investigating claims of abuse at the hands of the GOH, ranging from failure to deliver services to serious human rights violations, and has been a vocal critic of the excesses of the Honduran military. Since its founding, over 3,000 complaints have been received by CONADH. It is to CONADH that CONPAH brought the complaint filed by NABIPLA described previously.
- **Nongovernmental organizations**
  - *Fundación Vida.* This Honduran environmental NGO has received support from USAID and others for the National Environmental Protection Fund (NEPF). The NEPF was created in 1991 to stem the loss of biological diversity and watershed resources, launch pollution prevention and abatement programs, and promote environmental education. The fund is a partnership among the GOH, international donors, and nonprofit environmental groups in support of the country's conservation goals. It takes a decentralized approach to environmental protection by providing grants for small environmental subprojects that are designed and implemented exclusively by local and U.S. NGOs. *Fundación Vida* administers the fund and selects and oversees subprojects. Other development and environment NGOs actually formulate and carry out the subprojects. USAID has been supporting the effort since 1993 with a 7-year (FY 1993–1999), US$10 million grant. The Honduran government has provided US$5 million to the fund, and the UNDP has contributed US$680,000 to defray *Fundación Vida's* operating costs (http://www.info.usaid.gov). One of the approximately 10 subprojects funded through NEDA and *Fundación Vida* is the Sandy Bay-West End Management Plan.
  - **Confederation of Autochthonous Peoples of Honduras (CONPAH).** CONPAH is the major organization of indigenous peoples of Honduras. It is committed to protecting the human rights and resource rights of Honduras' aboriginal peoples and is most likely the organization that presents indigenous complaints to international bodies such as CIP and SAIIC. CONPPAH is composed of several smaller, ethnically specific organizations. The native peoples represented and the organizations that represent them include:
    The Chorti (*El Consejo Nacional Indigena Chorti de Honduras,* CONICHH)
    The Lenca (*El Consejo Civico de Organizaciones Populares e Indigenas,* COPIN)
    The Tolupanes (*La Federacion de Tribus Xicaques de Honduras,* FETRIXY)
    The Pech (*La Federacion de Tribus Pech de Honduras,* FETRIPH)
    The Miskitos (*La Moskitia Asla Takanka,* MASTA)
    The Garífuna (*La Organizacion Fraternal Negra Hondurena,* OFRAHEH)
    The English-Speaking Bay Islanders (The Native Bay Islands Professionals and Labourers Association, NABIPLA)

Although Garífuna make up the majority of the population in the Roatán community of Punta Gorda, the majority of Garífuna live in communities along the North Coast of Honduras. The English-Speaking Bay Islanders represented by NABIPLA are the most recent members of CONPAH. As discussed in previous chapters, the classification of the Bay Islanders as an autonomous ethnic and indigenous group was a difficult but significant step in Afro-Caribbean Islanders' process of self-identity and outside recognition.

Local Stakeholders

Chapter 4 considered the diverse local-level stakeholders by community as well as by ethnicity, nationality, gender, and socioeconomic class. That analysis is merely summarized here. Instead, this section concentrates on various local-level interest groups (stakeholders) involved in local government and NGOs.

- **Local Governments: The Municipalities (Roatán, Jose Santos Guardiola, Guanaja, Utila).** The municipal governments on the Bay Islands were significantly empowered with the passage of the Law of Municipalities. However, these local authorities, which include the departmental governor and municipal mayors, have many financial, technical, and logistical obstacles that hinder effective implementation of their responsibilities under the law, including enforcement of environmental regulations and management of protected areas. To date, none of the municipalities has taken effective steps to assume control over its natural resources, including establishing environmental offices as allowed under the law. The minimal official efforts to enforce the law have varied considerably among municipalities (Vega et al., 1993, p. 66).
- **Commission Pro Tourism Development of the Bay Islands (Commission).** The Commission is a public–private sector collaboration whose prime function is to oversee environmental and conservation efforts that maintain and/or enhance the potential for tourism. It is discussed in Chapter 4. Of great significance is that regulatory power is concentrated in the hands of national government officials (including the President of Honduras, the Minister of Government and Justice, and the Director of Tourism), departmental and municipal government officials (the governor of the Bay Islands and the mayors of the four island municipalities), representatives of the two major islands NGOs (BICA and APRODIB), and the owners of the largest hotels and other prominent businesses.
- **Nongovernmental Organizations (NGOs).** Three very different NGOs are significant actors regarding tourism development and conservation in the Bay Islands. The Bay Islands Conservation Association (BICA) and the Native Bay Islanders Professional and Labourers Association (NABIPLA) represent divergent segments of the local population and their respective interests. The Association Pro Development of the Bay Islands (APRODIB), although now defunct, was an important actor on the islands as a conduit of international foreign assistance to several environmental, conservation, and employment generation initiatives.
  - **Bay Island Conservation Association (BICA).** BICA is the most influential and well-funded NGO on the islands. It plays a leadership role in environmental issues and is a major link between public and private institutions at all

levels—from the international to the local. It was established in 1990 by a group of influential island residents concerned with environmental conservation on the islands. BICA'S main office is in Coxen Hole, Roatán but it has chapters on the islands of Guanaja and Utila. With the economic support of international environmental organizations such as WCS, governmental agencies, and the owners of island hotels, BICA collaborates in a number of activities including administering the management of the Sandy Bay-West End Marine Reserve. BICA also engages in a number of environmental education and beach and community clean-up projects in association with local schools. In these efforts, for several years BICA was assisted by a series of U.S. Peace Corps volunteers. In cooperation with the municipality of Roatán, BICA provides larger, tourist-dependent communities with garbage pick-up service on a weekly basis. The vast majority of BICA programs are aimed at maintaining an environment conducive to the promotion of tourism. For example, BICA's involvement with marine reserves is in prime tourist areas and its solid waste collection program services tourist rather than nontourist areas. Demarcation projects became a priority when freshwater needs of the tourism industry became critical (Seidl, 1996, p. 126). The wives of powerful island individuals dominate the leadership of BICA, including the wife of the owner of Cooper's Key Resort, the largest resort within the Sandy Bay-West End Marine Reserve, who is responsible for the environmental ills discussed in Chapters 4 and 5. They, foreign expatriates, and a few individuals who hold political office dominate BICA. Few Afro-Caribbean, ladino, poor, or lower middle-class residents of the islands are members of BICA—although they often are "targets" of BICA activities. On the other hand, with notable exceptions, most of the powerful "white" island elite are not members of BICA either. In his analysis of the performance features of BICA, Seidl concludes:

> BICA's membership does not reflect the socioeconomic, ethnic, or cultural profile of the Bay Islands. . . . BICA members are decidedly more middle class, educated, dependent upon the formal tourism economy, foreign, English speaking, secular, and prone to voluntary organization than the general population. The distinction between the member profile of BICA and the Bay Islands are observed to influence BICA's approach, program choice, and success (1996, p. 126).

The Sandy Bay West End Marine Reserve exemplifies BICA's control-centered approach to achieving its environmental goals. Demarcating protected areas, regulations, monitoring, and enforcement (sometime through coercive means in collaboration with the Honduran police) characterize the predominate activities of BICA. Seidl suggests that the propensity toward control-based solutions may be the result of class or cultural differences between the BICA membership and the majority of Bay Islanders (Seidl, 1996, p. 127). He further suggests that foreign expatriates from North America and Europe may have enkindled this approach because regulation is a favored tool of powerful minorities in those regions to control the behaviors of less powerful and unorganized majorities (Seidl, 1996, p. 127). Given its membership, overall strategy, and associated project activities it is not surprising that BICA is perceived as an organization that represents and furthers the interests of selective powerful players in the tourist industry. According to the conservation strategy for the Bay Islands conducted for USAID and *Paseo Pantera* in 1992:

> . . . the greatest barrier to broad popular support of marine conservation efforts in the Bay Islands is a common perception that BICA is first and foremost an instrument of the tourism industry and that proposed and existing conservation efforts are primarily designed to protect the interests and investments of that industry, even if at the expense of the poor. This perception is actively fueled by the existence of obvious, large-scale and long-standing violations of environmental/resource use regulations within the tourism industry. . . . Changing negative perceptions about existing and proposed marine conservation efforts will be difficult until these issues are addressed. Representatives of the many small communities comprising the base of the islands' populations must become an integral part of the planning and decision-making processes. . . . Particularly needed are exploration and enactment of mechanisms whereby the economic benefits to be realized from the development and management of the islands marine resources will be fairly shared by all the islands residents. (Alevizon, 1993, pp. 215–216).

It is significant that this astute assessment was not included among the major recommendations of the conservation strategy but only appeared in the final pages of the final appendix to the report.

• **Native Bay Islanders Professional and Labourers Association (NABIPLA).** In many ways, NABIPLA is the antithesis of BICA. Two young men from the Afro-Caribbean communities of Flowers Bay and Gravel Bay (located on the southwestern shore of Roatán) started NABIPLA in 1991 in response to, "the people from the mainland who were coming in and controlling everything" (President of NABIPLA, personal communication, 1997). Their attitude toward mainland efforts to assimilate the islands was expressed quite simply by a member of NABIPLA in 1997, "The government used to leave us alone. . . . It was the Islands for the Islanders. . . . If we didn't have the pressure from the government these islands would be much improved." By 1997, membership in NABIPLA had grown to several thousand and consisted in the main of poor and middle-class black islanders. According to NABIPLA's president, the grassroots organization now has a committee in virtually every community on all the islands. Fifteen women and men make up the board of directors—one for each major program area of the organization. Many of the leaders are pastors from the different Bay Islands' Protestant churches (Baptist, Church of God, Adventist, etc.).

— NABIPLA has a broad agenda that includes promoting social justice, maintaining black Bay Islanders' cultural and ethnic identity, protecting islanders' rights over land and other natural resources, enhancing human health, and conserving the islands' environment and natural resources. Its

major efforts, however, have been promoting bilingual education throughout the islands, which it feels is key to achieving its other objectives. The
organization wishes to collaborate with an educational institution, such as
the University of the West Indies, to establish a Center for Bilingual Education for the Bay Islands that would provide secondary school education for
islander youth. NABIPLA also is putting pressure on the GOH to implement
its recently enacted legislation allowing and facilitating bilingual education
among Honduras' diverse indigenous peoples.

— It was largely through the efforts of NABIPLA that "English-speaking Bay
Islanders" were recognized as an indigenous ethnic group in 1996. Since its
membership in CONPAH, NABIPLA has taken an increasingly activist
position as indicated by the human rights complaints it brought to national and international bodies over the last year. In their words, "We have
somewhat lost control of the islands. We are looking forward to taking it
back" (member of NABIPLA, personal communication, 1997).

— NABIPLA is quite interested in improving the day-to-day lives of Islanders.
In 1997, NABIPLA started a food cooperative in Flowers Bay as a way to
help poor islanders deal with the escalating cost of food on the islands.
NABIPLA began dealing directly with wholesalers on the mainland, thus
bypassing the supermarkets and food distribution channels controlled by
the island elite. Members get a 20% discount on all merchandise in the
store: meat, chicken, vegetables, canned goods, paper products, and other
manufactured items such as soap. Thought of as a pilot project, NABIPLA
hopes to establish a network of such cooperatives in other communities.

— NABIPLA also is thinking of ways to have islanders more directly benefit
from the growth of tourism. They have started a Board of Tourism to
control buses and taxis. The idea is to train islanders as tour guides for the
cruise ship passengers who now stop on Roatán once a week. Currently,
most cruise passengers visit West Bay Beach where they snorkel and picnic
at a new resort owned by the brother of the owner of the largest resort
located within the Sandy Bay-West End Marine Reserve. The Board of
Tourism also aims to set requirements for dive masters—most important
from the perspective of NABIPLA is that they be Honduran citizens.

— One of the major objectives of NABIPLA is to preserve islander ethnicity
and culture. To this end, one of their proposed projects is to build a
cultural village in the community of Gravel Bay. They are attempting to
raise US$40,000 to purchase a site for the project. The organization plans
to have the village show tourists how islanders used to live—their traditional foods (plantains, corn, dried plantain, salted fish, etc.), ways of
making a living, stories, songs, boats, and buildings.

— The attitude of NABIPLA toward environmental conservation initiatives on
the islands was conveyed quite forcefully in their first newsletter published in May 1995:

> We know that in every society laws and prohibitions are important but
> are we implementing them correctly? How can we stop a poor man

from selling the sand on his beach; and allow a rich man to dredge, fill
up our sea and terminate our mangrove? Is it fair to prohibit a poverty
stricken family from cutting down a tree in their back yard? When the
wealthy are destroying our flora by the thousands daily? Is it right to
construct roads that benefit the elite only and neglect the underprivi-
leged while they are stuck to [their] knees in mud? They want us to
clean and dispose of our litter. Where are the garbage collecting
trucks? . . . NABIPLA believes that for our islands to go forward successfully, biasness, corruption, political propaganda, unequal education, and
partiality on the whole must be eliminated. We must conserve our
children, our environment, our good customs, traditions and belief that
all men are created equally (NABIPLA, 1995, p. 3).

- **Association Pro Development of the Bay Islands (APRODIB).** APRODIB
  was founded in 1983 and existed until 1997. It organized a number of relatively unsuccessful projects around providing drinking water, environmental
  health, reforestation, small business development, and training. It was designated as the local-level NGO to implement the environmental sanitation
  aspects of the IDB Bay Islands Environmental Management Project. Its collaborative project with CARE/Honduras to introduce composting latrines to
  replace outhouses was discussed in Chapter 4. The demise of APRODIB
  further calls into question the eventual realization of the IDB project.
- **Communities.** The three communities where in-depth household surveys and
  interviews were conducted differ markedly in the types and degree of tourism
  development that has taken place.
  - **West End.** This community is characterized by a wide range of relatively
    small, budget to midscale enterprises predominantly owned by middle-class
    islanders and foreigners from the U.S. and Europe.
  - **Sandy Bay.** Sandy Bay encompasses a smaller number of more mid- and
    upscale hotels and is dominated by Cooper's Key Resort, the largest resort
    within the Sandy Bay-West End Marine Reserve which literally bisects the
    community.
  - **Flowers Bay.** The tourism industry is least developed in Flowers Bay, one of
    the oldest Afro-Caribbean community on the islands, although a significant
    proportion of households in the community are economically dependent on
    income earned from working in tourism and other businesses located else-
    where on Roatán. Members of the community have actively resisted the
    expansion of tourism into the community in its present dominant form.
  - **West End Beach.** During the 1990s, tourism skyrocketed in the West Bay
    Beach area, which currently has the most upscale accommodations available
    on the western shore of Roatán, most owned by islander elite or foreigners.
- **Ethnic Groups.** Ethnicity on the islands is very complex, as demonstrated in
  Chapter 2. Although the following classification into three major categories
  obscures the considerable diversity within each group, it is useful for analytical
  purposes.
  - **Islanders.** Islanders are differentiated into "white" and "black" subgroups on
    the basis of each group's self-identification, although according to assess-

Photo 6.1. Paradise for sale! Real estate development of the West Bay Beach area.

ments by outsiders, "white" islanders are more accurately described as
Creole.

— **"White" Islanders.** This group includes the large majority of the islands'
   powerful, traditional elite, the owners of the fishing fleets, packing plants,
   shipping companies, major hotels, construction businesses, and food
   services. They include individuals such as the owner of Cooper's Key.
   Evidence presented in Chapter 2 disclosed the extent to which this group
   historically has enjoyed the greatest social, political, and economic power
   on the islands.

— **Black, Afro-Caribbean Islanders—English-Speaking Bay Islanders.** Black
   islanders arrived on the islands from the Cayman Islands a few years after
   their white counterparts. By that time most of the best locations on
   shorelines near the largest population centers had been claimed by the
   earlier arrivals who also implemented land laws that forced many black
   islanders to found their own communities in more remote locations such
   as the western portion of Roatán. Socioeconmically, black islanders are
   quite diverse, ranging from a small number of upper middle-class families
   to a much larger number of middle-class and poor households. Wealthier
   black islanders own many smaller hotels and other tourist-related businesses, especially in West End.

• **Ladinos.** Until the early 1980s, ladinos made up a small minority of the
   islands' population. Since then, they have become a small majority on the

islands due primarily to massive migration from the Honduran mainland. Most
recent ladino immigrants are poor and are heavily dependent on income
earned from working in tourist-related businesses owned by others. In
addition, ladinos predominate in government administrative posts and as
teachers, police officers, and taxi drivers. Ladino children (between weaning
and 60 months of age) were the only group that demonstrated evidence of
chronic undernutrition. In addition, ladinos are at higher risk than either
islanders or foreigners for environmental health risks emanating from diminished water quality.

- **Socioeconomic Groups**
  - **The Wealthy.** Wealthy island residents consist of elite "white" islanders as
    well as recently arrived foreigners. Although foreigners may hold significant
    economic wealth, it is the islands' elite who continue to exercise the greatest
    political power.
  - **The Middle Class.** Black Bay Islanders make up a large proportion of the
    islands' middle class, which also consists of a much smaller number of ladinos
    from the mainland. To date, black islanders have enjoyed relatively low levels
    of political power compared to their white islander competitors.
  - **The Poor.** The islands' poor encompass both ladinos and black islanders,
    although black islanders are more able to deal with financial and food shortfalls
    because of larger, more established, social and family networks on the islands.
- **Gender Groups**
  - **Women.** Women constitute a much higher percentage of household heads on
    the islands than on the Honduran mainland, in part due to the traditional
    economic options of island men that required that they be gone for long
    periods of time. In general, both islander and ladina women earn approxi-
    mately half the amount of their male counterparts. Despite inequities in
    wages, islander women (and men) perceive tourism as a good thing that does
    not require long-term family separations—because it allows men and youth to
    stay on the islands to earn a living. In the present context of increased drugs
    and violence, women also believe that having their husbands at home aids
    them in supervising and controlling problems with their children. Very
    important questions pertaining to the extent to which a greater male pres-
    ence may affect gender roles, the relative power of men and women, and the
    family, remain to be investigated.
  - **Men.** A growing number of black islander men are choosing to remain on the
    islands and start small tourist-related businesses—many with savings earned
    while working as merchant sailors, cruise ships personnel, or as fishermen.
    Some have become middle-class business owners who are demanding a share
    of political power and decision making on the islands.
- **Nationalities**
  - **Hondurans.** Although Bay Islanders may not like to think of themselves as
    Honduran citizens, they do enjoy the benefits of citizenship. Honduran
    citizens enjoy considerable benefits under the law in terms of being able to
    own property and establish tourist businesses on the islands. As citizens,
    some black islanders have had some success exercising these rights. It

remains to be seen to what extent the recent revision of Article 107 of the Honduran Constitution will affect the ability of these English-speaking Bay Islanders to compete with foreign interests in the tourism industry.

- **Foreigners.** As discussed more fully elsewhere, foreigners sometimes have engaged in a number of devious and formally illegal activities in order to claim "ownership" of land for tourist enterprises. This may change presently in light of successful efforts to amend the Honduran Constitution. Foreigners constitute a heterogeneous group embodying individuals from the U.S. as well as several countries of Europe and the U.K. The majority of real estate developers have been from the U.S., while individuals from Italy and elsewhere in Europe have tended to start small businesses such as dive shops and restaurants.

Conflicts and Coalitions Surrounding Tourism and Conservation

Three major contending coalitions of stakeholders with interests in tourism, natural resources, and conservation have emerged on the islands (Table 6.1). The first (Coalition 1), the most economically and politically powerful, integrates the most influential interests at the international, national, and local levels. At the international level it includes the multilateral and bilateral funders (the UNDP, IDB, and USAID) and international environmental organizations (WCS). National-level stakeholders encompass the GOH, the national NGO *Fundación Vida*, and, to a minor extent, Honduran mainland elite. Departmental and local-level collaborators consist of the Commission, BICA, APRODIB, and a select group of influential elite and middle-class islanders. Through membership in BICA, this group also encompasses a number of influential foreign residents with business interests in the tourism industry and several islanders that hold, or have held, political office at the national, departmental, or local level. This faction generally does not include foreign real estate developers. This alliance promotes conservation efforts that support the growth and maintenance of the tourist industry. This group is linked through kinship as well as through relations of economic and political power. For example, the owner of the largest resort within the Sandy Bay-West End Marine Reserve is married to the president of BICA and wives of influential islanders dominate the leadership of BICA. Although many powerful, elite islanders may not formally be members of BICA and this coalition, their interests are served by the agenda and approach of the alliance. It is to the advantage of islander elite to have environmental laws and regulations enforced because they are powerful enough to ignore or circumvent those regulations. Foreigners and middle-class islanders are much more likely to be forced to comply with regulations affecting the digging of wells or the construction of business and residence properties than the traditional island elite. Island elite also are more likely to have ties to mainland government and private interests that ensure they are able to channel the benefits of tourism development and conservation to themselves while also exempting themselves from the rules. For example, the owner of the largest resort within the Sandy Bay-West End Marine Reserve, formerly a governor of the Bay Islands, was able to obtain a permit to construct a large, environmentally destructive, marina within the reserve. He also was able to get an exemption from the Honduran law prohibiting the capture of wild dolphins—on the basis that they were to be used for educational purposes.

Strikingly absent from Coalition 1 are most Afro-Caribbean islanders, ladinos, the poor, and most women—the majority of the islands' peoples. The founding of NABIPLA in 1991 coalesced the growing resentment and resistance among English-speaking Bay Islanders to the perceived loss of their culture, language, lands, and livelihoods. The second major coalition among stakeholders on the islands consists mainly of black islanders organized by NABIPLA. This group encompasses poor and middle-class islanders and to a certain extent women who are represented in the leadership as well as membership of NABIPLA. It also integrates local Protestant churches into the alliance as many of the leaders of NABIPLA are religious leaders in their communities. Christian ideals often are evoked by individual members as well as in the NABIPLA newsletter. Not surprisingly, this coalition is strongest in communities along the southwest shore of Roatán, including Flowers Bay, where the organization was founded, but it appears to be gaining strength among Afro-Caribbean islanders in other communities. NABIPLA's main office is in Coxen Hole—only a few blocks away from the office of BICA. The power of this alliance was enhanced significantly in 1996 when "English-speaking Bay Islanders" were formally recognized as an ethnically distinct, indigenous population in Honduras and NABIPLA became their representative in CONPAH. This enabled English-speaking Bay Islanders to claim land, language, and other indigenous rights under Honduran law. Their political power was further strengthened in 1997 when NABIPLA brought the killing of the youth in Sandy Bay by the marine reserve guard and the dispossession of the 12 islander families from their homes on Helene to the attention of CONPAH and the National Commissioner for Human Rights. The legitimization of "English-speaking Bay Islanders" as one of the indigenous peoples of the Americas was augmented when their human rights claims were taken up by SAIIC and CIP in 1997. It is noteworthy that recognition as a separate people largely stemmed from efforts within the black islander community with little outside support. While recent years have seen growing attention paid to the situation of Afro-Latin Americans (e.g., IDB, 1997a), this focus has ignored the Bay Islanders (e.g., Sieder, 1995). Although NABIPLA has become a growing cultural and social force on the islands and has garnered limited international attention, its political and economic power remain quite limited compared to that of the powerful members of Coalition 1.

An additional partnership (Coalition 3) on the islands is that between foreign (primarily U.S.) real estate developers and members of local and national government. Recall that the dispossession of black islanders from Helene came about because of the collusion between a foreign real estate developer and a Bay Islands' judge who not only found in favor of the developer against the islanders but also used the power of his office to bring in police from the mainland to enforce his ruling. The extent to which such collusion will continue in the future and whether such coalitions may eventually undermine the power of the islander elite remains to be seen. Also unknown is the degree to which the U.S. will direct events on the islands. Although current levels of U.S. foreign assistance to Honduras are meager compared to those of the 1980s, the U.S. still wields considerable political and economic power within the country. Overturning the decision of the municipal government of Guanaja to claim property "owned" by a U.S. citizen came about largely because of pressure from the U.S. embassy. It is not inconceivable that such pressure could be applied again in cases involving the growing number of U.S. developers and residents on the islands.

Glaringly absent from any of the above coalitions are poor ladinos—both men and women—yet they now comprise the majority of residents of the islands. At the same time they have benefited least from tourism and are at most risk from tourism's costs. It is inconceivable that tourism development or conservation initiatives could be judged successful without the advantageous integration of this group.

Current Trends in Conservation:
The Sandy Bay-West End Marine Reserve

The draft management plan for the Sandy Bay-West End Marine Reserve designed by WCS in collaboration with BICA, with funding from USAID and *Fundación Vida*, provides an opportunity to evaluate current trends in community-based participation in tourism and conservation. According to the draft, the major objectives of the proposed management plan are to:

- improve and preserve the quality of the environment inside the reserve;
- offer the public recreational opportunities that are not environmentally detrimental;
- promote the rational and sustainable use of marine resources among local residents;
- promote awareness by offering attractive environmental education programs that call for public involvement and/or community participation;
- promote scientific research;
- improve visitor information.

The Public Use Program

The public use aspect of the plan has the following objectives:

- incorporate the input of all stakeholders for an integral management of the reserve;
- ensure the cooperation and support of all concerned with the management;
- increase the production of fish and other marine organisms;
- create the conditions for future expansion of the reserve along the shoreline.

In order to realize these objectives the program calls for defining the limits of the reserve, strengthening its legal status through passage of a national decree, and establishing four use zones for recreation (diving, snorkeling, line fishing), multiple use (line fishing, diving, snorkeling, swimming, water-skiing, etc.), yachting, and fish recuperation. Major activities within this program include reaching consensus among users through a series of workshops to "advise and educate those involved regarding the Marine Reserve's current regulations."

Marine Resource Protection Program

Management objectives of this part of the plan include:

- control of erosion and sedimentation;
- permanent surveillance and control to avoid overexploitation of resources by permanent and occasional users;
- regulate and control the infrastructure development in the littoral shore;
- regulate recreational and tourism activities;
- establish closed season zones for fishing and extraction of marine resources;
- enforce legal regulations;
- establish a public user's fee and establish a trust for the collected funds and other donations to be administered by a council composed of:
    The Bay Islands Commission
    A representative of the Ministry of Tourism
    A member of AFE-COHDEFOR
    A representative of the municipality of Roatán
    BICA
    Three members from the business sector: a hotel owner, a dive operator, and one representative from another tourism firm.

The Users' Survey

In order to gather information on public attitudes and knowledge regarding specific issues related to the reserve, WCS and BICA administered approximately 100 surveys within the reserve. These were questionnaires, available in both English and Spanish, that were left at various businesses, offices, and elsewhere. The rate of return was very high (77%). The preliminary summary of results included with the draft management plan reveals that respondents were disproportionately biased in favor of foreigners, men, individuals with relatively high education and better jobs, and managers/owners of tourism businesses. Distributing questionnaires within the reserve was a methodologically flawed means of soliciting responses that were representative of the community of users, not to mention a strategy that eliminated from the sample anyone who was not literate enough to read and write responses. As a result, the "community" of users was not represented by the sample. Even though survey respondents were dominated by better off individuals with economic interests in the tourism industry, a majority of respondents (56%) reported that they did not support the reserve—a crucial result that was not discussed in the draft plan.

Discussion

Unfortunately, the draft management plan reinforces the coercive, regulatory, and enforcement-based conservation approach that has predominated on the islands. It is not a "community"-based management plan—unless "community" is conceptualized to consist overwhelmingly of better off business owners and others of their kind. Poorer members of the "community" (which include poor islanders, ladinos, women, children, and others) are considered only as "targets" who have to be informed, educated, and otherwise compelled (by regulations and guards) to make "rational" and "sustainable" use of the reserve. The draft plan does not understand or address "community" in terms of its extant heterogeneity, contending interest groups, and conflicts. Neither does the plan directly confront nor deal with the existing power structure, power relations, or coalitions among various power-holding groups—as difficult as this may be in a place as contentious and dangerous as the Bay Islands. Also missing from the plan is any consideration or discussion of how local people will benefit from the reserve in some definite way. It is insufficient to say the health of the reef will ultimately benefit everyone, as is claimed in the draft plan. Over the last several years, many people living in communities adjacent to the reserve have expressed serious doubts that this will happen. In this regard, the plan does not make explicit the linkages between tourism development and conservation—including diving, hotel construction, and road building, as well as vital sewerage, drinking water, and solid waste disposal systems. Here possible links with the IDB project are obvious though unmentioned in the WCS/BICA plan. It is impossible to put impenetrable boundaries around the reserve. Tourism is there to stay—at least until the reef dies and the water gets so contaminated that the tourists stop coming and find another "Paradise" elsewhere.

While it is generally a good idea to work with existing institutions when possible while designing and implementing conservation projects, the Bay Islands may be an exception. Because of BICA's close alliance with certain members of the tourist industry and the widespread perception that it represents those interests at the expense of the majority of island residents, a more representative collaborating organization (or organizations) than BICA may be preferable. Even the seemingly depoliticized environmental education and clean-up projects of BICA are not really apolitical because they reinforce the existing power relations. Who of the various stakeholders are responsible for the significant degradation of the area within the marine reserve—those who engage in rampant and unregulated development in order to increase profits or the poorer people (who according to the draft management plan, need environmental education projects to teach them the value of the reef) who use the resources for their sustenance? Organizations such as BICA play an insidious role in shifting the blame away from those significantly at fault and also toward the design of conservation policies, programs, and projects that cannot succeed because they do not address the root causes of problems.

One potentially crucial organization to participate in any management plans for the western portion of Roatán is NABIPLA. Although NABIPLA does not have the environmental expertise, experience, or contacts enjoyed by BICA, it does represent a large segment of the islands' population that heretofore has not played a significant part in conservation efforts—although crucially affected by the regulations and enforcement that have been part of such initiatives. NABIPLA has an important stake conserving the environment and natural resources of the Bay Islands while also maintaining islander culture and language, protecting resource rights, and improving islanders' lives. For NABIPLA, protecting island environments is part of a much larger agenda.

However, significant participation by NABIPLA in community-based conservation and development efforts would not integrate other important local stakeholders into those efforts. Conspicuously absent are the islands' many poor ladino residents. In fact, including NABIPLA could result in the further and systematic exclusion of ladinos given NABIPLA's strategy to actively exclude ladinos from Afro-Caribbean communities. Many ladinos, in fact, consider NABIPLA's activities to be segregationist and racist. To counter this, ladinos should be integrated into some new institutional context that fairly represents their interests. Ladinos throughout Honduras have been at the forefront of organizing peasant and worker movements for many decades (Stonich, 1993). It is likely that many recent immigrants to the islands have family histories and perhaps personal experience in organizing and mobilizing their peers. Including both ladinos and islanders into development and conservation projects would require direct efforts to resolve the longstanding, historical conflicts between these groups. One approach might include the formation of women's groups that included both ladino and islander members, similar to the hundreds of women's groups that are active on the mainland. This could not only bring women stakeholders together and into development and conservation efforts but also provide women an opportunity to discuss their common problems across ethnic lines.

Moving Toward Effective Community-Based Tourism Development and Conservation

The case of the Bay Islands suggests several recommendations to enhance the success of community-based tourism development and conservation initiatives. These recommendations are based on the argument that effective community participation essentially is based on an understanding of extant social relations.

1. Define and operationalize "participation." There are two main dimensions of participation: participation as a goal in itself that allows communities to have greater control over their lives and resources, and participation as a means of achieving improved social, economic, and/or environmental objectives. These two objectives are not mutually exclusive. In many cases the second dimension may prove impossible unless the first objective is achieved.

2. Realistically address the major weaknesses in many community-based initiatives. Some of the most important of these are:

    a. an unrealistic understanding of local social and cultural dynamics;

    b. lack of understanding of competing interest groups both within and outside the local community;

    c. ignorance of the larger political and economic structures that generate local competition and conflict.

3. Conduct a thorough, informed assessment of the meaning of the "local"—paying close attention to local–extra-local linkages.

4. Use sociocultural analysis to attain a realistic understanding of the "community" in terms of heterogeneity of nationality, ethnicity, class, and gender.

5. Identify relevant stakeholders at all levels—from the local through the global—including their ideologies, values, interests, and behaviors. The development and conservation literature is full of examples of unsuccessful efforts due to failure to collaborate with important interest groups or segments of the population. This involves:

   a. identifying major interest groups their motives, strategies, and behaviors;

   b. identifying conflicts among and between stakeholders over such things as jobs and resources.

6. Stipulate the structure of power and extant power relations among stakeholders.

7. Identify the benefits and costs/risks (the winners and losers) from current trends in development and conservation.

8. Collaboratively (i.e., with all stakeholders) identify feasible stages (from problem formation and design through implementation, monitoring, and evaluation), facilitating conditions (sharing, dispersing, and/or redistributing power among stakeholders), and actions/steps to ensure that power is distributed among stakeholders.

9. Collaboration among local, community, and extra-local stakeholders may involve establishing new institutions or enhancing existing ones.

10. Establish means to resolve conflicts.

11. Engage in direct and vigorous attempts to channel greater power and authority to less powerful local groups during processes of coalition building.

12. Establish networks among communities.

13. Ensure that local representatives of communities are truly representative and accountable.

14. Ensure that local people (especially the poor and women) benefit economically and in other ways from the development and conservation projects. Cases in which local communities in poor regions manage their resource base with the prime objective of conservation are virtually nonexistent.

15. Integrate cultural survival into community-based tourism development and conservation.

Conclusion

The Bay Islands present a considerable challenge for equitable tourism development and successful environmental conservation. The situation is exceedingly
complex and involves multiple, divergent interest groups formed into contending
coalitions within a context characterized by high levels of scientific uncertainty,
upside economic risk, and downside environmental risk. Although current conflicts
surround natural resources, they also encompass cultural concerns to a great
degree. To date, however, most local people, especially the poor and recent immigrants, have not been meaningfully involved in development or conservation
efforts. Significant differences among community stakeholders have not been
recognized, understood, or taken into account either in terms of tourism development or environmental conservation. The few attempts at mediation and dispute
resolution among contending stakeholders have been insufficient and ineffectual.
Movement toward development of a tourism industry that is beneficial to larger
segments of the community as well as toward effective conservation initiatives
must begin by facing past failures as well as the local reality of the Bay Islands.

Notes

[1]This discussion of the importance of sociocultural and stakeholder analysis is
based on a report prepared by Norman Schwartz, Anne Deruyttere, Sylvia Huntley,
Conrad Kottak, and myself for the IDB. The report presented a framework for
conducting community consultation/participation in the context of the IDB's
projects (Schwartz et al., 1996).

Chapter 7

The Political Ecology of Tourism and Conservation

For two centuries, Bay Islanders have been free to overharvest fish, jettison trash, even dredge and fill bays and inlets to build more commodious beachfront homes. . . . As a public official and resort owner [the owner of Cooper's Key Resort], was in a prime position to see that the economy of his island and the health of the reefs were intertwined. . . . A man of action, he bought a fiberglass skiff, recruited his own marine patrol, and set out to protect the dive sites within reach of his resort. And he gave his new "reef police" a strict mandate to hit poachers hard, with stiff sentences, including jail terms for repeat offenders. Fortunately, no one challenged the resort owner's authority to make his earliest arrests—statutory authority over the sanctuary now known as Sandy Bay Marine Reserve was only obtained this year. (Gordon, 1993).

For my patrol, I picked the guys who were out there spearing the fish, who were out there polishing the coral and selling it to the tourists . . . I'm the beneficiary of the reef. . . . The reef's beauty is what I sell, and I should be the person who pays for its upkeep. (Owner of Cooper's Key Resort, quoted in Gordon, 1993)

The above quotations are from an article entitled, "An Octopus' Garden: A Guide to Marine Parks and Reserves," that appeared in the December 1993 issue of *Hemispheres*, the onboard magazine of United Airlines. In it, the author points to the Sandy Bay Marine Reserve as a positive example of marine conservation. The first quotation is by the freelance reporter who investigated and wrote the article, based in part on interviews with BICA leaders and the owner of Cooper's Key Resort in Sandy Bay. The second statement is by the owner of Cooper's Key Resort. Together they disclose a great deal about the political ecology of tourism and conservation in the Bay Islands, as well as about media coverage and public perceptions of environmental problems and conservation initiatives. The reporter ascribes blame for the serious decline in the health of the islands' reefs to hundreds of years of overexploitation by Bay Islanders in general, who, according to him, have been free to engage in all sorts of environmentally destructive behaviors including overfishing, dredging, and construction of luxurious residences. He then attributes salvation of the reef to the efforts of a "man of action" who took it upon himself to save the reef by hiring his own "reef police" to guard the reserve and enforce its rules. The author asserts that it is fortunate that no one questioned this resort owner's authority since the "reserve" had not yet been designated as such by any local or national government authority. In his remark, the owner of Cooper's Key Resort, a member of the island elite, acknowledges that he benefits economically from a healthy reef and so is willing to pay to maintain its integrity. He also attests that he hired patrol guards from among those who exploited the reef for their own economic advantage.

The views presented in this article both reinforce and conflict with the analyses and concerns raised in this book. First, environmental degradation at its present level has not been going on for the last several hundred years—although the consequences of hundreds of years of human activities are detectable in the present landscape. The most severe environmental problems are the result of human activities that have occurred over the last few decades—the result of commercial fishing, migration from the mainland, and the unregulated growth of the tourism industry. Second, it is not all Bay Islanders who are responsible for the most egregious environmental problems; it is predominantly the island elite and foreign developers (including the owner of Cooper's Key Resort). Third, the reporter is correct in saying that the resort owner was on shaky ground—fining and arresting "poachers"—because his attempt to privatize a national/public/communal resource was both illegal and unconstitutional. The reporter's remarks expose the coercive nature of the marine reserve and its oligarchic control by the powerful resort owner. It recalls the observation made by Jane Houlson in 1934, quoted in Chapter 2, that white island elite, "ruled with a feudal right unquestioned" (Houlson, 1934). The comments by the owner of Cooper's Key Resort reinforce this. To him, the "reef police" are "my patrol." Through his remarks, the owner appears to claim "ownership" of the reserve and its resources even though shoreline and inshore areas cannot be privatized according to Honduran law. He also seemingly takes credit for establishing the reserve, although the notion of the reserve initially came from environmentally concerned community members. While it is true that the resort owner provided the majority of funding for the reserve for several years, as he said, he was a major beneficiary of the reserve. Moreover, his financing stopped when management of the reserve expanded to include other business owners and community members who questioned his authority and behavior.

The article also evinces the power of this individual to frame the understanding of the islands' environmental problems as well as their potential solutions for the international media—who in turn communicate this framework to the public. To diving enthusiasts, Cooper's Key Resort is one of the best known diving resorts in the Caribbean and is widely respected as environmentally concerned and involved. Professionals, as well as the public, have constructed their perceptions of the islands predominantly on the basis of the images, views, and perspectives of island elite, government officials, or travel writers with very short-term experience. For example, the team of consultants who authored the conservation strategy for the Bay Islands prepared for USAID and *Paseo Pantera*, which is cited often in this book, acknowledge the assistance of BICA and the owner of Cooper's Key Resort with "logistics and advice on how to approach the relevant conservation and development issues in the islands" (Vega et al., 1993, p. 7). In addition, a growing number of conservation organizations, environmental scholars, and their students, many associated with prestigious universities, have used the research facilities available at the resort's, for-profit, marine science center. Members of the media, consultants, researchers, and students, like thousands of tourist divers, apparently are unaware of the environmental and social controversies that have surrounded the resort and its owners or of the larger political ecological context in which tourism and conservation on the islands are situated.

In part to fill this void, this chapter begins with a summary discussion of the political ecology of tourism and conservation in the Bay Islands. It extends this analysis and summarizes obstacles to community-based tourism development and conservation and the importance of considering extant power relations, history, and cultural survival in order to enhance local participation. It evaluates the viability of tourism as an economic development strategy in Central America in light of the present global economy and ongoing constraints within the region, including the effects of Hurricane Mitch. It concludes with a series of recommendations for more comprehensive, informed, and just tourism and conservation policy.

The Political Ecology of Tourism and Conservation in the Bay Islands

Among the central objectives of this book were to use political ecological analysis to demonstrate the distributional aspects of tourism and conservation efforts in the Bay Islands. This involved determining the benefits and costs and the related winners and losers stemming from current trends in tourism and conservation. Chapter 5 showed that the Bay Islands' poor ladinos, poor islanders, and women were receiving the least benefits from tourism as measured by levels of income, patterns of consumption, food security, and nutritional status. It identified recently arrived poor ladinos to be most in jeopardy in terms of these measures. Moreover, although all island residents as well as tourists currently face escalated risks from diseases associated with declines in the quality of fresh, brackish, and seawater, the risks to recent ladino immigrants are the most serious. For poor ladinos and poor islanders, insufficient benefits from employment in the tourist sector have been exacerbated by reduced access to previously available natural resources through the establishment of protected areas such as the Sandy Bay-West End Marine Reserve. For some islanders the expansion of tourism has resulted in dispossession from their homes due to collusion between foreign developers, Honduran elite, and government officials.

Understanding the relationships between tourism development and conservation efforts requires understanding the interrelationships among diverse stakeholders as detailed in Chapter 6. In the case of the Bay Islands, the GOH certainly is a major stakeholder, not only regarding its historical relationship to the Bay Islands but also in terms of the effects of its current incentives to promote tourism. Other important stakeholders include international donors, lenders, and environmental organizations; foreign investors; government agencies and national NGOs; Honduran elite; extremely poor ladinos on the mainland; local nongovernmental organizations such as BICA and APRODIB; grassroots organizations such as NABIPLA; the ethnically and economically diverse Bay Island population; and the escalating number of tourists. It is important to point out that the Bay Islands are not an example of the consequences of excessive foreign investment in the tourism industry. In fact, Bay Island elite contributed significantly to the current tourism boom on the islands. Moreover, in many instances, the interests of island elite are more akin to those of foreign investors than to those of their less affluent neighbors. Rather than being determined entirely by external forces, the present tourism sector has been shaped by a complex mix of local and extra-local forces and actors.

Many residents, especially those from predominantly Afro-Caribbean communities such as Flowers Bay, feel that they have been intentionally excluded from benefiting from tourism development by the GOH, international interests, and island elite who control the development opportunities. Island elite and middle-class business owners engage in environmentally destructive activities while they simultaneously extol the virtues of environmental conservation, attend international tourism conferences, and support the protection of marine reserves at the expense of poor ladinos and islanders. However, without the collaborative support of stakeholders, from the least to the most powerful, there is little chance that the existing reserves or the proposed Bay Islands National Marine Park will succeed in their conservation goals over the long term. No single stakeholder or the various coalitions of actors are in complete control over all the forces and actors that are at play in the islands.

At present, unregulated tourist development appears to be accelerating through the construction of upscale hotels and resorts by island elite, Honduran elite from the mainland, and well-capitalized foreign investors; the expansion of small-scale hotels, rooms for rent, and other tourist-related businesses by middle-class islanders and less well-capitalized foreigners; and the increased parcelization of remaining areas of tropical forests, upland areas, and prime beach property, which is being sold principally to foreigners from the U.S. and elsewhere. The influx of a large number of less educated, less healthy, and desperately poor ladinos, along with unbridled development and increased pressures on resources from tourists, affects the environmental quality of the islands, the environmental health of the population, and the long-term viability of the tourism industry itself. The inability of the GOH, the IDB, the USAID, and the variety of NGOs to ameliorate the negative environmental effects and associated human costs of tourism command the meaningful involvement of local people in all facets of the tourism industry, not just as workers at the lowest rung of employment. These failures are not merely problems of enforcement of existing environmental laws and regulations. This is one of the most important policy lessons to be learned from this case study. The emergence and expansion of NABIPLA beyond Flowers Bay to other parts of Roatán and the insistence of the residents of West End to have community control of their marine reserve demonstrate that the less empowered on the islands want to share in the benefits of development and are likewise committed to sustaining the environment and natural resources on which an alternative vision or model of tourism can be based.

Obstacles to Community Participation, Development, and Environmental Conservation

The uncontrolled growth of tourism that is occurring simultaneously with internationally funded environmental management plans and conservation initiatives emphasizes the underlying discord between the goals of economic development and environmental conservation on the islands. Even within the tourism sector, the Bay Islands present a case of unresolved contradictions between the desired models of tourism along with their respective environmental requirements—from mass tourism on the one hand to academic, adventure, and ecotourism on the other. At the community level, effective community-based conservation and development also conflict with the interests of the state, the island elite, and foreign investors. In this context, the coercive approach of the Sandy Bay-West End Marine Reserve may intensify with the creation of the Bay Islands National Marine Park. The integration of the Sandy Bay-West End Marine Reserve (as it is currently conceived and managed) with the Bay Islands National Marine Park may strengthen the GOH's control over the islands' natural resources and people. The mandate of the GOH to protect the country's environment and natural resources, along with its monopolization of legitimate force, could combine to facilitate state control as well as exacerbate current levels of resistance, conflict, and violence. The GOH, in collaboration with unrepresentative NGOs such as BICA and island elite, is likely to use conservation dogma to defend coercion in the name of conservation. Sanctioned violence in the name of resource defense also facilitates the control of people—especially less affluent black islanders, including members of NABIPLA, who challenge the state's claims to natural resources as well as its hegemony in other areas.

Enhancing Local Participation

The politics of environmental conservation and development largely have been ignored by international donors and NGOs with interests in the Bay Islands. These politics include not only relations of power concerning material resources but cultural politics as well. Yet, conservation and development projects fundamentally promote new social relations among stakeholders—in addition to establishing new mechanisms for controlling the allocation, access, and use of resources. In the Bay Islands' case such initiatives have tended to reinforce and augment the power of the most influential segments of society. Power among relevant stakeholders is extremely unequal and vigorously defended by the most powerful social actors. Although this book has argued that issues of power must be addressed at every stage of development and conservation efforts—from problem framework through project design, implementation, monitoring, and evaluation—any attempts to balance or redistribute power among stakeholders are likely to be contested. It is probable that traditional power-holding groups on the islands will resist redistribution and do all they can to hamper efforts at local participation and community collaboration among legitimate stakeholders. As suggested in Chapter 1, asymmetries of power are not simply obstacles to be overcome through better facilitation mechanisms. They are central to the processes of development and conservation and frequently determine why such efforts succeed or fail.

Integrating Cultural Survival Into Tourism and Conservation

The emergence of NABIPLA provides a chance to examine how cultural survival might enhance the success of conservation efforts and promote tourism that is more beneficial to local people. NABIPLA certainly does not represent all of the islands' less affluent residents. In fact, the organization intentionally excludes ladinos. However, NABIPLA does represent a significant portion of the islands' population that until now has been left out of conservation efforts. Because NABIPLA is closely linked to the islands' Protestant churches it also provides an opportunity to integrate local people into conservation and tourism projects through widely accepted religious beliefs, moral values, and existing organizations. Among the islanders' major objections to tourism are the perceived immoral behaviors and dress of tourists and the associated loss of longstanding islander values among their youth. In these and more material ways, members of NABIPLA feel that they have paid the price rather than reaped the benefits of tourism. Currently, NABIPLA is attempting to establish a number of projects that would augment their participation in the tourist industry in ways that they see appropriate—including training as tour guides, purchasing tourist vans, and creating a cultural village to highlight islander traditions. In part, their efforts to establish a bilingual secondary school is a bid to ensure islanders have English language skills sufficient for better jobs in the tourist industry. Among their major concerns are declines in the quality and quantity of potable and seawater and the related effects on human health. To date, however, the organization has not had sufficient funding to implement projects to address these problems. Neither can it afford a desired program to promote the cultivation of agricultural crops for home consumption as well as for sale to the growing tourist market. However, NABIPLA has sought to confront food insecurity and rising food prices by establishing food cooperatives in local communities. For NABIPLA, environmental conservation efforts are inextricably linked to the preservation of their ethnicity, culture, lands, and livelihoods. Although representatives of NABIPLA have attended a number of island workshops and meetings, the organization has not been integrated into ongoing development or conservation efforts in any meaningful way.

The Role of History

Achieving tourism development that is more equitably beneficial to the Bay Islands' diverse population as well as environmentally sound requires more than confronting present structures and relations of power. The islands' history as well as its power structure will shape its future. Considering the islands' fascinating history leads to a comprehension of its current social, cultural, economic, and political complexity—the context in which contemporary tourism is taking place. The Bay Islands are a tiny place, a former outpost of the British Empire, a haven for pirates, and home to farmers, freed slaves, scoundrels, and sailors, and a popular tourist destination. The Bay Islands' existing complexity provides a lesson for other potential tourist destinations—most of which have their own intricate histories. Yet, most tourism policy and practice, regardless of place, have failed to consider the complex context in which tourism occurs.

The islands' economic history demonstrates a series of dependencies—on subsistence and export agriculture, boat building, seafaring, smuggling, fishing, and now tourism. Weighty evidence from throughout the world has demonstrated the notorious instability of tourism earnings and its unreliability as an exclusive economic development strategy. The unpredictability of tourism is due to a number of factors: economic recessions and downturns; seasonality, bad weather, and natural disasters; high degrees of competition; political instability in tourist locales; high crime rates; tourists' changing tastes; etc. Despite the historical evidence that the islands have the capacity to engage successfully in a diverse array of economic activities, presently there is no concerted attempt at integrated development that would diversify the islands' economy and reduce the growing singular dependence on the tourism sector. Notwithstanding the islands' potential (and the existing desire of NABIPLA to promote agricultural production for the tourist sector), there have been no forcible efforts to link the islands' tourism, fishing, and agricultural sectors, even though such efforts could lead to enhanced economic opportunities and greater food security for less affluent island residents.

Perhaps, most importantly, the islands' history contributes significantly to current tensions among the many social and cultural actors both on and off the islands. Contemporary frictions between the GOH, Spanish-speaking ladino mainlanders, and islanders are the latest demonstration of 400 years of Anglo–Hispanic conflict. Despite attempts over the last 100 years to integrate the islands more closely into the nation state, never before has the GOH tried as forcefully to assimilate the islands into the mainland polity, economy, society, and culture. While the combined strengths of nationalism, tourism development, conservation initiatives, mainland poverty, and massive migration may result in national integration, the costs may be extravagant. The price may include the unrecoverable destruction of the biophysical environment and the natural resources on which all island residents depend, a declining standard of living for large segments of the islands' people, and the significant loss of Bay Islanders' culture. Rather than promoting social, cultural, and economic equity, the current patterns of tourism development, along with conservation efforts, are exacerbating long-term struggles, enhancing existing inequalities, and promoting cultural and social conflict. These critical costs threaten the long-term viability of the tourism industry itself.

Tourism as Economic Development in the Bay Islands and Central America

> When I got here in 1978, Central America, in the public perception, was a toilet. Our marketing job was to position Costa Rica as an oasis. (Costa Rican ecotourism pioneer originally from U.S., quoted in Weir, 1997)

> The point is that how the world perceives a city or country is a key component in developing the destination touristically. . . . Honduras could use a good dose of "good image," we need to show the world what we've got to be proud of. (Rosenzweig, 1998a)

> Coming into Mitch, tourism ranked behind bananas, coffee, and shrimp in revenue generation for Honduras. Now we must carry the load. (Norman Garcia, Honduran Ministry of Tourism, press release, January 20, 1999)

Given the many obstacles to local participation, equitable development, and environmental conservation, how viable is tourism as an economic development strategy in the Bay Islands, Honduras, and Central America more broadly—particularly given the current crisis in the global economy as well as the ongoing constraints within the isthmus including the repercussions of Hurricane Mitch? During the 1990s, enlarging international tourism has been a major development goal for all the countries of Central America in their attempts to integrate and diversify their economies. Currently all the countries of the region have in place a variety of tourism policies, programs, incentives, legislation, and regulations, many of which involve the use of terrestrial and marine resources. All countries of the isthmus also have established a number of public and private protected areas in the forms of national parks and reserves. The overriding aim of these efforts has been to increase the number of international tourist arrivals in order to augment foreign exchange earnings. During the decade, all Central American countries have shown increases in tourist arrivals and earnings—a few countries like Belize and Costa Rica have demonstrated outstanding growth in these areas. In contrast, with the arguable exception of Costa Rica, environmental protection for its own sake remains a low priority for national governments. Unfortunately, the contradictions between tourism development and environmental conservation goals noted for the Bay Islands exist throughout the region—including Costa Rica and Belize. A recent example of this occurred in Costa Rica in mid-1998. In August, the Costa Rican Tourism Institute, via a presidential decree, launched a certification procedure along the lines of the hotel rating system, to grade the "sustainability" of tourist accommodations, giving higher rankings to environmentally friendly developments. Shortly thereafter, the Costa Rican president publicly defended a controversial tourism complex on Costa Rica's northern Pacific coast being built by the Spanish hotel chain, Barceló, allegedly without construction permits. The proposed holiday villa and golf course is being built adjacent to the company's existing 400-room hotel on Playa Tambor and according to critics is likely to cause considerable environmental damage. The Costa Rican English language newspaper, *The Tico Times*, quotes President Miguel Angel Rodrigez as saying, "Who hasn't destroyed a little bit of nature to build the foundations of his house?" (Escofet, 1998b).

As discussed in Chapter 1, no countries within the isthmus show strong commitments to community-based conservation and tourism development—despite the considerable rhetoric (and projects) to the contrary. National governments throughout Central America, like the majority of communities throughout the Third World, engage in environmental conservation only when they see some economic or other material benefit from doing so. However, like NABIPLA in the Bay Islands, local community members are attempting to wrest control of tourism development and reshape it along lines that they feel are more in harmony with community needs and objectives. Again using a Costa Rican example, business owners and residents of the area adjacent to Manual Antonio National Park recently protested plans for a US$4 million tourism development project under construction on beachfront property close to the entrance of the park. The Italian owned project, *Olas del Pacifico*, includes nine, three-story, time-share apartment buildings and a shopping center, less than 100 meters from the beach and 250 meters from the park entrance within an endangered wetland area. Critics claim that building permits were acquired illegally and that both health and environmental rules are being violated. As of late 1998, the scheme was under investigation by the Costa Rican Prosecutor's Office of Ecological Crimes for alleged anomalies in the concession of building permits (Escofet, 1998a). Another example comes from the community of Cahuita located along Costa Rica's Caribbean coast. Reminiscent of NABIPLA's nascent struggles on the Bay Islands, the predominantly Afro-Caribbean and foreign residents of Cahuita are engaged in a variety of efforts to create a style of tourism stemming from their vision of community-based tourism. Residents have begun a number of projects to counter Cahuita's image as a dangerous place for tourists because of mounting drugs and crime, to construct necessary infrastructure (paved roads and sanitation systems), to advertise (through publication of tourist maps and magazines that are distributed to travel agencies), to train local residents as ecotourist guides, and to implement a series of cultural activities (short courses, dramatic events, brochures) designed to inform tourists about the community's residents. In 1995, the community won the right to administer and manage a portion of Cahuita National Park and obtained funding to build changing rooms and provide security guards for visiting tourists (Weir, 1998).

Stock markets around the world recently fell precipitously as the economic crisis that affected Asia in 1997 and Russia early in 1998 expanded to Latin America. In the 2 months from July 17 to September 18, 1998, the U.S.-based Dow Jones financial index fell 15%—from 9338 to 7896 points. Despite the subsequent upturn in the Dow, many economic forecasters are predicting a global economic slowdown for the foreseeable future, especially in so-called emerging markets. This could have unfortunate consequences on the expansion of international tourism and environmental conservation in Central America, particularly coupled with the ongoing decline in the prices of natural resource-based commodities upon which the region's economies also are heavily dependent. It is likely that dwindling export revenues would lead to declining national-level capacities to maintain existing conservation projects and to enforce tourism regulations. In all probability, a significant economic downturn also would intensify the exploitation of the region's natural resources through tourism and other sectors in an attempt to increase foreign exchange. These concerns are applicable to Central America as well as to other emerging markets.

These considerations are amplified in post-Mitch Central America, especially in the hardest hit country, Honduras, where tourism is regarded as the primary means of economic recovery. If the recent revision of the Honduran constitution does attract US$500 million in foreign investments in the Bay Islands and the North Coast as predicted, recent history suggests that adequate environmental regulation is unlikely. It is probable that the magnitude of such investments will further displace many Bay Islanders from their land and the coastal resources on which they depend—in the name of economic development and the reconstruction of their country. This, in turn, may exacerbate the already high level of conflict surrounding the growth of the tourism industry on the islands. It is profoundly ironic that the Bay Islands, which for so long were so marginal and antagonistic to Honduran polity, economy, society, and culture, should become the hope of Honduran economic recovery. If increased tourism is to advance national reconstruction and result in a "New Honduras" (using the phrase of the Honduran president, Carlos Flores) it must not only contribute to Honduras' foreign exchange earnings but also do so in a way that enhances the livelihoods of the majority of Honduran citizens and conserves the natural environment.

Depending on tourism as the principal means of economic recovery in Honduras and as a major avenue to economic growth throughout the isthmus is made more problematic in light of a number of persistent regional- and national-level obstacles. Among the most important of these is the continuing perception that Central America is a dangerous place for tourists, not only because of the prevalence of natural disasters, civil wars, political violence, and risks to human health but also because of rising crime. Not only in the Bay Islands has crime become a major concern. The U.S. State Department's Consular Information Sheets contain warnings about increasing crime and violence against tourists for every country in the isthmus: pickpocketing, house and car break-ins, robberies, and muggings are most prevalent but more violent crimes, such as carjackings, rapes, kidnappings, and even murders, are increasing as well (http://travel.state.gov). Although the level of violence against tourists is greatest in countries with higher overall levels of crime (i.e., Honduras, Guatemala, and El Salvador), growing crime also affected tourism in Costa Rica, perceived as the most politically stable country in the region. Rising crime and police corruption, including the murder and kidnappings of tourists, contributed to a serious drop in the number of international tourists to Costa Rica in 1996. The following year, Costa Rica initiated a system of T-shirt-clad "tourist police" to patrol the country's major resort areas and a 24-hour telephone hotline for tourists to report crimes.

In addition to rising crime, a deterioration of human rights in Central America has been noted by groups such as the Central American Human Rights Commission

(CODEHUCA). This has triggered a new wave of protests by local, regional, and international human rights groups, which fear a return to the violence of the 1980s. Violations of basic rights, especially the right to life, are becoming more frequent in Guatemala, Honduras, and El Salvador, according to the president of CODEHUCA. In Costa Rica, Panama, and Nicaragua violations mainly involve economic and social rights. In their latest annual report, Amnesty International identified Guatemala, El Salvador, and Honduras as the Central American countries with the worst human rights records (Amnesty International, 1998). Despite the efforts of the tourist operators quoted at the beginning of this section, Central America has done little to permanently counter its widespread image of political and social instability. Declining economies within and outside the region, enhanced internal poverty and desperation, and rising crime, violence, and human rights violations present major obstacles to the growth of Central America's tourist sector.

Recent research in the Caribbean on the effects of government incentives to encourage investment in the tourist sector suggest that such efforts play a smaller role in affecting new investment than generally believed (Mather & Todd, 1993). Rather, the primary concerns of potential investors include political stability, economic stability, labor unrest, customs duties on imported supplies and equipment, the costs of training, and seasonality of demand (Arthur Young Ltd., 1988). These conclusions have implications for Central American countries in terms of identifying the primary regional and national constraints to be eliminated or minimized if further investment is desired. Most national incentives already include generous tax and customs advantages for potential investors. Attempts at regional economic integration and the promotion of various types of tourism within the region also have begun to address problems of seasonality in tourist demand. As suggested above, however, the persistent and widespread constraints related to political instability and social unrest (and the associated images of Central America that these arouse among potential tourists) remain resistant to amelioration.

Toward More Comprehensive Tourism Policy

According to David Edgell (1987), most tourism policy has extremely narrow objectives: to maximize the number of international tourists and international tourist receipts in order to augment foreign exchange earnings and improve balance of payments. The much broader outcomes of tourism development, however, insinuate that tourism policy must be more comprehensive. This book raises a number of crucial questions related to tourism and conservation policy in the Bay Islands as well as in other ecologically fragile and politically complex areas of the Third World.

Important Questions

- What role should tourism play in national economies? In light of the unpredictability of tourism as an economic development strategy, how can tourism become part of more integrated development?

- Are there limits to the growth of tourism in light of the sector's dependence on high levels of environmental quality?
- Is the government of Honduras justified in promoting tourism on the Bay Islands in the name of national unity and economic growth? What are the implications of the Bay Islands' case for similar situations in which national governments attempt to encourage tourism in areas inhabited by independent and recalcitrant minorities?
- How best might governments reconcile national economic interests with local sociocultural, environmental, and ecological needs?
- In regard to local people, how might poorer islanders and ladino immigrants overcome several hundred years of ethnic animosity and sometimes violent conflict in order to collaborate to increase their power in affecting tourism development and conservation on the Bay Islands? Can participation in community-based tourism and conservation contribute to empowerment, increasing democracy, and improvement of the quality of life of local people in tourist areas while also maintaining the health of the environment?
- What is the role of international donors and NGOs in contexts of state-sponsored or sanctioned human rights abuses related to tourism and conservation efforts?

Policy, Planning, and Project Considerations

- **Limits to growth.** The accelerating growth of the tourism industry on the Bay Islands is a conspicuous example of short-term gain at the price of the long-term sustainability of the industry. The islands represent a case in which tourism growth (in combination with migration) likely has exceeded the maximum desirable level given the islands' current infrastructural development. This is suggested by the degree of environmental decline that has occurred as well as by the perceptions of tourists and many local people. The islands' are an example of the need for government, perhaps in collaboration with international donors and NGOs, to set limits on the growth of the industry—at least temporarily.
- **Reconcile contradictions between tourism development and environmental conservation.** Setting limits on the growth of tourism would be a step toward reconciling the conflicts between development and environmental goals on the islands. This contradiction is part of a broader deficiency in specifying the goals of tourism and conservation efforts, including the intended beneficiaries of such endeavors.
- **Increase collaboration among international funders, the state, and local communities.** There is a conspicuous need to integrate not only policy but also planning and projects. Tourism is a complex phenomenon that produces diverse and often contrary repercussions. The Bay Islands' example illustrates that tourism policy and planning must involve social, cultural, economic, political, gender, and environmental factors. Tourism is also a multilevel phenomenon that integrates social and cultural actors at many scales from the local to the global. These linkages must also be addressed by tourism policy and planning. Together

the multiple factors and levels of analysis that are part of the tourism process suggest the essential integration of actors at various levels and with various kinds of expertise, responsibility, and authority.

- **Promote community-based conservation and tourism.** Chapter 6 includes a series of recommendations designed to enhance community-based conservation and tourism development on the Bay Islands and elsewhere. The current state of the global economy, declining levels of foreign assistance, and other constraints insinuate the pragmatic necessity of community control. Such efforts should integrate existing local-level organizations and institutions when appropriate and also establish new institutions when necessary in order to ensure that all local-level stakeholders are represented.

- **Address the local reality.** Chapter 6 also emphasized the requirement that recognition of local complexity, history, and extra-local linkages be the foundation of tourism and conservation policy, planning, and projects. The Bay Islands are a diverse site, but other potential tourist locations also embody their own heterogeneity. The existence of place-specific diversity in itself advises that tourism development and conservation initiatives must be site specific. They require the integration and coordination of diverse values, interests, goals, and stakeholders. In the Bay Islands' case this implies that different projects, or aspects of project, would be appropriate for specific groups (poor islanders, ladinos, women, middle-class islanders, youth, etc.) and that different groups would have different roles in such initiatives.

- **Should assistance come with strings attached?** The Bay Islands are an example of tourism promotion in a region that heretofore was relatively independent of national polity, society, culture, and economy. Similar examples are found throughout Central America and other parts of the Third World, where tourism is promoted in locales inhabited largely by ethnic minorities or indigenous peoples who have antagonistic relationships with national governments. Unfortunately, in many tourist locations the resource rights of minorities often are not considered or respected. Many times the human rights of local inhabitants are violated. In the Bay Islands and elsewhere, foreign assistance (in constructing roads, airports, sanitation systems, etc.) often provides the initial foundation for the industry as well as facilitates its continued growth. What is the responsibility of international donors, assistance agencies, and NGOs in such instances? Faced with their own contradictory policies (working through national governments and also promoting local participation) in the context of the continuing reluctance of the GOH to devolve authority to the local level (despite the Law of Municipalities) and the clear exclusion of large segments of the islands' peoples, the IDB's involvement in the Bay Islands presents an important example of such a discordant situation.

While it is apparent that tourism development and conservation initiatives are political processes, policies and practical recommendations often do not go beyond this assertion. An alternative is to treat power and politics with appropriate respect by identifying the various groups involved in the processes: assessing their influence; tracing the linkages among them; and prescribing ways to negotiate conflicts and mobilize support. The probability of effective interventions would rise if contending forces were candidly addressed during the process of policy design and implementation through this kind of applied political ecological analysis.

Appendix: Research Methodology

The research results presented in this book are from a collaborative study of the related human (social, economic, nutritional, and health) and environmental effects of tourism development in the Bay Islands. The overall project uses a political ecology approach to analyze human–environmental interactions in three neighboring communities—Sandy Bay, West End, and Flowers Bay—located on the western end of Roatán. These communities were chosen for a number of reasons. First, at the time research began in 1991, that section of Roatán was a "hot spot" where tourism was growing explosively. Thus, the findings from these communities could be used to predict subsequent repercussions on other parts of the islands and elsewhere. Second, although tourism was growing rapidly, it appeared to be affecting communities quite differently (e.g., in terms of the degree and style of tourism). During the first year of the project, rapid assessment techniques (i.e., interviews with individual and focus groups; compilation of documentary, statistical, and technical reports; and field reconnaissance) were used to acquire initial information about the characteristics of the tourism industry as it was developing on Roatán. A small pilot study was carried out in order to test household-level survey instruments that were modifications of household surveys previously administered to men and women householders on the Honduran mainland. The second year of the project, 1992, field research emphasized the collection of baseline data through in-depth ethnographic and survey research in the three communities. Because national census data appeared inaccurate and out of date, research in each community began with preparing a base map and community census that served as sampling frames from which a 50% random sample of households was chosen for survey work. The preliminary community census also enabled researchers to determine more accurately the population of each community and to identify specific Spanish- and English-speaking households. Appropriate Spanish or English versions of the semistructured surveys were administered separately to women and men heads of households. Both the women's and men's surveys contained questions regarding attitudes toward tourism development. In addition, the surveys administered to men householders included questions regarding the economic options available to men and men's use of land, marine, and other natural resources. The women's surveys included a more detailed household census, a reproductive history, a material culture inventory of household goods, questions related to the economic activities (including domestic tasks) of women, family dietary patterns and nutritional problems, and a family health history. A specific section of the instrument included questions related to access, use, and treatment of water resources. A total of 249 interviews were administered. These interviews were essential not only for the collection of baseline data but also to help identify individuals for life history interviews. These were people who were especially well informed about their communities and the recent history of the Bay Islands. Audio tape-recorded oral histories were elicited from six individuals (two in each community) in order to document their unique perspectives on changes in the Bay Islands. Two additional types of semistructured survey instruments were administered the first and subsequent years of the project: a tourist survey administered to approximately 200 tourists per year, and a business survey that documented the annual growth of tourist-related businesses in the three communities.

In 1993 the project expanded to include a more specific nutritional study carried out in association with a second household survey that was administered to 225 householders. This was an abridged version of the survey administered the previous year. In collaboration with the St. Luke's Cornerstone Medical Mission and other local health care providers, anthropometric data from 168 children 5 years old and younger were collected in the study communities. A parent was also interviewed about dietary habits of each child. These data were linked with specific households via the household surveys.

Most recently the project expanded to include a water quality and environmental health component (Stonich, 1998). A critical addition was the investigation of the quality and quantity of potable water and of seawater quality near sites of human habitation. Although several water quality tests had been done previously, these had concentrated on seawater near prime dives sites and major resorts, in order to determine potential risks for tourists, rather than on potable water available to island residents and tourists alike or on seawater adjacent to local communities. With the assistance of Dr. Becky Myton, Professor of Biology at the National Autonomous University of Honduras (UNAH) and technical advisor to the recently created Honduran Ministry of Tourism (SEDA), a simple, but reliable, methodology and system for determining total coliform and fecal coliform (*Escherichia coli*) contamination of potable water and seawater was set up at project headquarters (for water testing methods used see HACH, 1993). More than 200 water samples from all available sources of potable water (community wells, private wells, rain water cisterns, natural springs [seeps]) and at selected points throughout the communities' water lines were collected and analyzed. Samples of "purified" bottled water were also analyzed. In addition, samples of seawater from shoreline sites adjacent to human settlements and beach areas were also collected and analyzed. Drinking water from all sources available in the three communities were tested for the presence and absence of total coliforms and *E. coli* on the theory that any presence of these bacteria was unacceptable (World Health Organization, 1993). Sufficient sampling of seawater was done to calculate the density of these bacteria using the method of "most probable number" (MPN) (HACH, 1993).

As assessment of human environmental health related to water quality was made based on analysis of diagnoses included in the more than 2,000 computerized patient records from the island's only no-fee, nongovernmental, primary care clinic, St. Luke's Medical Mission, located in Sandy Bay. Analysis focused on determining the extent to which fecal–oral water-borne infections (e.g., diarrheas, dysenteries, and enteric fevers), water-washed skin and eye infections, and water-related insect vector diseases (e.g., malaria and dengue fever) were affecting the local and tourist populations.

Bibliography

Adams, R. N. (1956). Cultural components of Central America. *American Anthropologist, 58,* 881-907.

Adams, R. N. (1957). *Cultural surveys of Panama, Nicaragua, Guatemala, El Salvador, Honduras.* (Scientific Publication No. 33). Washington, DC: Pan American Sanitary Bureau, Regional Office of the World Health Organization.

Alevizon, W. S. (1993). An ecological assessment of two marine reserves in the Bay Islands, Honduras. *Watersheds, wildlands, and wildlife of the Bay Islands, Honduras: A conservation strategy* (Appendix 5, pp. 203-216). Gainesville, FL: Tropical Research & Development, Inc.

Alexander, S. E., & McKenzie, K. L. (1996). *The ideal vs. the real: Conceptualizing ecotourism as a Third World development option in Belize.* Paper presented at the Society for Applied Anthropology, Baltimore, MD.

Allen, L. (1988, February 21). The Bay Islands of Honduras. *New York Times,* pp. xx19(N), xx19(L).

Amnesty International. (1998). *1998 annual report: A year of broken promises: Amnesty International.* http://www.amnesty.org.

Anderson, B. (1991). *Imagined communities.* New York: Verso.

Andrews, K. R. (Ed.). (1959). *English privateering voyages to the West Indies, 1588-1595* (Vol. III). Cambridge: Cambridge University Press.

Andrews, K. R. (Ed.). (1964). *Elizabethan privateering: English privateering during the Spanish War, 1585-1603.* Cambridge: Cambridge University Press.

Annis, S. (Ed.). (1992). *Poverty, natural resources, and public policy in Central America.* Washington, DC: Transaction Books.

Annis, S., & Hakim, P. (1988). *Direct to the poor: Grassroots development in Latin America.* Boulder, CO: Lynn Rienner.

Aquarium of the Americas. (1991). *Bacterial contamination in waters in and around Roatán, Islas de la Bahía, Honduras, Central America.* New Orleans: Author.

Aquarium of the Americas. (1992). *Bacterial contamination in waters in and around Roatán, Islas de la Bahía, Honduras, Central America.* New Orleans: Author.

Aquarium of the Americas. (1993). *Bacterial contamination in waters in and around Roatán, Islas de la Bahía, Honduras, Central America.* New Orleans: Author.

Arthur Young Ltd. (1988). *A study of the impact of tourism investment incentives in the Caribbean Region: Report for the Caribbean Development Bank.* Bahamas: Author.

Ascher, W. (1995). *Communities and sustainable forestry in developing countries.* San Francisco: ICS Press.

Barzetti, V., & Rovinski, Y. (Eds.). (1992). *Toward a green Central America: Integrating conservation and development.* West Hartford, CT: Kumarian Press.

Basch, H. (1992, January 12). Honduras' Treasure Island in world of its own. *Los Angeles Times,* pp. L10, L11, L18.

Bay Islands Conservation Association. (1997). *Conserving biodiversity in the Sandy Bay-West End Marine Reserve on Roatán and the Turtle Harbour Wildlife Refuge on Utila* [press release]. Roatán: Author.

Bjorndal, K.A., & Bolten, A. B. (1992). Spatial distribution of Green Turtle nests at Tortuguero, Costa Rica. *Copeia*, 45-53.

Bjorndal, K. A., Bolten, A. B., & Lagueux, C. J. (1993). Decline of the nesting population of Hawksbill Turtles at Tortuguero, Costa-Rica. *Conservation Biology, 7*(4), 925-927.

Bjorndal, K. A., & Carr, A. (1989). Variation in clutch size and egg size in the Green Turtle nesting populations at Tortuguero, Costa Rica. *Herpetologica*, 181-189.

Blaikie, P. (1985). *The political economy of soil erosion in developing countries.* London: Longman.

Blaikie, P., & Brookfield, H. (1987). *Land degradation and society.* London/New York: Methuen.

Blank, U. (1989). *The community tourism imperative: The necessity, the opportunities, its potential.* State College, TX: Venture Publishing.

Boo, E. (1992). *The ecotourism boom: Planning for development and management* (Vol. 2). Washington, DC: World Wildlife Fund, Wildlands and Human Needs.

Breaking out of the tourist trap—part one. (1990a). *Cultural Survival Quarterly*, 14(2).

Breaking out of the tourist trap—part two. (1990b). *Cultural Survival Quarterly*, 14(2).

Briguglio, L., Archer, B., Jafari, J., & Wall, G. (Eds.). (1996). *Sustainable tourism in islands and small island states: Issues and policies* (Vol. 1). London/New York: Pinter.

Briguglio, L., Butler, R., Harrison, D., & Filho, W. L. (Eds.). (1996). *Sustainable tourism in islands and small island states: Case studies* (Vol. 2). London/New York: Pinter.

Britton, R. (1979). The image of the Third World in tourism marketing. *Annals of Tourism Research, 6*, 318-329.

Britton, S. G. (1982). The political economy of tourism in the Third World. *Annals of Tourism Research, 9*, 331-358.

Britton, S. (1987). Tourism in small developing countries. In S. Britton & W. C. Clarke (Eds.), *Ambiguous alternative: Tourism in small developing countries* (pp. 167-194). Suva: University of the South Pacific.

Britton, S. (1989). Tourism, dependency and development: A mode of analysis. In T. V. Singh, H. L. Theuns, & F. M. Go (Eds.), *Towards appropriate tourism: The case of developing countries* (Vol. 11, pp. 93-116). Frankfurt am Main/Bern/New York/Paris: Peter Lang.

Britton, S., & Clarke, W. C. (Eds.). (1987). *Ambiguous alternative: Tourism in small developing countries.* Suva: University of the South Pacific.

Brohman, J. (1996). New directions in tourism for Third World development. *Annals of Tourism Research, 23*(1), 48-70.

Brown, M., & Wyckoff-Baird, B. (1992). *Designing integrated conservation and development projects.* Washington, DC: Biodiversity Support Program of the World Wildlife Fund, The Nature Conservancy, and the World Resources Institute.

Brown, V. L. (1922). *Anglo-Spanish relations in America in the closing years of the Colonial era* (Vol. 5). Baltimore: Williams & Wilkins.

Bruner, G. Y. (1993). *Evaluating a model of private-ownership conservation: Ecotourism in the Community Baboon Sanctuary in Belize.* Atlanta: Georgia Institute of Technology.

Bryant, R. L. (1992). Political ecology: An emerging research agenda in Third World studies. *Political Geography, 11*(2), 12-36.

Bulmer, M. (1985). The rejuvenation of community studies? Neighbors, networks, and policy. *Sociological Review, 33*(3), 430-448.

Carr, A. Z. (1963). *The world and William Walker.* New York/Evanston/London: Harper & Row Publishers.

Castonguay, G., & Brown, A. (1993). "Plastic surgery tourism" proving a boon for Costa's surgeons. *Canadian Medical Association Journal, 148*(1), 74-76.

Central American presidents draw up joint plan to develop regional tourism industry. (1996). *Latin America Data Base, 1*(3).

Cernea, M. (1985). *Putting people first: Sociological variables in rural development.* London and New York: Oxford University Press.

Cernea, M. M. (1992). *The building blocks of participation: Testing bottom-up planning* [World Bank Discussion Papers]. Washington, DC: World Bank.

Chambers, R. (1983). *Rural development: Putting the last first.* London: Longman.

Chambers, R. (1993). *Challenging the professions: Frontiers for rural development.* London: Intermediate Technology Publications.

Chambers, R. (1994a). The origins and practice of participatory rural appraisal. *World Development, 22*(7), 953–969.

Chambers, R. (1994b). Participatory rural appraisal (PRA): Analysis of experience. *World Development, 22*(9), 1253–1268.

Chambers, R. (1994c). Participatory rural appraisal: Challenges, potentials, and paradigms. *World Development, 22*(10), 1437–1454.

Chambers, R. (1995). *Poverty and livelihoods: Whose reality counts?* (Report DP 347). Brighton, England: Institute of Development Studies.

Chambers, R. E., & McBeth, M. K. (1992). Community encouragement: Returning to the basis for community development. *Journal of the Community Development Society, 23*(2), 20–38.

Chant, S. (1992). Tourism in Latin America: Perspectives from Mexico and Costa Rica. In D. Harrison (Ed.), *Tourism and the less developed countries* (pp. 85–101). London: Belhaven Press.

Checchi, V. (1959). *Honduras: A problem in economic development.* New York: Twentieth Century Fund.

Cheung, W. H. S., Hung, R. P. S., Chang K. C. K., & Kleevens, J. W. L. (1991). Epidemiological study of beach water pollution and health-related bathing water standards in Hong Kong. *Water, Science, and Technology, 23*, 243–252.

Christensen, J. A., & Robinson, J. W. (1980). *Community development in America.* Ames: University of Iowa Press.

Clark, J. R., & Smith, A. H. (1988). *Coastal resources management program for the Bay Islands, Honduras.* Washington, DC: Peace Corps, Honduras, Central America and the Office of Training and Program Supports.

Clark, S. (1946). *All the best in Central America.* New York: Dodd, Mead & Company.

Coffey, B. (1993). Investment incentives as a means of encouraging tourism development: The case of Costa Rica. *Bulletin Latin American Research, 12*(1), 83–90.

Cohen, E. (1978). The impact of tourism on the physical environment. *Annals of Tourism Research, 5*, 215–237.

Cohen, J., & Uphoff, N. (1977). *Rural development participation: Concepts and measures for project design, implementation, and evaluation.* Ithaca, NY: Rural Development Committee, Cornell University.

Conroy, M. E., Murray, D. L., & Rosset, P. M. (1996). *A cautionary tale: Failed U.S. development policy in Central America.* Boulder/London: Lynn Rienner.

Crossette, B. (1998, April 12). Surprises in the global tourism boom. *The New York Times*, pp. WK 5.

Dalling, J. (1779). *Some observations on the probability of success in case an attack should be made on . . . Nicaragua, Honduras, and Guatemala.* London: British Museum Manuscript.

Davidson, W., & Counce, M. (1989). Mapping the distribution of Indians in Central America. *Cultural Survival Quarterly, 13*(3), 37–40.

Davidson, W. V. (1974). *Historical geography of the Bay Islands, Honduras.* Birmingham: Southern University Press.

Dieke, P. U. C. (1993). Tourism and development policy in The Gambia. *Annals of Tourism Research, 20,* 423–449.

Dulin, P. (1979). *Natural resources conservation and watershed management in Roatán, Bay Islands, Honduras.* Tegucigalpa, Honduras: Watershed Management Unit, Department of Forestry, Honduran Forestry Development Corporation.

Duncan, M. (1990). *The Bay Islands or the gentle art of cutting the painter* (Occasional Papers in Caribbean Studies). Warwick: Centre for Caribbean Studies, University of Warwick.

Eadington, W. R., & Smith, V. L. (1992). Introduction: The emergence of alternative forms of tourism. In V. L. Smith & W. R. Eadington (Eds.), *Tourism alternatives: Potentials and problems in the development of tourism* (pp. 1–12). Philadelphia: University of Pennsylvania Press.

Edgell, D. L. (1987). The formulation of tourism policy — a managerial approach. In J. R. B. Ritchie & C. R. Goeldner (Eds.), Travel, tourism, and hospitality research (pp. 23–33). New York: John Wiley & Sons.

Edwards, F. (Ed.). (1988). *Environmentally sound tourism in the Caribbean.* Alberta, Canada: The University of Calgary Press.

Edwards, M., & Hulme, D. (1992a). *Making a difference: NGOs and development in a changing world.* London: Earthscan Publications.

Edwards, M., & Hulme, D. (1992b). Scaling up NGO impact on development: Learning from experience. *Development in Practice, 2*(2), 77–91.

Edwards, M., & Hulme, D. (Eds.). (1996a). *Beyond the magic bullet: NGO performance and accountability in the Post-Cold War World.* West Hartford, CT: Kumarian Press.

Edwards, M., & Hulme, D. (1996b). Too close for comfort? The impact of official aid on non-governmental organizations. *World Development, 24*(6), 961–973.

Egret Communications. (1999). *The official Honduras tourism response to Hurricane Mitch.* http://www.hondurasmitch.com.

Enloe, C. (1989). *Bananas, beaches, and bases.* Berkeley: University of California Press.

Escofet, G. (1996, December 27). Boosts, setbacks for the environment. *Tico Times, II*(52). http://ticotimes.co.cr/.

Escofet, G. (1998a, May 29). Development raises storm. *Tico Times, IV*(20). http://ticotimes.co.cr/.

Escofet, G. (1998b, September 4). Mixed signals on tourism. *Tico Times, IV*(34). http://ticotimes.co.cr/.

Evans, D. K. (1966). *The people of French Harbour: A study of conflict and change on Roatán Island.* Doctoral dissertation, University of California, Berkeley, CA.

Evans-Pritchard, D. (1993). Mobilization of tourism in Costa Rica. *Annals of Tourism Research, 20*(4), 778–779.

Faber, D. (1992). *Environment under fire.* New York: Monthly Review Press.

Firmen convenio para construir hotel de la cadena Holiday Inn. (1997, January 24). *La Prensa* (online edition). http://www.laprensahn.com/econoarc/9701/e24003.html.

Fodor, E., & Fisher, R. C. (Eds.). (1977). *Fodor's Caribbean, Bahamas, and Bermuda.* New York: McKay.

Foer, G., & Olsen, S. (Eds.). (1992). *Central America's coasts: Profiles and agenda for action.* Narragansett: University of Rhode Island.

Frehsee, R. (1997, October). The Bay Islands: A paradise of sand and sea. *Skin Diver, 46*(10), 86–94.

Frink, S. (1994, May). Aggressor's Caribbean fleet. *Skin Diver, 43*(5), 80–93.

Fussell, P. (1980). *Abroad: British literary traveling between the wars.* New York: Oxford Press.

Getino, O. (1990). *Turismo y desarrollo en America Latina* (1st ed.). Mexico: Editorial Limusa.

Ghimire, K. B., & Pimbert, M. P. (1997). Social change and conservation: An overview of issues and concepts. In K. B. Ghimire & M. P. Pimbert (Eds.), *Social change and conservation: Environmental politics and impacts of national parks and protected areas* (pp. 1–45). London: Earthscan.

Gobierno de Honduras/Programa de las Naciones Unidas para el Desarrollo. (1992a). *Estudio de factibilidad tecnica y economica del ordenamiento ambiental de desarrollo de las Islas de la Bahia: Volumen III—Evaluacion financiera y socio-economica.* Tegucigalpa: Author.

Gobierno de Honduras/Programa de las Naciones Unidas para el Desarrollo. (1992b). *Estudio de factibilidad tecnica y economica del ordenamiento ambiental de desarrollo de las Islas de la Bahia: Volumen IV—Manejo de recursos marinos y costeros.* Tegucigalpa: Author.

Godfrey, H. F. (1970). *Your Central American guide.* New York: Funk and Wagnalls.

Gollin, J. D., & Mader, R. (1998). *Honduras: Adventures in nature.* Santa Fe, NM: John Muir Publications.

Gomara, F. L. d. (1966). *Cortez, the life of the conqueror by his secretary, Francisco Lopez de Gomara* (L. B. Simpson, Trans./Ed.). Berkeley/Los Angeles: University of California.

Gonzalez, N. L. S. (1969). *Black Carib household structure: A study of migration and modernization.* Seattle/London: University of Washington Press.

Gonzalez, N. L. (1979). From Black Carib to Garifuna, the coming of age of an ethnic group. *42nd International Congress of Americanists Proceedings, 6,* 577–588.

Goodenough, W. H. (1966). *Cooperation in change: An anthropological approach to community development.* New York: Wiley.

Gordon, D. G. (1993, December). An octopus' garden: A guide to the world's marine parks and reserves, the sanctuaries of the sea. *Hemispheres,* 68–80.

Gormsen, E. (1988). Tourism in Latin America: Spatial distribution and impact on regional change. *Applied Geography and Development, 32,* 65–80.

Government of Honduras. (1997). *Executive Order: Bay Islands National Marine Park* (Executive order Number 28279, June 7). Tegucigalpa: Author.

Graham, R. (n.d.). *The Bay Islanders: Evolution of a cultural identity* [manuscript]. University of the West Indies.

Green, H., & Hunter, C. (1992). The environmental impact assessment of tourism development. In P. J. a. B. Thomas (Ed.), *Perspectives in tourism policy.* London: Mansell.

Griffin, W. (1998a, January 5). Honduran sailors come home from the sea. *Honduras This Week* (Online edition 87). http://www.marrder.com/htw/.

Griffin, W. (1998b, February 9). Traditional (Bay Island) island homes in jeopardy. *Honduras This Week* (Online edition 92). http://www.marrder.com/htw/.

Gruson, L. (1988, October 11). On scorned isles they'd have Victoria whipped. *New York Times,* pp. 4(N), A4(L).

Guha, R. (1990). *Unquiet woods.* Berkeley: University of California Press.

Guha, R., & Martinez-Alier, J. (1997). *Varieties of environmentalism: Essays North and South.* London: Earthscan.

Gunson, P. (1996, September 28). Marketing men put curse of tourism industry on Maya. *The Guardian,* p. 14.

HACH Corporation. (1993). *HACH analytical procedures: Coliform procedures.* Loveland, CO: Author.

Halcrow and Partners. (1983). *Plan de control ambiental de la Isla de Roatán.* Tegucigalpa, Honduras: Direccion General de Urbanismo/SECOPT.

Harris, B. (1996, March 8). Charges filed in parkland road construction. *The Tico Times, II*(10). http://infoweb.magi.com/calypso/ttimes.html.

Harrison, D. (1996). Sustainability and tourism: Reflections from a muddy pool. In L. Briguglio, B. Archer, J. Jafari, & G. Wall (Eds.), *Sustainable tourism in islands and small states: Issues and policies* (Vol. 1, pp. 69–89). London/New York: Pinter.

Haylock-Sanabria, J. R., Reina, M., & Matute, F. L. (1994). *Estudios Iniciales de Impacto Ambiental en Las Areas Protegidas del Litoral Atlantico.* La Ceiba, Honduras: Programa Ambiental y de Apoyo al Desarrollo de la Red Ambiental de Canada (PAAD), Union Quebescence para La Conservacion de la Naturaleza (UQCN), Grupo Regional de Apoyo a las Areas Protegidas del Litoral Atlantico (GRAPLA), Proyecto de Reforzamiento e Integracion de Instituciones Conservacionistas de la Costa Norte de Honduras GRAPLA-UQCN.

Hill, C. (1990). The paradox of tourism in Costa Rica. *Cultural Survival Quarterly, 14*(1), 14–19.

Hitchcock, R. K. (1995). Centralization, resource depletion, and coercive conservation among the Tyua of the Northeastern Kalahari. *Human Ecology, 23*(2), 169–199.

Holtz, C., & Alexander, S. (1995). *Ecotourism development in Belize: A critical review and policy analysis* [manuscript]. Baylor University.

Honduras Tourist Board. (1985). *Bay Islands* [pamphlet], Tegucigalpa, Honduras: Author.

Horowitz, M., & Painter, T. (1986). *Anthropology and rural development in West Africa.* Boulder, CO: Westview Press.

Horwich, R. H. (1990). How to develop a community sanctuary: An experimental approach to the conservation of private lands. *ORYX, 24*(2), 95–102.

Horwich, R. H., & Lyon, J. (1998). Community-based development as a conservation tool: The Community Baboon Sanctuary and the Gales Point Manatee Reserve. In R. B. Primack, D. B. Bray, H. A. Galletti, & I. Ponciano (Eds.), *Timber, tourists, and temples: Conservation and development in the Maya Forest of Belize, Guatemala, and Mexico* (pp. 343–364). Washington, DC: Island Press.

Houlson, J. H. (1934). *Blue Blaze: Danger and delight in strange islands of Honduras.* London: Duckworth.

Hulme, D. (1994). Social development research and the third sector: NGOs as users and subjects of social inquiry. In D. Booth (Ed.), *Rethinking social development: Theory, research, and practice* (pp. 251–279). Harlow, England: Longman Scientific & Technical.

Hunter, C., & Green, H. (1995). *Tourism and the environment: A sustainable relationship?* London/New York: Routledge.

Inter-American Development Bank. (1992). *Honduras: Bay Islands environmental management project (HO-0028) loan proposal.* Washington, DC: Author.

Inter-American Development Bank. (1994). *Programa de manejo ambiental de las Islas de la Bahia.* Washington, DC: Author.

Inter-American Development Bank. (1996). *Bay Islands environmental management project—summary.* http://www.iadb.org

Inter-American Development Bank. (1997a). *Latin America's invisible challenge: Afro-Latin Americans are finding a political voice.* http://www.iadb.org/IDB/Text/THEIDB/Jan97/invisib.html.

Inter-American Development Bank. (1997b). *Resource book on participation.* http://www.iadb.org/english/policies/participate/.

International Monetary Fund. (various years). *Balance of payments statistics yearbook.* Washington, DC: Author.

Island Resources Foundation. (1996). *Tourism and coastal resources degradation in the wider Caribbean.* http://www.irf.org/irunep.htm.

Jackson, N. B. (1970, March 8). Bay Islands: Adventure for the hardy. *New York Times*, Travel and Resorts, pp. 29.

Jacobson, S. K., & Lopez, A. F. (1994). Biological impacts of ecotourism: Tourists and nesting turtles in Tortuguero National Park, Costa Rica. *Wildlife Society Bulletin, 22*(3), 414–419.

Jacobson, S. K., & Robles, R. (1992a). Ecotourism, sustainable development, and conservation education—development of a tour guide training program in Tortuguero, Costa-Rica. *Environmental Management, 16*(6), 701–713.

Jacobson, S. K., & Robles, R. (1992b). Ecotourism, sustainable development, and conservation education: Development of a tour guide training program in Tortuguero, Costa Rica. *Environmental Management, 16*(6), 701–714.

Jamal, T. B., & Getz, D. (1995). Collaboration theory and community tourism planning. *Annals of Tourism Research, 22*, 186–204.

Jefferys, T. (1970). *A description of the Spanish Islands and settlements on the coast of the West Indies.* New York: AMS Press. (Original work published 1792, St. Martin's Lane, near Charing Cross, London)

Johnson, T. (1994a, January 1). Americans' loss of Honduras properties irks D.C. *Miami Herald*, p. 20A.

Johnson, T. (1994b, December 4). Outdoors beckons in Central America. *Miami Herald*, p. 1F.

Jones, D. R. W. (1970). The Caribbean coast of Central America: A case of multiple fragmentation. *The Professional Geographer, 12*(5), 260–266.

Jones, D. W., & Glean, C. A. (1971). The English speaking communities of Honduras and Nicaragua. *Caribbean Quarterly, 17*(2), 50–61.

Jukofsky, D. (1993). Ecotourism: Eco-worries for Costa Rica. *Landscape Architecture, 83*(10), 49.

Keenagh, P. (1937, January 16). A ceded British colony, the Bay Islands. *The Times-London*, pp. 13–14.

Keenagh, P. (1938). *Mosquito Coast: An account of a journey through the jungles of Honduras.* Boston: Houghton Mifflin Co.

Kilbracken, L. (1967, March). I found Treasure Island. *Argosy*, 65, 122.

Kottak, C. P. (1995). Participatory development: Rhetoric and reality. *Development Anthropologist, 13*(1–2), 1, 3–8.

Krok, J. (1988, August). Using Z Score as a descriptor of discrete changes in growth. *Nutritional Support Services, 6*(8), 14–21.

Laarman, J. G., & Perdue, R. R. (1989). Science tourism in Costa Rica. *Annals of Tourism Research, 16*, 205–215.

Lanfant, M.-F., & Graburn, N. H. H. (1992). International tourism reconsidered: The principal of the alternative. In V. L. Smith & W. R. Eadington (Eds.), *Tourism alternatives: Potentials and problems in the development of tourism* (pp. 88–112). Philadelphia: University of Pennsylvania Press.

Larson, P., Freudenberger, M., & Wyckoff-Baird, B. (1997). *Lessons from the field: A review of World Wildlife Fund's experience with integrated conservation and development projects 1985–1996.* Washington, DC: World Wildlife Fund.

Leach, M. (1961). Jamaican duppy lore. *Journal of American Folklore, 74*, 207–215.

Lee, D. N. B., & Snepenger, D. J. (1992). An ecotourism assessment of Tortuguero, Costa Rica. *Annals of Tourism Research, 19*(2), 367–370.

Levy, D. E., & Lerch, P. B. (1991). Tourism as a factor in development: Implications for gender and work in Barbados. *Gender & Society, 5*(1), 67–85.

Li, T. M. (1996). Images of community: Discourse and strategy in property relations. *Development and Change, 27*, 501–527.

Lindberg, K. (1991). *Policies for maximizing nature tourism's ecological and economic benefits.* Washington, DC: World Resources Institute.

Lindberg, K., & Enriquez, J. (1994). *An analysis of ecotourism's economic contribution to conservation and development in Belize* [summary report]. University of Virginia.

Lindberg, K., Enriquez, J., & Sproule, K. (1996). Ecotourism questioned: Case studies from Belize. *Annals of Tourism Research, 23*(3), 543-562.

Little, P., & Horowitz, M. (1987). Social science perspectives on land, ecology, and development. In P. Little & M. Horowitz (Eds.), *Lands at risk in the Third World: Local level perspectives* (pp. 1-16). Boulder: Westview.

Little, P. D. (1994). The link between local participation and improved conservation: A review of issues and experiences. In D. Western, R. M. Wright, & S. C. Strum (Eds.), *Natural connections: Perspectives in community-based conservation* (pp. 347-372). Washington, DC/Covelo, CA: Island Press.

Long, E. H. (1949). *O. Henry: The man and his work.* Philadelphia: University of Pennsylvania Press.

Lord, D. G. (1975). *Money order economy: Remittances in the island of Utila.* Doctoral dissertation, University of California, Riverside, CA.

Love, A. R. (1991). Participatory development and democracy. *OECD Observer, 173,* 4-6.

Luttinger, N. (1997). Community-based coral reef conservation in the Bay Islands of Honduras. *Ocean & Coastal Management, 36*(1-3), 11-22.

Lynch, O. J., & Talbott, K. (1995). *Balancing acts: Community-based forest management and national law in Asia and the Pacific.* Washington, DC: World Resources Institute.

Marin, M. (1993). *Status of the natural resources of the Bay Islands.* Washington, DC: Inter-American Development Bank.

Mascia, M. (1998, August 31). *Marine parks and protected areas in the wider Caribbean.* http://www.irf.org/irmascia.html.

Mather, S., & Todd, G. (1993). *Tourism in the Caribbean.* London: Economist Intelligence Unit.

Mathieson, A., & Wall, G. (1982). *Tourism: Economic, physical and social impacts.* New York: John Wiley & Sons, Inc.

McNeely, J., & Miller, K. (1984). National parks, conservation, and development: The role of protected areas in sustaining society. *Proceedings of the World Congress on National Parks*, Bali, Indonesia, 11-22 October 1982. Washington, DC: Smithsonian Institution Press.

McNeely, J. A. (Ed.). (1995). *Expanding partnerships in conservation.* Washington, DC/Covelo, CA: Island Press.

Michell, R. C. (1850, August). A statistical account and description of the island of Ruatan. *Colburn's United Service Magazine and Naval and Military Journal,* 541-546.

Mieczkowski, Z. (1995). *Environmental issues of tourism and recreation.* Lanham/New York/London: University Press of America, Inc.

Miller, M. L., & Auyong, J. (Eds.). (1990). *Proceedings of the 1990 Congress on Coastal and Marine Tourism. Volumes I and II.* Honolulu, HI/Newport, OR: National Coastal Resources Research & Development Institute.

Miller, M. L., & Auyong, J. (1991). Coastal zone tourism: A potent force affecting environment and society. *Marine Policy, 15*(2), 75-99.

Mitchell-Hedges, F. A. (1954). *Danger my ally.* (1st ed.). Boston/Toronto: Little, Brown and Company.

Murphy, P. (1985). *Tourism: A community tourism approach.* New York: Methuen.

Nance, J. V. (1970). *Resources for tourism on the island of Roatán, Republic of Honduras.* Master of Arts thesis, University of Colorado, Boulder, CO.

Native Bay Islanders Professional and Labourers Association. (1995, May). *Bay Islanders' Echo: The Way We See Things, 1*(1), 1-20.

Neider, C. (1952). Philip Ashton's own account (1722). In C. Neider (Ed.), *Great shipwrecks and castaways: Authentic accounts of adventures at sea.* New York: Harper & Brothers Publishers.

Neighbors to aid Mayan ruins. (1991, June 27). *New York Times*, p. 20.

Nelson, J. G., Butler, R., & Wall, G. (Eds.). (1993). *Tourism and sustainable development: Monitoring, planning, managing* (Vol. 37). Waterloo: University of Waterloo.

Neumann, R. P. (1992). Political ecology of wildlife conservation in the Mt Meru area of northeast Tanzania. *Land Degradation and Rehabilitation, 3*, 85-98.

Newton, A. P. (1914). *The colonising activities of the English Puritans.* New Haven: Yale University Press.

Norris, R., Wilber, J. S., & Marin, L. O. M. (1998). Community-based ecotourism in the Maya Forest. In R. B. Primack, D. B. Bray, H. A. Galletti, & I. Ponciano (Eds.), *Timber, tourists, and temples: Conservation and development in the Maya Forest of Belize, Guatemala, and Mexico* (pp. 327-342). Washington, DC: Island Press.

Oliver-Smith, A. (1999, April). Environment and disaster in Honduras: The social construction of Hurricane Mitch. *Newsletter-Anthropology and the Environment Section, 1*, http://dizzy.library.arizona.edu/ej/ipe/anthenv/newsletter/9904.html.

Oliver-Smith, A., Arrones, F. J., & Arcal, J. L. (1989). Tourist development and the struggle for local resource control. *Human Organization, 48*(4), 345-350.

Olson, M. S. (1994, October 16). Honduras puts itself on the map; Caribbean beaches, offshore islands and bargain prices attract more and more visitors. *New York Times*, pp. xx12(N), xx18(L).

Painter, M., & Durham, W. (Eds.). (1995a). *The social causes of environmental destruction in Latin America.* Ann Arbor: University of Michigan Press.

Painter, M., & Durham, W. R. (1995b). Introduction. In M. Painter & W. Durham (Eds.), *The social causes of environmental destruction in Latin America.* (pp. 1-24). Ann Arbor: University of Michigan Press.

Pan American Health Organization. (1994). Honduras. In *Health conditions in the Americas—volume 2* (pp. 252-265). Washington, DC: Author.

PANOS. (1995). *Ecotourism—part 1.* http://www.oneworld.org/panos/panos_eco2.html

Parsons, J. J. (1954). English speaking settlement of the western Caribbean. *Yearbook of the Association of Pacific Coast Geographers, 16*, 3-16.

Pattullo, P. (1997). *Last resorts: The cost of tourism in the Caribbean.* London: Cassell.

Pearce, D. (1989). *Tourist development* (2nd ed.). Harlow: Longman Scientific & Technical.

Peet, R., & Watts, M. (1993). Introduction: Development theory and environment in an age of market triumphalism. *Economic Geography, 69*(3), 227-253.

Peluso, N. (1993). Coercing conservation: The politics of state resource control. *Global Environmental Change, 3*(2), 199-218.

Peluso, N. L. (1992). *Rich forests, poor people: Resource control and resistance in Java.* Berkeley: University of California Press.

Peluso, N. L., Vandergeest, P., & Potter, L. (1995). Social aspects of forestry in Southeast Asia: A review of postwar trends in the scholarly literature. *Journal of Southeast Asian Studies, 26*(1), 196(23).

Pettrie, G. H. (1996, August/September). Bay Islands: Honduran paradise buys U.S. products. *AgExporter*, 20-21.

Pigram, J. J. (1980). Environmental implications of tourism development. *Annals of Tourism Research, 7*, 554-583.

Pi-Sunyer, O., & Thomas, R. B. (1997). Tourism, environmentalism, and cultural survival in Quintana Roo. In B. R. Johnston (Ed.), *Life and death matters: Human rights and the environment at the end of the millenium* (pp. 187-212). Walnut Creek/London/Delhi: Altamira Press.

Place, S. (1995). Ecotourism for sustainable development: Oxymoron or plausible strategy. *GeoJournal, 35*(2), 161-173.

Place, S. E. (1988). The impact of national park development on Tortuguero, Costa Rica. *Journal of Cultural Geography, 9*(1), 37-52.

Place, S. E. (1991). Nature tourism and rural development in Tortuguero. *Annals of Tourism Research, 18*(2), 186-201.

Plans for sustainable development: Foundation names board of directors, representatives elected to presidential commission. (1993, October/November). *Coconut Telegraph, 8,* 3.

Pleumarom, A. (1994). The political economy of tourism. *The Ecologist, 24*(4), 142-148.

Poirier, R. A., & Wright, S. (1993). The political economy of tourism in Tunisia. *Journal of Modern African Studies, 31*(1), 149-162.

Porter, W. S. (1904). *Cabbages and kings.* New York: McClure, Phillips.

Presidents push for tourism integration. (1996, May 12). *Central American News.* http://infoweb.magi.com/crica/news/ca10.html.

Primack, R. B. (Ed.). (1998). *Timber, tourists, and temples: Conservation and development in the Maya Forest of Belize, Guatemala, and Mexico.* Washington, DC: Island Press.

Princen, T., & Finger, M. (1994). *Environmental NGOs in world politics: Linking the local and the global.* London/New York: Routledge.

Rahnema, M. (1993). Participation. In W. Sachs (Ed.), *The development dictionary: A guide to knowledge as power* (pp. 116-131). London/New York: Zed Books.

Reed, M. (1997). Power relations and community-based tourism planning. *Annals of Tourism Research, 24*(3), 566-591.

Rijsberman, F. (n.d.). *Conflict management and consensus building for integrated coastal management in Latin America and the Caribbean* (draft report). Delft, The Netherlands: Resource Analysis.

Ritchie, L. H., Fothergill, W. R., Oliver, R. R., & Wulfing, M. E. (1965). *A regional study of tourist development in Central America.* Tegucigalpa, Honduras: Central Bank for Economic Integration.

Rivas, C. A. (1990, November/December). The Mayan World: For the development of Central American tourism. *Aboard, 14,* 68-72.

Roberts, H. (1979). *Community development: Learning and action.* Toronto: University of Toronto Press.

Roberts, O. W. (1827). *Narrative of voyages on the East Coast and in the interior of Central America.* Edinburgh: Constable and Company.

Rocheleau, D. E., Slayter, B. P., & Wangari, E. (1996). *Feminist political ecology: Global issues and local experience.* London/New York: Routledge.

Rodman, S. (1966). *The road to Panama.* New York: Hawthorn Books, Inc.

Rose, R. H. (1904). *Utila: Past and present.* Dansville, NY: F. A. Owen Publishing Co.

Rosenzweig, H. (1998a, September 14). Copan update (images of Honduras). *Honduras This Week* (Online edition 123). http://www.marrder.com/htw/.

Rosenzweig, H. (1998b, March 19). Copan update (tourism I). *Honduras This Week* (Online edition 97). http://www.marrder.com/htw/.

Rosenzweig, H. (1999, February 15). Article 107's reform could bring more tourist bucks to Honduras. *Honduras This Week* (Online edition 145). http://www.marrder.com/htw/.

Royte, E. (1992). Imagining *Paseo Pantera. Audubon, 94*(6), 76-89.

Sauer, C. O. (1966). *The early Spanish Main.* Berkeley/Los Angeles: University of California Press.

Schmink, M., & Wood, C. (1987). The political ecology of Amazonia. In P. D. Little & M. M. Horowitz (Eds.), *Lands at risk in the Third World: Local perspectives.* Boulder: Westview Press.

Schmitt, E. (1998, January 7). Senators' tour includes 2 nights at island resort. *New York Times,* pp. A12(N), A15(L).

Schwartz, N., Deruyttere, A., Huntley, S., Stonich, S., & Kottak, C. (1996). *Community consultation, sustainable development and the Inter-American Development Bank: A concept paper.* Washington, DC: Inter-American Development Bank.

Schwartz, N. B. (1981). Anthropological views of community and community development. *Human Organization, 40*(4), 313-322.

Secretaria de Educacion Publica. Direccion General de Educacion Primaria. Servicio de Alimentacion Escolar de Honduras/Instituto de Nutricion de Centro America y Panama. (1987). *Primer censo de talla en escolares de primer grado de educacion primaria de la Republica de Honduras.* Tegucigalpa, Honduras: Author.

Secretaria de Planificacion, Coodinacion y Presupuesto. (1989). *Censo nacional de poblacion y vivienda.* Tegucigalpa, Honduras: Author.

Secretaria de Estado en los Despachos de Recursos Naturales y Ambiente/Proyecto Manejo Ambiental Islas de la Bahia. (1997). *Expediente tecnico-administrativo para la creacion del area protegida marina de las Islas de la Bahia, Honduras.* Tegucigalpa, Honduras: Author.

Seidl, A. (1996). *Performance features of a local nongovernmental organization in natural resource management: The case of the Bay Islands Conservation Association.* Doctoral dissertation, University of Florida, Gainesville, FL.

Selin, S., & Beason, K. (1991). Interorganizational relations in tourism. *Annals of Tourism Research, 18*, 639-652.

Sieder, R. (1995). Honduras. In M. R. Group (Ed.), *No longer invisible: Afro-Latin Americans today* (pp. 235-242). London: Minority Rights Publication.

Staging post: Honduras. (1997, March 29). *Economist, 342*(8010), 50.

Slater, S., & Basch, H. (1997, July 20). Southern hospitality on Norwegian Star. *Los Angeles Times*, p. L7.

Sletto, B. (1993). Crosscurrents to the mainland: The Honduran Bay Islands build bridges between two cultures. *Americas, 45*(5), 6-13.

Sorensen, J. C. (1993). *A plan to establish, develop and manage the Bay Island National Marine Park.* Gainesville: Tropical Research and Development, Inc. (Originally published 1992)

Southgate, D. (1998). *Tropical forest conservation: An economic assessment of the alternatives in Latin America.* London/New York: Oxford University Press.

Stephens, J. (1989). Retreat to Roatán Island. *Aboard, 13*(4), 44-57.

Stevens, S. (Ed.). (1997). *Conservation through cultural survival: Indigenous peoples and protected areas.* Washington, DC: Island Press.

Stone, D., & Lange, F. (1984). *The archeology of lower Central America.* Albuquerque: University of New Mexico Press.

Stonich, S. C. (1989). The dynamics of social processes and environmental destruction: A Central American case study. *Population and Development Review, 15*(2), 269-296.

Stonich, S. C. (1991). The promotion of nontraditional exports in Honduras: Issues of equity, environment, and natural resources management. *Development and Change, 22*(4), 725-755.

Stonich, S. C. (1992). Struggling with Honduran poverty: The environmental consequences of natural resource-based development and rural transformations. *World Development, 20*(3), 385-399.

Stonich, S. C. (1993). *I am destroying the land! The political ecology of poverty and environmental destruction in Honduras.* Boulder: Westview Press.

Stonich, S. C. (1995). The environmental quality and social justice implications of shrimp mariculture in Honduras. *Human Ecology, 23*(2), 143-168.

Stonich, S. C. (1998). Water, power, and environmental health in tourism development: The

Bay Islands, Honduras. In J. M. Donahue & B. R. Johnston (Eds.), *Water, culture, and power: Local struggles in a global context* (pp. 263–285). Washington, DC/Covelo, CA: Island Press.

Stonich, S. C., Sorensen, J. H., & Hundt, A. (1995). Ethnicity, class, and gender in tourism development: The case of the Bay Islands, Honduras. *Journal of Sustainable Tourism, 3*(1), 1–28.

Strong, W. D. (1934). *An archeological cruise among the Bay Islands of Honduras, explorations and field-work of the Smithsonian Institution in 1933* (pp. 49–53). Washington, DC: Smithsonian Institution.

Strong, W. D. (1935). *Archaeological investigations in the Bay Islands, Spanish Honduras* (Vol. 92). Washington, DC: Smithsonian Institution.

The Caribbean islands of the Maya World. (1994). *Mundo Maya, 2*(2), 36–48.

The tourist trap—who's getting caught. (1982, Summer). *Cultural Survival Quarterly, 6*, 3.

Thomlinson, E. (1994). *The Business of ecotourism: Company and environmental relations in the context of el Mundo Maya, Central America.* Master of Business Administration thesis, The University of Calgary, Alberta.

Thrupp, L. A. (1990). Environmental initiatives in Costa Rica: A political ecology perspective. *Society and Natural Resources, 3*, 243–256.

Thrupp, L. A. (1995). *Bittersweet harvests for global supermarkets: Challenges in Latin America's agricultural export boom.* Washington, DC: World Resources Institute.

Trigano, G. (1984). *Tourism and the environment: The Club Méditerranée experience* (United Nations Environment Programme: Industry and Environment, Vol. 7, No. 1). Paris: United Nations Publication.

Trowbridge, F. L., Marks, J. S., Romana, G. L. d., Madrid, S., Boutton, T., & Klein, R. D. (1987). Body composition of Peruvian children with short stature and high weight-for-height: Implications for the interpretation of weight-for-height as an indicator of nutritional status. *American Journal of Clinical Nutrition, 46*, 411–418.

Tsartas, P. (1992). Socioeconomic impacts of tourism on two Greek Isles. *Annals of Tourism Research, 19*, 516–533.

Underwater wilds.: Nature unveils itself in Roatán's marine parks. (1994, February/March). *Coconut Telegraph, 10*, 1, 34.

United Nations. (1998). *1996 demographic yearbook* (Vol. 48). New York: Author.

United Nations Environment Programme, International Union for Conservation of Nature and Natural Resources, World Wildlife Fund, Food and Agriculture Organization of the United Nations, & Unesco. (1980). *World conservation strategy: Living resource conservation for sustainable development.* Gland, Switzerland: IUCN.

United Nations Environment Programme: Industry and Environment. (1995). *Environmental codes of conduct for tourism* (Vol. 29). Paris: Author.

Uphoff, N. (1985). Fitting projects to people. In M. Cernea (Ed.), *Putting people first: Sociological variables in rural development* (pp. 359–395). New York: Oxford University Press.

Uphoff, N. (1996). Why NGOs are not a third sector: A sectoral analysis with some thoughts on accountability, sustainability, and evaluation. In M. Edwards & D. Hulme (Eds.), *Beyond the magic bullet: NGO performance and accountability in the Post-Cold War world* (pp. 23–39). West Hartford, CT: Kumarian Press.

Utting, P. (1994). Social and political dimensions of environmental protection in Central America. *Development and Change, 25*, 231–259.

van Willigen, J., & Finan, T. L. (Eds.). (1991). *Soundings: Rapid and reliable research methods for practicing anthropologists.* Washington, DC: National Association for the Practice of Anthropology.

Vandergeest, P. (1996). Property rights in protected areas: Obstacles to community involvement as a solution in Thailand. *Environmental Conservation, 23*(3), 259-268.

Vandergeest, P., & Peluso, N. L. (1995). Territorialization and state power in Thailand. *Theory and Society, 24*(3), 385-426.

Vega, A., Alevizon, W., Dodd, R., Bolauos, R., Villeda, E., Cerrato, C., & Castro, V. (1993). *Watersheds, wildlands, and wildlife of the Bay Islands, Honduras: A conservation strategy* (Vol. 1). Gainesville, FL: Tropical Research & Development, Inc.

Waddell, D. (1959). Great Britain and the Bay Islands, 1821-1861. *The Historical Journal, 2*(1), 59-77.

Wallstrom, T. (1955). *A wayfarer in Central America.* London: Arthur Barker, Ltd.

Watt, I. (1973). *The historical development of settlement, Bay Islands, Honduras.* Masters of Arts thesis, University of Calgary, Calgary.

Wauchope, R. (1962). *Lost tribes & sunken continents: Myth and method in the study of American Indians.* Chicago/London: University of Chicago.

Webb, J. H., Jr. (1954). The Bay Islands of Honduras. *Americas, 6,* 16-19; 43-45.

Week in Review. (1998, June 8). Mayor restrict visits to Guanaja. *Honduras This Week* (Online edition 109). http://www.marrder.com/htw/.

Weir, C. (1997, February 7). Tourism pioneer speaks out. *Tico Times, III*(6). http://ticotimes.co.cr.

Weir, C. (1998, March 6). Cahuita unites for a fight. *Tico Times, IV*(9). http://ticotimes.co.cr.

Wells, M., Brandon, K., & Hannah, L. (1992). *People and parks: Linking protected area management with local communities.* Washington, DC: The World Bank, World Wildlife Fund, U.S. Agency for International Development.

West, P. C., & Brechin, S. R. (Eds.). (1991). *Resident peoples and national parks: Social dilemmas and strategies in international conservation.* Tucson: University of Arizona Press.

Western, D., & Wright, R. M. (1994). The background to community-based conservation. In D. Western, R. M. Wright, & S. C. Strum (Eds.), *Natural connections: Perspectives in community-based conservation* (pp. 1-12). Washington, DC/Covelo, CA: Island Press.

Western, D., Wright, R. M., & Strum, S. C. (Eds.). (1994). *Natural connections: Perspectives in community-based conservation.* Washington, DC/Covelo, CA: Island Press.

Wetzel, M. (1998, August 10). Bay Islands named to Skin Diver Travel Hall of Fame. *Honduras This Week* (Online edition 118). http://www.marrder.com/htw.

Wildlife Conservation Society. (1998). *Proposed management plan: Sandy Bay-West End Marine Reserve* (Draft). Gainesville, FL: Author.

Wilensky, J. M. (1979). *Cruising guide to the Bay Islands.* Stanford: Wescott Cove Publishing Company.

Wilkinson, P. (1989). Strategies for tourism in island microstates. *Annals of Tourism Research, 16,* 153-177.

Williams, R. (1986). *Export agriculture and the crisis in Central America.* Chapel Hill: University of North Carolina Press.

Wolf, E. (1972). Ownership and political ecology. *Anthropological Quarterly, 45*(3), 201-205.

Wong, P. P. (Ed.). (1993). *Tourism vs. environment: The case of the coastal areas* (Vol. 26). Dordrecht/Boston/London: Kluwer Academic Publishers.

World Bank. (1996). *The World Bank participation sourcebook.* Washington, DC: Author.

World Health Organization/United Nations Environment Programme. (1977). *Health criteria and epidemiological studies related to coastal water pollution.* Copenhagen: WHO Regional Office for Europe.

World Resources Institute, United Nations Environment Programme, United Nations Development Bank, & The World Bank. (1996). *World resources, 1996-97.* New York/Oxford: Oxford University Press.

World Tourism Organization. (1993). *Yearbook of tourism statistics* (Vol. 1). Madrid: Author.

World Tourism Organization (1994). *Yearbook of tourism statistics* (Vol. 1). Madrid: Author.

World Tourism Organization. (1996). *Yearbook of tourism statistics* (Vol. 1). Madrid: Author.

World Tourism Organization. (1997a, November). Travel to surge in the 21st century. *WTO News*.

World Tourism Organization. (1997b). *Yearbook of tourism statistics* (Vol. 1). Madrid: Author.

World Travel & Tourism Council. (1998a, April 8). *Sustainable travel and tourism infrastructure and jobs: A 21st century virtuous circle* [news release]. http://www.wttc.org/WTTCGATS.NSF/.

World Travel & Tourism Council. (1998b, April 8). *WTTC key statistics 1998* [news release]. http://www.wttc.org/WTTCGATS.NSF/.

Wright, I.A. (1929). *Spanish documents concerning English voyages to the Caribbean, 1527-1568* (Vol. 62). London: Hakluyt Society.

Wright, I.A. (1932). *Spanish documents concerning English voyages to the Spanish Main, 1569-1580* (Vol. 71). London: Hakluyt Society.

Wright, I.A. (1964). *Further English voyages to Spanish America, 1583-1594* (Vol. 99). London: Hakluyt Society.

Yost, J. (1992). Worlds of blue in Roatán. *Aboard, 16*(4), 52-59.

Index

Tourism Dynamics Book Series

TOURISM POLICY & PLANNING:
Case Studies from the Commonwealth Caribbean

By Paul F. Wilkinson
1997, 250 pp.
ISBN 1-882345-12-6 (hardbound)   **$35.00**
ISBN 1-882345-13-4 (softbound)   **$26.00**

CASINO GAMBLING IN AMERICA:
Origins, Trends, and Impacts
Edited by
Klaus Meyer-Arendt and Rudi Hartmann
1998, 270 pp.
ISBN 1-882345-16-9 (hardbound)   **$38.00**
ISBN 1-882345-17-7 (softbound)   **$30.00**

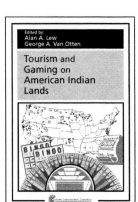

TOURISM AND GAMING ON AMERICAN INDIAN LANDS
Edited by
Alan A. Lew and
George A. Van Otten
1998, 260 pp.
ISBN 1-882345-21-5 (softbound) $30.00

Tourism Tourism

INFORMATION TECHNOLOGY & TOURISM

Applications • Methodologies • Techniques

Editor-in-Chief and Founding Editor: Hannes Werthner
Volume 1, 1998 ISSN: 1098-3058
Published 4 numbers per annum beginning Volume 2, 1999

Subscription Term	Price US & Canada	Price ROW
Inaugural Volume 1	$115.00	$130.00
Volume 2, 1999	$135.00	$150.00
Vols. 1&2 98/99	$225.00	$270.00
Professional Rate, Vol. 1	$65.00	$75.00
Professional Rate, Vols. 1&2	$120.00	$135.00

TOURISM, CULTURE & COMMUNICATION

Edited by: Brian King and Lindsay W. Turner
Volume 1, 1998   ISSN: 1098-304X
Vol 1: Published 2 numbers per annum
Vol 2: Published 3 numbers per annum

Subscription Term	Price US & Canada	Price ROW
Volume 1, 1998	$95.00	$115.00
Volume 2, 1999	$125.00	$145.00
Vols 1&2 98/99	$198.00	$234.00
Professional Rate, Vol. 1	$40.00	$55.00
Professional Rate, Vols. 1&2	$72.00	$100.00

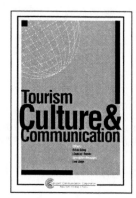

TOURISM ANALYSIS

An Interdisciplinary Journal

Editors-in-Chief: Muzaffer Uysal and Richard R. Perdue
Volume 4, 1999   ISSN: 1083-5423
Published 4 numbers per annum

Order Code	Subscription Term	Price US & Canada	Price ROW
	Volume 4, 1999	$125.00	$150.00
	Professional Rate	$40.00	$55.00

Back volumes 1, 2, & 3 are available @$125.00 + shipping per volume.

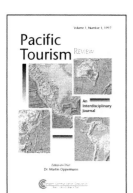